"Mutie's meticulous and logical analysis of Baur's false theories puts the study of church history back on a correct and logical path once again. This book should be required reading at all seminaries for those doing church-history studies."

—BOB FREIBERG,
Central Baptist Theological Seminary

"In this penetrating study, Mutie . . . persuasively demonstrates that the church always set a demarcation between what it knew as orthodoxy and heresy. In so doing, the ancient faith was never reinvented but remained as that 'once for all delivered to the saints' (Jude 3). I highly commend this balanced 'quest' for an early-church historiography that accounts for all the available data."

—CORY M. MARSH,
Southern California Seminary

"Mutie has written a systematic and comprehensive book on the historiography of the early church. It is a voice of clarity amid confusion of our time and a must-read for every student of church history."

—SOHRAB RAMTIN,
Southern California Seminary

"Mutie carefully and clearly divides truth from error, orthodoxy from heresy, early Christian historiography from modern historiographies that are pale reflections of their researchers. . . . Mutie convincingly demonstrates that orthodoxy emerged from the New Testament, was guarded by the apologists, and was solidified in the councils. I strongly recommend this book to anyone interested in the New Testament, the fathers, orthodoxy, heresy, historiography, and Christology."

—JUSTIN W. BASS,
author of *The Bedrock of Christianity: The Unalterable Facts of Jesus' Death and Resurrection*

"Jeremiah Mutie's valuable study offers an important context for understanding the popularity of biblical critics such as Bart Ehrman. Mutie skillfully shows that ideas have roots, and the roots of modern biblical skepticism go back for centuries. I commend the author for this clear and insightful contribution to Christian historiography."

—MARK SHAW,
Africa International University

"Did the Christian faith gradually emerge through the early centuries, a final triumph of one option over competing formulations? Or was there a singular, consistent rule of faith, an unsullied apostolic deposit that alone is found in the canonical Scriptures? . . . This is the one book I would read if I was concerned to understand the flow of the more recent history on the subject. Obviously, Mutie seeks to defend the integrity of the witness of Holy Scripture and the apostolic rule of faith."

—JOHN D. HANNAH,
Dallas Theological Seminary

"In an era when scholars view faith commitments in historical writings as suspicious, Mutie shows that early church histories can still be recognized as credible and genuine. A *regula fidei* is restored here as central to an early Christianity which is multifaceted and diverse. Yet, it is also safeguarded, unified, and orthodox, and Mutie salutes it as he calls for a workable early church historiography that is balanced and refreshing."

—W. BRIAN SHELTON,
Asbury University

The Quest for Early Church Historiography

The Quest for Early Church Historiography

*From Ferdinand C. Baur
to Bart D. Ehrman and Beyond*

JEREMIAH MUTIE

Foreword by James I. Fazio

WIPF & STOCK · Eugene, Oregon

THE QUEST FOR EARLY CHURCH HISTORIOGRAPHY
From Ferdinand C. Baur to Bart D. Ehrman and Beyond

Copyright © 2022 Jeremiah Mutie. All rights reserved. Except for brief quotations in critical publications or reviews, no part of this book may be reproduced in any manner without prior written permission from the publisher. Write: Permissions, Wipf and Stock Publishers, 199 W. 8th Ave., Suite 3, Eugene, OR 97401.

Wipf & Stock
An Imprint of Wipf and Stock Publishers
199 W. 8th Ave., Suite 3
Eugene, OR 97401

www.wipfandstock.com

PAPERBACK ISBN: 978-1-6667-1144-8
HARDCOVER ISBN: 978-1-6667-1145-5
EBOOK ISBN: 978-1-6667-1146-2

AUGUST 15, 2022 8:39 AM

This book is dedicated to the memory of my parents, Mr. Job Mutie Musoi and Mrs. Monicah Yula Mutie, as well as my mother-in-law, Mrs. Lena Kavemba Muli, who are all now in the presence of the Lord Jesus Christ. You all showed me what a disciplined Christian life looks like. *Soli Deo Gloria.*

Contents

Foreword by James I. Fazio | ix

Preface | xi

Acknowledgments | xiii

A Note on Terminology | xv

    Introduction | 1

Chapter 1
    Competing Early Church Historiographies | 7

Chapter 2
    Christian Ferdinand Baur and His Contemporaries: "Hegelian" Historiography | 22

Chapter 3
    Adolf Von Harnack and His Posterity: "Hellenistic" Historiography | 47

Chapter 4
    Walter Bauer and the "Priority of Heresy" Historiography: The Emergence of the "Bauer Thesis" | 73

CHAPTER 5
  THE HISTORIOGRAPHY OF BART EHRMAN
  AND HIS CONTEMPORARIES: EXTREME HISTORICISM | 121

CHAPTER 6
  DETERMINATION OF ORTHODOXY AND HERESY
  IN EARLY CHRISTIANITY: THE QUEST FOR CRITERIA | 151

CONCLUSION
  TOWARD AN EARLY CHURCH HISTORIOGRAPHY | 200

Bibliography | 205

Index | 219

Foreword

IN EVERY GENERATION THE church is confronted with challenges that Christians must rise to meet. One could find irony in the fact that just as contentions arose in the earliest centuries of the church over how the last days should be interpreted, so in these days Christians find themselves contending over how to interpret the earliest centuries of the church. This is the question that this book seeks to answer. Or, if you prefer, this is the *quest* upon which this book embarks. To press the imagery a bit further, it could be said that this *quest* bears similarities to those concocted by the great storytellers of the past, replete with twisted labyrinths, fire-spitting dragons, and a damsel in need of rescue from the jaws of her afflicters. It could otherwise be said that this book places the reader before a well-trodden maze while shining a spotlight on the footprints of those who have traversed it, over the past few centuries, to mark out a path. At this point you may ask, "Why embark on this journey at all? Why trouble yourself with such an arduous *quest*?" The answer is that we have not chosen this *quest* at all . . . the *quest* has fallen to us.

In the introduction, Jeremiah Mutie refers to Hugh Turner's appraisal of those branded as heretics in the early church, noting that they were motivated by "a restless quest for novelty."[1] One cannot help but hear that phrase echo throughout each subsequent chapter as Mutie traces a path from Ferdinand Christian Baur (1792–1860), the pioneer of the Tübingen school of theology in nineteenth-century Protestant Germany, that winds up to the extreme historicism of Bart D. Ehrman (1955–) in the present day.

After leading readers by the hand through centuries of *questing*, Mutie raises the horn to his lips and gives the clarion blast that cuts through the rumbling; alighting a beacon on the New Testament writings

1. Turner, *The Pattern of Christian Truth*, 6.

that signals the path ascending out of the labyrinth. In his typical charitable style, with grace and armed with sound reason, Mutie demonstrates the need for an early church historiography akin to the methodological scope and framework outlined by Richard Muller.[2] The historiography which Mutie models in the concluding chapter stands out as particularly refreshing against the morass of "Hegelian", "Hellenistic," "Hybrid," and other competing historiographies. Indeed, Jeremiah Mutie has done us a great favor of drawing up a road map that can guide readers through *The Quest for Early Church Historiography*.

—James Fazio
Dean of Bible and Theology and Professor of Biblical Literature
Southern California Seminary

---

2. Cf. Muller, *Post-Reformation Reformed Dogmatics*. A succinct description of his method can be found in Bradley and Muller, *Church History*.

Preface

THIS STUDY IS THE CULMINATION of years of my interest in the subject of early church historiography. The initial impetus was a doctoral seminar that I took at Dallas Theological Seminary in the fall of 2007 under the renowned early church historian and my eventual *Doktorvater*, Dr. D. Jeffrey Bingham, on the development of Christian doctrine. About three years later, I attended a debate on the reliability of the New Testament documents between Dr. Daniel B. Wallace and Dr. Bart D. Ehrman at Southern Methodist University.[1] As I keenly followed the debate, it became clear that the issue they were tangling over was more *historiographical* than *textual* in nature. In other words, how does one read the documents in question?

Indeed, with the passing of time, scholarly interest in early church historiography continues to grow. With this increase, proposed historiographies have also been on the increase. One very recent example of these historiographies is Markus Vinzent's *Writing the History of Early Christianity: From Reception to Retrospection* (Cambridge: Cambridge University Press, 2019). In this volume, Vinzent argues that the best way to fill up the gaps in reading early church documents is to read them retrospectively (that is, approaching history from the present and reading it back to the past). Vinzent's work serves to illustrate the continued need for a helpful early church historiography.[2]

However, many other approaches to the reading of early church texts have been characterized by extreme historicism. An example here is

---

1. I am forever grateful to my friend Dr. Justin Bass for not only inviting me to this debate but also graciously paying for my ticket.

2. Vinzent, *Writing the History of Early Christianity*, 3. See also Laing, *Retrieving History*. Laing's focus (and that of the entire series) is to find a way to retrieve church histoy and make it meaningful to the present church.

Bart Ehrman's *Lost Christianities: The Battles for Scripture and the Faiths We Never Knew* (New York: Oxford University Press, 2003), in which he argues, as Bingham summarizes, that the history of early Christianity is the story of "a movement from an originally broad variety of Christianities, ideologically in conflict with Proto-orthodoxy, to a later, but strategically superior 'orthodoxy.'"[3] This work, instead of seeing the debates in the early church as between proto-orthodox and heresy (as the classical historiography has understood them over hundreds of years), sees them as competing "Christianities" with the prescribed "early Catholicism" winning the day. But how did we get the historiography of such scholars as Ehrman? What are the historiographical trajectories that led us to this point?

It is this last question that is the focus of this book. The main thesis of this book, therefore, is that, rather than having suddenly appeared, the extremely skeptical historicism of such scholars as Bart Ehrman is instead the fruition of a long process that stared with the Hegelian early church historiography of Ferdinand Christian Baur (1792–1860) of Tübingen University. As such, the historiographical trajectory (obviously, with some twists and turns), will be traced as the chapters of the book unfold. Finally, a suggested historiography of the early church will be offered (modified classicism).

Finally, I will be fooling myself if I do not clearly acknowledge the daunting nature of this kind of a project. Honestly, I have thought about this project perhaps more than any other one in my career. However, when the push finally came to the shove, I had to take courage in the words of Jeane Leavy, who, as quoted by Robert W. Yarbrough, famously declared that "You don't need to know everything to write the truth. You just need to know enough."[4] With this understanding, the final hesitation faded away.

---

3. Bingham, "Development and Diversity," 59.
4. Yarbrough, *The Salvation Historical Fallacy*, xiv.

Acknowledgments

In the process of writing of books, as all authors know, there is an endless list of people involved in various ways and stages. Thus, it is practically impossible to mention by name all of my friends who gave me helpful insights and all kinds of encouragement in the process of writing this book. To all of you, I am eternally grateful.

First, I am grateful for my mentor, Dr. D. Jeffrey Bingham, who created in me an insatiable interest in the area of early church historiography. *Second*, I want to thank my esteemed colleagues here at Southern California Seminary for the many conversations that we had around the ideas presented in this book. While not limited to these two, mention must be made of my dean, Dr. James Fazio, who went out of his way to accommodate my stretched work schedule, ensuring the timely completion of the book, and Dr. Cory Marsh with whom we fruitfully conversed over the book's ideas—conversations that sometimes went on until late hours of the evening. Indeed, I am truly grateful for the prayers and support that I received from the entire SCS leadership. In the same vein, I want to express my immeasurable gratitude to all of our librarians both at SCS and San Diego Christian College who went out of their way to make sure that I had all my needed resources in a very timely manner. A special thanks to Jennifer Ewing, Kathleen Russel, Matt Owen, and Mona Hsu. Your reward in heaven will be great!

Third, I want to also express my gratitude to our students, with whom the ideas in this book were tried during its various stages of writing. This is true of both the ThM and DMin students. Thank you for accepting to act as the proverbial "guinea pigs" for the project. The same is true of my friends Drs. Bob Freiberg and Sohrab Ramtin, with whom I brainstormed some of the key ideas for the book in its earliest stages. I owe a great deal of gratitude to both of you.

Fourth and finally, more than anyone else, I want to thank my dear family for their help and support. I am extremely grateful to my precious wife, Eunice Jeremiah, my life's partner and soul mate, for her unending love, prayers, and support even when I felt like not going on with the project. She continuously supported me and cheered "her man" up. Love, your reward before our heavenly Father is great. Thanks also to our children, Jackson and Cynthia Jeremiah, who always made sure to check with Dad to see how his "project" was progressing as well as what they can do to make the process easier for me. Thank you! Finally, I want to thank my father-in-law, Mr. Jackson Muli Katiitii, for his unending love and support. I cannot count the times that he called to check on the "project." The Lord will reward you mightily.

Soli Deo Gloria!

A Note on Terminology

The term "quest," as used in this work, primarily refers to the attempts that historians of early Christians have made over the years to understand the history of earliest Christianity. It is used, in this sense, to refer to the dueling paradigms that have been proposed and defended since the second century. Thus, it is being used in a manner akin to the way Albert Schweitzer used it in his *The Quest of the Historical Jesus: A Critical Study of its Progress from Reimarus to Wrede*. However, in another sense, the term is also used to refer to the quest for an early church historiography that, as best as possible, accounts for the available data. As with everything else, the reader will be able to decipher these usages from the *context*.

Introduction

ONE OF THE MOST fascinating disciplines of study is history. Among other reasons, part of the fascination with history is due to the attitudes and emotions that the subject matter usually evokes. Indeed, just like philosophers, who have been caught lampooning their own discipline by defining it as "a group of blind men in a dark room looking for a black cat—that isn't [even] there,"[1] historians have also made fun of their own discipline of inquiry because of the fascination that the subject matter brings to the table. For example, while sometimes historians define history as a "record of past events and people," others find fun in defining it as "a game we play on the dead."[2] And, perhaps, a game it is—and everything depends on how the game is played.

Understood this way (a game), much of the reading of history involves the art of interpretation. Indeed, speaking of *interpretation*, it is always important to remember that, for the most part, interpretation is dependent on the interpreter's own philosophy of interpretation. That is, interpretation is never done in a vacuum. Rather, it brings with it the interpreter's worldview—that set of presuppositions that act as the fundamental basis for the interpretation. In fact, it is in this aspect—the interpretation of history—where some of the fiercest battles of the discipline have been fought.

Technically speaking, that aspect of the discipline of history that deals with the interpretation of history is known as *historiography*. Mark Shaw notes concerning historiography: "Because we all look at the world and its historical past from a different perspective, it is important to find as much as we can about the values and perspectives of authors when we

---

1. Gustafson, *Quest for Truth*.
2. Or, as Voltaire jibed, "History is a pack of lies we play on the dead." Although this quote is attributed to Voltaire, the exact source seems untraceable.

read their work."³ He adds that "the study of how historians think and write about history is called historiography."⁴ Indeed, as historian David Hackett Fischer notes, in order for a historian to write history objectively, he needs to have a "tacit logic of historical thought."⁵ Fischer further explains:

> The Logic of historical thought is not a formal logic of deductive inference. It is not a symmetrical structure of Aristotelian syllogisms, Ramean dialectics, or Boolean equations. Nor is it precisely an inductive logic, like that of Mill or Keynes or Carnap. It consists neither in inductive reasoning from the general to the particular. Instead, it is a process of adductive reasoning in the simple sense of adducing answers to specific questions so that a satisfactory explanatory "fit" is obtained. The answers may be general or particular as the questions may require. History is, in short, a problem-solving discipline. A historian is someone (anyone) who asks an open-ended question about past events and answers it with selected facts which are arranged in the form of an explanatory paradigm. These questions and answers are fitted to each other by a complex process of mutual adjustment: a statistical generalization, or a narrative, or a causal model, or a motivational model, or a collectivized group-composition model, or maybe an analogy. Most commonly it consists not in any one of these components but in a combination of them. Always, it is articulated in the form of a reasoned argument.⁶

What Fischer is getting to is the usually unstated fact that, in order for a historian to be able to function successfully in his/her discipline of inquiry, he/she must have a clear logic of historical thought. Often referred to as a "paradigm," this is a set of (sometimes unspoken) rules of historical scholarship without which, although a person may be doing something in the name of history, he probably is not "doing history." Fischer notes that "there are some very strict tautological rules of historical scholarship which are rather like the rules of chess."⁷ He adds that "When a chess player sits down to a game, he must respect a rule which requires him to move his bishops on a diagonal. Nobody will arrest him if he doesn't. But if he refuses to play that way, then he isn't exactly playing

---

3. Shaw, *Kingdom of God in Africa*, 1.
4. Shaw, *Kingdom of God in Africa*, 1.
5. Fischer, *Historians' Fallacies*, xv.
6. Fischer, *Historians' Fallacies*, xv.
7. Fischer, *Historians' Fallacies*, xix.

chess."[8] The question before us, therefore, is whether or not early church historians are playing chess.

The situation has been exacerbated by the current epistemological climate of postmodernity. "It is now commonplace for historians," writes Alan Munslow, capturing this current climate, "philosophers of history and others interested in narrative to claim we live in a postmodern age wherein the old modernist certainties of historical truth and methodological objectivity, as applied by disinterested historians, are challenged principles."[9] He further makes the key clarification that, "specifically, the impact of postmodernism on the study of history is seen in the new emphasis placed on its literary or aesthetic aspect, but not as before only as stylistic presentation, but now as a mode of explanation not primarily dependent upon the established empiricist paradigm."[10] Thus, if there was any time when historians had to pay careful attention to their historiographies, this would be that time. As such, a good historiography helps safeguard historians from falling into what Fischer and others call "historians' fallacies." "Among my colleagues," writes Fischer, "it is common to believe that any procedure is permissible as long as its practitioner publishes an essay from time to time and is not convicted of a felony."[11] He quips; "The resultant condition of modern historiography is that of the Jews under the Judges: every man does that which is right in his own eyes."[12] Certainly, Christians (and specifically, church historians) are not exempt from these noted scenarios.

While Fischer's concern is historiography as it applies to historians in general, the concern of this work is the historiography of history of the early church. But the standards of doing history are similar, and "rules of the game," if the results are to be deemed credible, are similar as well. In fact, here would be a good place for one to ask whether or not church historians have fared any better in their historiography. While more will be said in the succeeding chapter, it would suffice to answer, regrettably,

---

8. Fischer, *Historians' Fallacies*, xix.

9. Munslow, *Deconstructing History*, 1. Carl R. Trueman makes the same observation, writing: "There has been a trend over recent decades toward a kind of epistemological nihilism that has so relativized everything that acess to the past in any meaningful way is virtually denied" (Trueman, *Histories and Fallacies*, 18). Trueman's work helpfully highlights historiographical fallacies in doing history generally.

10. Munslow, *Deconstructing History*, 19.

11. Fischer, *Historians' Fallacies*, xix.

12. Fischer, *Historians' Fallacies*, xix.

in the negative. For example, addressing historical fallacies pertaining to the study of early Christianity—itself the key subject of this work—Donald Carson notes that it has been plagued by, among others, fallacies of causation. He writes:

> Granted that Edwin M. Yamauchi and others are right in arguing that there is no evidence of full-blown Gnosticism in the pre-Christian period, it is difficult to resist the conclusion that a great many of the connections drawn by scholars (especially those of the "history of religions school") who believe Christianity is an off-shoot of Gnosticism are nothing more than examples of *pro hoc, propter hoc*, the worst kind of causal fallacy.[13]

By *pro hoc, propter hoc*, it is meant "this mistaken idea that if event B happened after event A, it happened because of event A."[14] Thus, while specific responses to this and other related historical fallacies that have accrued in the reading of church history will be offered in the following chapter, the point being emphasized here is that a proper historiography is *sine qua non* to the study of the history of the church. This point will become clearer as the work progresses.

In terms of the book's roadmap, chapter 1, entitled "Competing Early Church Historiographies," in addition to setting up the need and parameters of the work, will present an overview of the main historiographies of the early church. This will lay the ground for more detailed treatment in the following chapters. Chapter 2, entitled "Christian Ferdinand Baur and His Contemporaries: 'Hegelian' Historiography," explores how F. C. Baur utilized Hegelianism in his study of the emergence and development of the early church. In addition, the chapter will trace the adoption and influence of Hegelianism from Baur to Schleiermacher, developments that happened in quick succession.

A key question that early church historiographers contend with is the influence of the F. C. Baur thesis in the scholarly climate immediately following Baur himself. This is the subject of chapter 3, entitled "Adolf Von Harnack and His Posterity: 'Hellenistic' Historiography." This chapter traces the developments from Schleiermacher to Harnack. As the reader will notice, even though the views of Baur continue to influence the study of early Christianity, focus now shifts to the question of how the new "thesis" position (i.e., Hellenism) resulted in a regression and

---

13. Carson, *Exegetical Fallacies*, 13–14.
14. Fischer, *Historians' Fallacies*, 166.

Introduction

not progression in the development of early Christianity. The pinnacle of this approach is Harnack's work entitled *What Is Christianity?* As it will be demonstrated, however, even in this approach, there is no clean break from Baur's Hegelianism. Instead, historiography enters a new "thesis" status after the previous "thesis-antithesis-synthesis" cycles.

Chapter 4, entitled "Walter Bauer and the 'Priority of Heresy' Historiography: The Emergence of the 'Bauer thesis,'" explores the movement from Harnack's historiography to the paradigmatic historiographical shift that the so-called "Bauer thesis" infused in this thread. While not significantly noticed in the English-speaking world, Bauer's *Rechtgläubigkeit und Ketzerei im ältesten Christentum Beiträge zur historischen*, published in 1934, proved to be extremely influential in the study of the early church. His main thesis was that in many early centers of Christianity, what we know as "heresy" preceded orthodoxy. With his work, the final transition to the historiography of Bart Ehrman is complete. Ehrman refers to this work as "arguably the most important book in the history of early Christianity to appear in the twentieth century."[15] Its importance in the progression of this historiographical thread will be demonstrated in this chapter of the work.

According to Bart Ehrman, "If anything, early Christianity was even less tidy and more diversified than he [Bauer] realized."[16] However, in between Bauer and Ehrman, there were other key proponents of Bauer who helped import his views to America. Attention, therefore, will be focused on such thinkers as James Robinson and Helmut Koester, both students of Rudolf Bultmann. The tracing of these developments will be the subject of chapter 5, entitled "The Historiography of Bart Ehrman and His Contemporaries: Extreme Historicism." Finally, the historiography of Bart Ehrman, who is the most eloquent and effective popularizer of the Bauer thesis in America and beyond, will be explored. Of course, other current historians of similar thought, such as Einar Thomassen, Elaine Pagels, Karen King and Rebecca Lyman, Daniel Boyarin, and Virginia Burrus, will also be addressed.

Finally, chapter 6 concludes the work and adduces some lessons from this historiographical trajectory. My goal is to propose a modified historiography which insists that although there were detectable "Christianities" in the early church, overall the church recognized and put a

---

15. Ehrman, *Lost Christianities*, 173.
16. Ehrman, *Lost Christianities*, 176.

demarcation between orthodoxy (however rudimentary it may have been conceived) and heresy. Indeed, in doing so, the church was not inventing anything. Rather, she was following clearly-set-out criteria of determining these, set forth in the New Testament, and often introduced by such creedal formula as πιστὸς ὁ λόγος ("This is a trustworthy saying") or similar language.

CHAPTER 1

Competing Early Church Historiographies

JEFFREY BINGHAM BEGINS HIS article by summarizing the current status of the history of early Christianity, which sees this as the story of "a movement from an originally broad variety of Christianities, ideologically in conflict with proto-orthodoxy, to a later, but strategically superior 'orthodoxy.'"[1] In other words, this is how it has been argued in some key early historiographical circles today. According to Bart Ehrman, for example, "it is widely thought today that proto-orthodoxy was simply one of many competing interpretations in the early church."[2] On the other hand, instead of understanding these so-called varieties of Christianities as such, these are rather to be understood as heretical groups that were, for the most part, subsequent to orthodox Christianity.

Both of these views on both ends of the early church historiographical continuum alert the reader to the several approaches that scholars have adopted in the study of early Christianity. Consistent with other areas of study, current trends tend to emphasize doctrinal and social diversity rather than uniformity in earliest Christianity. Thus, in an age that is incessantly fascinated with the idea of diversity and unity like ours, it is no surprise that the possibility of a tolerable existence of diverse groups (Christianities) in the early church has generated such as level of interest. Again, arguing for diversity in early Christianity, Ehrman notes that the

---

1. Bingham, "Development and Diversity," 59. It should be noted, however, that Bingham is summarizing Bart Ehrman's views here.
2. Ehrman, *Lost Christianities*, 176.

present ecclesial scenario is easily comparable to the that of early Christianity. He writes:

> It may be difficult to imagine a religious phenomenon more diverse than modern-day Christianity. There are Roman Catholics missionaries who devote themselves to voluntary poverty for the sake of others, and evangelical televangelists who run twelve-step programs to ensure financial success. There are New England Presbyterians and Appalachian snake handlers. There are Greek Orthodox priests committed to the liturgical service of God, replete with set prayers, incantations, and incense, and fundamentalist preachers who view high church liturgy as a demonic invention. There are liberal Methodist political activists intent on transforming society, and Pentecostals who think that society will soon come to a crashing halt with the return of Jesus. And there are followers of David Koresh—still today—who think the world has already started to end, beginning with the events at Waco, a fulfillment of prophecies from Revelation. Many of these Christian groups, of course, refuse to consider other such groups Christian.[3]

In response to his question, Ehrman sees Christianity in the ancient world as the only "more diverse" situation than this "variegated phenomenon." According to him, "during the first three centuries, the practices and beliefs found among people who called themselves Christian were so varied that the differences between Roman Catholics, Primitive Baptists, and Seventh-Day Adventists pale by comparison."[4] Bingham further notes that "Questions of orthodoxy and heresy, tolerance and intolerance, exclusivity and syncretism, are [now] common to both Roman Hellenism and [early] Christianity."[5] Operating from a different historiographical orientation, Bingham casts these early Christian doctrinal diversities as "the struggle to define truth and communities," a process that "was a common concern of groups in the second and third centuries."[6] However, while Ehrman and others contend that these diversities are what historians have come to realize, the question still remains: Has this been the standard interpretation of early Christianity? If not, when and why did historians begin to read early Christian history this way? Even more

---

3. Ehrman, *Lost Christianities*, 1.
4. Ehrman, *Lost Christianities*, 1.
5. Bingham, "Development and Diversity," 47.
6. Bingham, "Development and Diversity," 47.

pertinent is the issue of whether or not this is a demonstrably justifiable historiography of early Christianity.

While many of these questions are the subject of the subsequent inquiry here, the focus of this chapter is on the first question: Has this been the standard interpretation of early Christianity? Historians of earliest Christianity agree that seeing these early movements as "varieties" of Christianities has not been the standard interpretation of early Christianity. Rather, these relationships were explained using the "classical view" of early Christian history. This has been the standard explanation of the relationship between orthodoxy and heresy in earliest Christianity.[7]

THE QUEST FOR EARLY CHURCH HISTORIOGRAPHY: THE CLASSICAL THEORY

In order to be in a position to intelligently trace the early church historiography that emerged in the thought of F. C. Baur, it is imperative that we briefly recite the historiography that had been held to tenaciously up to that point: the classical theory. A view assumed throughout most of the history of Christianity, its name was coined and fully elucidated by H. E. W. Turner in his 1954 work aptly entitled *The Pattern of Christian Truth: A Study of the Relations between Orthodoxy and Heresy in the Early Church*.[8] After declaring that his approach to early church historiography was "neither uncritically conservative nor uncompromisingly liberal,"[9] Turner turns his attention to what he calls the classical theory of early church historiography. He summarizes the classical view thusly:

---

7. The focus of this work is early Christian historiography. For those interested in Christian historiography in general, a good source is Green, *Christian Historiography*.

8. Turner, *Pattern of Christian Truth*. In a way, the present work is patterned after Turner's. However, while Turner's work focuses on the classical theory and its main challenger, the theory of Walter Bauer, this work, rather, treats Bauer's thesis as part of an early church historiographical trajectory that concretized in the thought of Ferdinand Christian Baur and continues to take shape in the works of such present-day historians as Bart Ehrman and Elaine Pagels, among others. Of course, the work does not treat this as a lineal progression *per se* as there are notable turns and twists in the process. However, it seeks to demonstrate a seminal relationship between Baur's historiography and this succeeding generation of historians who argue for historiographies that are opposed to Turner's classical theory. Thus, the work differs from Turner's both in its beginning point and its *terminus ad quem*. And, in its treatment of the turns and twists while not losing the synthetic connection of these historiographies, the work is akin to that of Albert Schweitzer (see Schweitzer, *Quest of the Historical Jesus*).

9. Turner, *Pattern of Christian Truth*, ix.

> The Church originally kept unsullied and undefiled the teaching of our Lord and the tradition of the Apostles. Thus Hegesippus, the first writer known to us to examine the problem of heresy with close attention, speaks of the Church of Jerusalem in the following terms, 'For this reason they call the Church a virgin because she had not yet been corrupted by vain teaching. But Thebutis because he was not made bishop began secretly to corrupt her from the seven sects among the people to which he himself belonged.'[10]

According to this theory, therefore, the church kept pure the Lord's and the apostles' teaching. Further, as Turner argues, the theory sees orthodoxy as temporally prior to heresy. Heresy, according to this theory, "was a crooked deviation from orthodoxy, a heretic [is] the one who departed from the truth."[11] For Turner, this was the position of the church from her earliest days. Thus, the essence of this view, otherwise known as the "traditional view," is that truth preceded error in early Christianity.[12]

Turner outlines a number of key lines of evidences in support of this theory. *First*, he notes, as explained above, that the "Church originally kept unsullied and undefiled the teaching of the Lord and the tradition of the apostles."[13] No wonder the early church chronicler Hegesippus would speak of the church in Jerusalem as a virgin "because she had not yet been corrupted by vain teaching."[14] *Second*, according to this theory, the "temporal priority of orthodoxy to heresy is everywhere assumed."[15]

Indeed, according to Hegesippus (ca. 100–180 CE, as recorded by Eusebius), the church remained a pure virgin as long as the apostles were

---

10. Turner, *Pattern of Christian Truth*, 3.

11. Bingham, "Development and Diversity," 48. Bingham further summarizes the classical view this way: "Originally, in this theory, the Church kept the Lord's teaching and the apostolic tradition untainted and pure. It understood orthodoxy as temporally prior to heresy. Heresy was a crooked deviation from orthodoxy, a heretic one who departed froth the truth. Orthodoxy's temporal priority could be seen in Scripture's prophecies of heresy while the crookedness of the heretics' doctrine was believed to follow from the adulterous, factious, criminal intent of their motives. They preferred to choose novelty rather than to receive that which was handed down" (Bingham, "Development and Diversity," 48–49).

12. Bingham, "Development and Diversity," 48n22. See also Hultgren, *Rise of Normative Christianity*, 7–8.

13. Turner, *Pattern of Christian Truth*, 3.

14. Turner, *Pattern of Christian Truth*, 3.

15. Turner, *Pattern of Christian Truth*, 3–4.

still alive. However, this changed after their deaths. He writes, elucidating this point further:

> But when the sacred college of apostles had suffered death in various forms, and the generation of those that had been deemed worthy to hear the inspired wisdom with their own ears had passed away, then the league of godless error took its rise as a result of the folly of heretical teachers, who, because none of the apostles was still living, attempted henceforth, with a bold face, to proclaim, in opposition to the preaching of the truth, the "knowledge which is falsely so-called."[16]

Thus, although this issue will be fully explored in chapter 4 as the staunchest challenger to the classical view (viz the Bauer thesis, itself the main subject of Turner's work), it would suffice here to note that the view that orthodoxy preceded heresy in earliest Christianity was held by all the early church fathers who spoke on it. This is certainly the case with both Irenaeus and Tertullian, as will be demonstrated later.

Another corollary point that Turner raises is the understanding among many in early Christianity that not only did heresy chronologically come after orthodoxy, but it was itself an offshoot of orthodoxy and clearly predicted in the New Testament. "Heresy was thus originally an offshoot of orthodoxy," writes Turner, "and the leading heresiarchs [founders of heresy] are regarded as *catholiques manqués*."[17] Therefore, according to this theory, in terms of chronology, error followed truth; heresy followed orthodoxy. Heresy, therefore, as Jude says, was a departure from "faith which was once for all handed down to the saints" (Jude 3 NASB). Indeed, a few years before Hegesippus wrote, Clement of Rome had made the same observations concerning the order of the reception of the gospel. Writing around ca. 96 CE, Clement provides this order in terms of the transfer of truth in *1 Clement* 42:1–4:

> The Apostles received the Gospel for us from the Lord Jesus Christ; Jesus Christ was sent forth from God. So then Christ is from God, and the Apostles are from Christ. Both therefore came of the will of God in the appointed order. Having therefore received a charge and having been fully assured through the resurrection of our Lord Jesus Christ and confirmed in the word of God with full assurance of the Holy Ghost, they went forth

---

16. Eusebius, *HE* 3.32.8. For this work, I am using Eusebius and Crusé, *Eusebius' Ecclesiastical History*.

17. Turner, *Pattern of Christian Truth*, 4.

with the glad tidings that the kingdom of God should come. So preaching everywhere in country and town, they appointed their first fruits, when they had proved them by the Spirit, to be bishops and deacons unto them that should believe.[18]

Thus, for this early father, the order of the transmission was very simple: "the gospel was given by Jesus to the apostles, who appointed bishops and deacons after testing them—presumably in order to guard the gospel in its purity."[19] Therefore, rather than error (heresy) developing either earlier or concurrent with truth (orthodoxy), it was instead a later development, an impure innovation, needing to be rejected strongly.

One of the most elaborate demonstration of how heresy was considered an offshoot of orthodoxy is in the brief summary of the presumed religious pilgrimage of the second-century apologist Tatian by Irenaeus (ca. 130–202 CE), bishop of Lyons. According to Irenaeus, after the martyrdom of Tatian's teacher, Justin Martyr, he left the church and became a heretic. In fact, Irenaeus discusses the "fall" of Tatian in the context of some heretical offshoots from early orthodoxy. He writes in *Adv. Haer.* 1.28.1:

> Many offshoots of numerous heresies have already been formed from those heretics we have described. This arises from the fact that numbers of them—indeed, we may say all—desire themselves to be teachers, and to break off from the particular heresy in which they have been involved. Forming one set of doctrines out of a totally different system of opinions, and then again others from others, they insist upon teaching something new, declaring themselves the inventors of any sort of opinion which they may have been able to call into existence. To give an example: Springing from Saturninus and Marcion, those who are called Encratites (self-controlled) preached against marriage, thus setting aside the original creation of God, and indirectly blaming Him who made the male and female for the propagation of the human race.[20]

Before mentioning Tatian directly, who he sees as having become an Encratite himself, Irenaeus explains that adherents of this kind of teaching also abstained from animal food, "thus proving themselves ungrateful

---

18. *1 Clem* 42.1–4. For this work, I am using Holmes, *Apostolic Fathers*.
19. Hultgren and Haggmark, *Earliest Christian Heretics*, 5.
20. Irenaeus, *Adv. Haer.* 1.28.1. For this work, I am using Irenaeus, *Against Heresies*.

to God, who formed all things."²¹ Then, after noting that the same group of people reject salvation, he explains how Tatian became a member of this group after the death of Justin. He continues:

> They deny, too, the salvation of him who was first created. It is but lately, however, that this opinion has been invented among them. A certain man named Tatian first introduced the blasphemy. He was a hearer of Justin's, and as long as he continued with him he expressed no such views; but after his martyrdom he separated from the Church, and, excited and puffed up by the thought of being a teacher, as if he were superior to others, he composed his own peculiar type of doctrine. He invented a system of certain invisible Æons, like the followers of Valentinus; while, like Marcion and Saturninus, he declared that marriage was nothing else than corruption and fornication. But his denial of Adam's salvation was an opinion due entirely to himself.²²

Whether Tatian himself turned to heresy continues to be a debated issue in scholarship.²³ While it seems that Irenaeus was a pastor who was overly concerned about heresy in his beloved flock at Lyons, his accusation of heresy on the part of Tatian was understandably picked up by his successors. It was repeated by such fathers as Clement of Alexandria (ca.

---

21. Irenaeus, *Adv. Haer.* 1.28.1.

22. Irenaeus, *Adv. Haer.* 1.28.1. Elsewhere, Irenaeus writes concerning the genealogical origins of heresies this way: "For prior to Valentinus, those who follow Valentinus had no existence; nor did those from Marcion exist before Marcion; nor, in short, had any of those malignant-minded people, whom I have above enumerated, any being previous to the initiators and inventors of their perversity. For Valentinus came to Rome in the time of Hygius, flourished under Pius, and remained until Anicetus. Cerdon, too, Marcion's predecessor himself arrived in the time of Hyginus, who was the ninth bishop. Coming frequently into the Church, and making public confession, he thus remained, one time teaching in secret, and then again making public confession; but at last, having been denounced for corrupt teaching, he was excommunicated from the assembly of the brethren. Marcion, then, succeeding him, flourished under Anicetus, who held the tenth place of the episcopate. But the rest, who are called Gnostics, take rise from Menander, Simon's disciple, as I have shown; and each one of them appeared to be both the father and the high priest of that doctrine into which he has been initiated. But all these (the Marcosians) broke out into their apostasy much later, even during the intermediate period of the Church" (*Adv. Haer.* 3.4.3). Irenaeus's understanding, therefore, is that heresy was a novelty which came after orthodoxy.

23. For a recent treatment of the Tatian's presumed heresy, see Hunt, *Christianity in the Second Century*.

150–215 CE), Hippolytus (ca. 160–235), Eusebius (ca. 260–339 CE), and Epiphanius (ca. 315–402 CE).[24]

While the goal here is not to resolve this enduring debate on the orthodoxy or lack thereof of Tatian, it is significant to note that some solutions have been based on the understanding that what is known as "orthodoxy" is a later consolidation rather than an early development (as the classical view insists). Hunt, for example, after assessing the question in great depth, bluntly concludes:

> I believe that in Irenaeus' charge of Valentinianism and Encratism, we are faced with political propaganda rather than a true representation of Tatian's views. At the end of the second century some fairly major changes were happening within western Christianity; the stream that was to become known as "orthodoxy" was beginning to achieve dominance, and the consolidation of that power involved an increasing intolerance towards more extreme Christian groups and a formalization of the content of mainstream Christian teaching. It may well have been Tatian's disillusionment with the direction that the mainstream church was taking that led him to leave Rome. At any rate, Irenaeus' claim of apostasy seems a convenient way to discredit Tatian whilst retaining the teaching of Justin for orthodoxy.[25]

It is clear from Hunt's conclusion that she sees Irenaeus's charge as being motivated by political convenience rather than an actual apostasy on the side of Tatian.[26] Hunt's historiography, itself a reflection of historiographies that challenge the classic theory, is not the only solution to this issue.

A fair assessment of the actions of both Irenaeus and Tatian must be conducted within the ecclesiological climate in which they both operated.

---

24. Hunt, *Christianity in the Second Century*, 20–21. See also Clem. *Strom.* 3.82.2; Hipp. *Refutation of all Heresies* 8.16; 10.8; Eus. *EH* 4.29.3, and Epiph. *Panarion* 46.1.6–7. See also Koltun-Fromm, "Re-Imagining Tatian." For a current defense of the presumed Tatian's apostasy, see Grant, "The Heresy of Tatian," 62–68.

25. Hunt, *Christianity in the Second Century*, 177.

26. Hunt, *Christianity in the Second Century*, 177. Hunt further explains: "The Tatian of the heresiological literature thus became a tool to discredit the extreme asceticism of the East, in much the same way that the legendary Paul of Acts and the Pastoral Epistles became a tool to reclaim the historical Paul. Tatian, who was not present to defend himself, has therefore been remembered as the conceited and mutinous pupil of Justin Martyr, who followed the teachings of orthodoxy whilst his master was alive but was drawn towards heresy after Justin's death, and in his arrogance returned to his homeland to set up his own school" (Hunt, *Christianity in the Second Century*, 178).

As L. W. Barnard has demonstrated, the best way to resolve this issue is to take a closer look at some of the chronological issues in Tatian's life that proponents of the Tatian "arch-heretic" utilize to reach their conclusions. Based on a critical remark made by Eusebius in *HE* 4.16.7 concerning the timing of the martyrdom of Justin as well as Tatian's composition of the *Oratio*, he argues that the composition of this work can be dated around ca. 160 or a few years before.[27] That is, while most current scholars give a late date for the Tatian's composition of *Oratio*, itself the assumed indication of his changed theology, Barnard joins an older generation of scholars who argue for an early date of the work. These scholars dated the work earlier (same time as Justin Martyr's I *Apology*, ca. 150–55).[28] He writes:

> In contrast to this later date for Tatian's *Oratio* an older generation of scholars held that the work was composed about the same time as Justin Martyr's I *Apology* (c. 150–155) and was, therefore, evidence for his views while he was still a member of the Church in Rome. In considering this divergence it is worth while to examine what Tatian and Eusebius actually say. In *Orat.*, xix Tatian says: "Crescens, who made his nest in the great city, surpassed all men in unnatural love, and was strongly addicted to the love of money. Yet this man, who professed to despise death, was so afraid of death, that he endeavoured to inflict on Justin and, indeed, on me, the punishment of death, as being an evil (ἐδεδίει τὸν θάνατον ὡς καὶ Ἰουστίνον καθάπερ καὶ ἐμὲ ὡς κακῷ τῷ περιβαλεῖν πραγματεύσασθαι)." Because by proclaiming the truth he (i.e. Justin) convicted the philosophers of being gluttons and cheats.[29]

The point that Barnard makes here is pivotal. He argues that those who make the case that the *Oratio* was written later when Tatian apostatized after Justin's death are misreading this key phrase: καθάπερ καὶ ἐμὲ ("and indeed, on me"), a phrase that Eusebius evidently *omits* in his retelling the story. "Whereas Tatian says that Crescens was plotting Justin's death," writes Barnard, "*and, indeed his own*, Eusebius admits [omits, rather], καθάπερ καὶ ἐμὲ."[30] He further notes that the "reason for this

---

27. Barnard, "The Heresy of Tatian—Once Again," 3.

28. Barnard, "The Heresy of Tatian—Once Again," 2. See also Zahn, *Forschungen Zur Geschichte Des Neutestamentlichen Kanons*.

29. Barnard, "The Heresy of Tatian—Once Again," 2. For a recent evaluation of the so-called "Tatian heresy," see Mutie, *Death in Second-Century Christian Thought*, 138–41. For Tatian, I am using Chadwick and Whittaker, *Tatian: Oratio Ad Graecos*.

30. Barnard, "The Heresy of Tatian—Once Again," 2–3.

omission is not far to seek. He wished to show that Tatian actually referred to Justin's death (which Justin had anticipated in II *Apol.*, iii) whereas καθάπερ καὶ ἐμὲ, in *Orat.*, xix, by linking Justin and Tatian together as subjects of Crescen's machinations, implied that Justin (like Tatian) was still alive."[31] Thus, according to Barnard, rather than seeing *Oratio* as having been written after the death of Justin, a critical reconstruction of his life places its authorship to a time when both Tatian and Justin were still alive. Barnard clarifies that Tatian, in this comment, "does not say that Crescens succeeded in effecting that death of Justin, but only that he was *endeavouring* to bring this about."[32] But what does one make of Irenaeus's accusation and its subsequent mentions?

Once again, Barnard's reconstruction of Tatian's life leads to the conclusion that, contrary to Hunt's argument, "Irenaeus' accusation of heresy on the part of Tatian is based on ignorance and not politics." Indeed, Barnard doubts this clear-cut ascription of heresy on Tatian by Eusebius, given what Eusebius himself understands the personage of Tatian to be. He writes:

> This clear-cut theory of Tatian's heresy, however, runs somewhat counter to Eusebius's statement that Tatian had been the teacher of Rhodon, after the death of Justin—and that Rhodon combated Marcion's heresy—and that Tatian had also written a book of questions in which he promised he would explain what was hidden and obscure in the biblical writings, which no doubt included the Old Testament. Rhodon himself had promised that he would give solutions to these questions in a book of his own (Eus., *H.E.*, v. 13). This is very odd if Tatian was an arch-heretic and follower of Marcion's brand of Gnosticism for there is no suggestion that Rhodon and Tatian held divergent views. Then Eusebius (*H.E.*, v. 28) quotes an author opposed to the heresy of Artemon who mentions Tatian as one of the brethren older than Victor's time who wrote in defence of the truth and against the heresies then prevailing.[33]

Thus, from both Tatian's correct biographical chronology as well as Eusebius's comments elsewhere, it is clear that Tatian can be exonerated from his presumed descent to heresy after the death of his teacher, Justin. As for Irenaeus, again, Barnard is correct in observing that it is

---

31. Barnard, "The Heresy of Tatian—Once Again," 3.
32. Barnard, "The Heresy of Tatian—Once Again," 2.
33. Barnard, "The Heresy of Tatian—Once Again," 3.

better to suggest that Irenaeus, "who knew that on leaving Rome Tatian had embraced extreme views, had no real knowledge when the *Oratio* had been written and assumed that it belonged to the time when Tatian had defected, after Justin's death, from what Irenaeus believed was a once 'orthodox' faith which he had learnt from Justin."[34] Of course, this conclusion is a far cry from ascribing malice or political motivation as the basis for Irenaeus's accusation. As I argue elsewhere, "if we understand Irenaeus correctly, it is incorrect to argue that only ecclesial politics were behind his accusation of heresy on the side of Tatian."[35] Indeed, as Brian Daley explains, "Irenaeus' theology is essentially a plea for the validity of ordinary Christian life and tradition."[36] And, therefore, "anything that seems to threaten this proposition is treated with suspicion by him." And, for Tatian, it is clear that he was concerned with holiness in the church as well.

The goal of this brief exposé is to illustrate how the early church developed and held tenaciously to the classical theory of early church history. In addition to both Clement and Irenaeus, perhaps the best proponent of this theory in the early church was Tertullian. For example, this was the key theme in his apologetic against Marcion, who, according to him, "lost the God Whom he had found by the extinction of the light of his own truth. [Thus] He was a deserter before he became a heretic."[37] Further, Tertullian made it clear that this order, that is, truth preceding heresy, was actually prophesied in the Scriptures. As Turner explains, Tertullian "evidently has in mind passages like our text from the farewell sermon of St. Paul to the elders of the church of Ephesus."[38] Again, "In line with passages like 1 Corinthians xi, 19, he can even find a place for heresy within the economy of the Divine Providence as an instrument for the testing and approving of Christians."[39] Thus, not only was this chronological order predicted in the Scriptures, but, as such, it also plays a role in the outworking of God's divine purposes, argues Tertullian.

Another tenet of this theory that Turner brings up, and which is very much consistent with the other points, pertains to perceived motives

---

34. Barnard, "The Heresy of Tatian—Once Again," 3–4.
35. Mutie, *Death in Second-Century Christian Thought*, 141.
36. Daley, *Hope of the Early Church*, 141.
37. Tertullian, *Adv. Marc.* 1.1., quoted in Turner, *Pattern of Christian Truth*, 5.
38. Turner, *Pattern of Christian Truth*, 5.
39. Turner, *Pattern of Christian Truth*, 5.

of the heretics. That is, as far as this theory is concerned, the fathers of the church could just as easily identify the motives of the heretics as well. According to them, the heretics "were motivated by a spirit of faction, or a restless quest for novelty."[40] Thus, the heretics "are puffed up with pride or intoxicated by the position accorded to a Christian leader."[41] Indeed, according to the fathers, heresy "is adultery, and their doctrines adulterous or adulterated."[42] However, not all church fathers were on board with this simplistic explanation, by Tertullian, of the motives for the heretics in the early church. That is, "where Tertullian discovers a vicious principle, Origen finds a right principle misapplied."[43] However, novelty, as a key motive for the heretics, is a consistent theme among these early heresiologists.

Two more other salient points deserve mention here. The first point pertains to the comparative spread of heresy in the early church. According to Turner, this theory argues that heresy was restricted to relatively few places in the early church, "whereas the Catholic Church, as the name implies, is world wide."[44] However, as it will be pointed out, this claim has been a major point of contest among scholars of early Christianity. Turner comments that while "it [the argument] could be used with telling effect against the Donatist schism, a second-century Marcionite or fourth-century Arian would have found it less convincing."[45] Thus, as St. Jerome is noted as complaining pertaining to Arianism, "the Nicene

---

40. Turner, *Pattern of Christian Truth*, 5.

41. Turner, *Pattern of Christian Truth*, 5.

42. Turner, *Pattern of Christian Truth*, 5. Turner further elucidates Tertullian's arguments concerning the roots of heresy: "The root of heresy is personal choice exercised in matters where it does not apply. The personal system of the heresiarchs are contrasted with the teaching of the Apostles who had 'no faith of their own' and did not choose what they believed. In his apologetic against Marcion the term *electio* becomes almost a synonym for heresy. The other motive to which he calls special attention is the spirit of restless curiosity concerning the faith. Here the heretics seem to have claimed scriptural support from the Domical precept, 'Seek and ye shall find' (St. Matt. Vii, 7; Luke xi, 9), or the injunction to search the Scriptures recorded in the Fourth Gospel (St. John v, 39). In each case Tertullian restricts the range of the saying to the immediate Gospel context; it is simply addressed to the Jews who during the ministry of our Lord were uncertain whether He was the Messiah" (Turner, *Pattern of Christian Truth*, 6; see also Tertullian, *Praescr.* 8–12).

43. Turner, *Pattern of Christian Truth*, 6.

44. Turner, *Pattern of Christian Truth*, 7.

45. Turner, *Pattern of Christian Truth*, 7.

Competing Early Church Historiographies 19

Faith stood condemned by acclamation. The whole world groaned, and was astonished to find itself Arian."[46] This issue will be revisited later.

Finally, and consistent with the other points raised, Turner's most significant point pertains to the early church's perception of the origin of heresy. For many of the church fathers, heresy emerged from the philosophers. While a lot more will be said on this, especially as Gnosticism is considered, Tertullian's comments, once again, should be brought to bear here. Concerning Valentinianism (one school of Gnosticism), Tertullian comments, "Indeed the heresies are themselves instigated by philosophy. From this source came the Æons, and the Trinity of man in the system of Valentinus, who was of Plato's school."[47] Tertullian, then, cleverly shows the origins as well and the genealogical spread of Marcionism based on the classical theory, as he writes:

> From the same source came Marcion's better god, with all his tranquillity; he came of the Stoics. Then, again, the opinion that the soul dies is held by the Epicureans; while the denial of the restoration of the body is taken from the aggregate school of all the philosophers; also, when matter is made equal to God, then you have the teaching of Zeno; and when any doctrine is alleged touching a god of fire, then Heraclitus comes in. The same subject-matter is discussed over and over again by the heretics and the philosophers; the same arguments are involved. Whence comes evil? Why is it permitted? What is the origin of man? And in what way does he come? Besides the question which Valentinus has very lately proposed—Whence comes God? Which he settles with the answer: From *enthymesis* and *ectroma*. Unhappy Aristotle! Who invented for these men dialectics, the art of building up and pulling down; an art so evasive in its propositions, so far-fetched in its conjectures, so harsh, in its arguments, so productive of contentions—embarrassing even to itself, retracting everything, and really treating of nothing! Whence spring those "fables and endless genealogies."[48]

Tertullian concludes his discussion concerning the philosophical sources of heresy by offering his widely-quoted and often misunderstood

---

46. Jerome, *Dial. adv. Lucif.* 19. For this, I am using Jerome and Fremantle, *The Principal Works of St. Jerome*.

47. Tertullian, *Praescr.* 7. For Tertullian's work here, I am using Tertullian, Roberts, and Donaldson, *Latin Christianity: Its Founder, Tertullian: I*.

48. Tertullian, *Praescr.* 7.

and misapplied caution against relying too much on the philosophies for knowledge of God. He writes:

> What indeed has Athens to do with Jerusalem? What concord is there between the Academy and the Church? What between heretics and Christians? Our instruction comes from the porch of Solomon, who had himself taught that the Lord should be sought in simplicity of heart. Away with all attempts to produce a mottled Christianity of Stoic, Platonic, and dialectic composition! We want no curious disputation after possessing Christ Jesus, no inquisition after enjoying the gospel! With our faith, we desire no further belief. For this is our palmary faith, that there is nothing which we ought to believe besides.[49]

In other words, Tertullian wrote these terms as part of a larger section dealing with the genealogy and progression of heresies. As Nicholas Wolterstorff argues, rather, Tertullian's comments were part of his rhetorical argument against the deception of heretics, since, according to him, Greek philosophy was at the root of all heresies.[50] "Were Tertullian living in our own day," Wolterstorff continues, "his list would be much longer: be done with Kantianized Christianity, with Hegelianized Christianity, with deconstructionist Christianity. Be done with them all. The stance of the Christian toward all attempts at 'worldly wisdom' must be unrelenting opposition."[51] And, therefore, as already argued, Tertullian addressed the question of the origin, priority, and spread of early heresy using the classical theory.

CONCLUSION

As this chapter concludes, it is clear that what Turner named the "classical view" was the view of the early church fathers who dealt with the question of the origin, priority, and spread of heresy in the early church. For these church fathers, heresy originated from the unguarded study

---

49. Tertullian, *Praescr.* 7. For a recent analysis of this comment by Tertullian, see Wolterstorff, "Tertullian's Enduring Question." See also Eusebius, *EH*, 5.28.14, where Hippolytus seems to have made the same point when he wrote in so-called Little-Labyrinth as follows; "To study Euclid is for some of them [the Artemonites] a labour of love. Aristotle and Theophrastus are reverenced; even Galen in like manner is worshipped by some of them" (quoted in Turner, *Pattern of Christian Truth*, 8).

50. Wolterstorff, "Tertullian's Enduring Question," 283.

51. Wolterstorff, "Tertullian's Enduring Question," 283.

of all kinds of Greek philosophy. While the question of the origins of especially Gnosticism, the most significant heresy in the early church, will be dealt with later, according to these fathers, in keeping up with the classical view, heresy "was thought to be an alloy forged from Hellenistic philosophy and apostolic tradition."[52] This is the essence of the classical view: heresy was the distortion of truth, was always subsequent to it in terms of its priority, and, finally, it was the minority position as far as its spread is concerned.

However, while the classical view had been the standard historiography of the early church for the most part, some fissures began to be noticed especially with the rise of modern historical and critical methods of reading both Scripture and early church history, a development that has been most observable in the last five hundred years. Even Turner himself, while evaluating the classical view, noted that some proponents of the classical view understand that orthodoxy was actually not static in those earliest times. Rather, "orthodoxy demonstrated aspects of fluidity; therefore heresy cannot be defined essentially as a deviation from an unchanging norm."[53] However, the nature of these aspects of fluidity and how to account for them have been major bones of historiographical contention. Frankly, this is what occupies the remainder of this book. However, instead of treating them as isolated themes, this book traces these historiographies in a historical manner in the following chapters. It begins with Ferdinand Christian Baur (1792–1860) and ends with Bart Ehrman (1955–). Additionally, as will be demonstrated, there seems to be an attempt to move beyond Ehrman in the field of early church historiography. This attempt will also be highlighted.

---

52. Bingham, "Development and Diversity," 49.

53. Bingham, "Development and Diversity," 48n22. Bingham further explains that modern interpreters see the classical theory as having failed to account for doctrinal development even within orthodoxy itself. He writes: "The classical position is also challenged by orthodoxy's development. Shorter, simpler affirmations gave way to fuller statements; theologians revered in one age were replaced by the theological rock stars of another; doctrinal emphases normative at one time and place were assessed as intolerably imbalanced by another. Therefore, what appeared to Turner as such obvious diversity and development in early Christian thought brought him to the following perspective. The patristic theological journey to decipher the meaning of the One and the Many in relation to the Christian God (the problems of Trinity and Christology) indicates shifts in the composition of orthodoxy. Orthodoxy in the fourth and fifth century differed from that in the second. Even in the same century measurements of orthodoxy for different doctrines varied in terms of degrees of completeness and debate" (Bingham, "Development and Diversity," 48n22).

CHAPTER 2

CHRISTIAN FERDINAND BAUR AND HIS CONTEMPORARIES

"Hegelian" Historiography

INTRODUCTION

THE PREVIOUS CHAPTER BRIEFLY examined the early church historiography that had dominated Christianity for her first 1500 years and which Turner named the "classical theory." However, as it was observed, major historiographical fissures began to emerge, especially in the last five hundred years. Indeed, scholars in this area have justifiably noted increased attention to the question of early church history, especially on the question of the relationship between orthodoxy and heresy since the emergence of modern historical-critical methods of reading Scripture. Expectedly, these methods have spilled over to other, related areas such as early church history.

As a result of these developments, there have been many studies whose main goal is to respond to these changes. However, as one peruses the available literature, it becomes clear that the majority of these tend to pick up the discussion from the extremely influential "Bauer thesis" (see chapter 4).[1] Very few works seem to establish and analyze what seems to be an early church historiographical trajectory which, although it

---

1. While a complete list of works relating to the "Bauer thesis" is provided in chapter 4, some works need to be highlighted here. These include (but are not limited to): Köstenberger and Kruger, *Heresy of Orthodoxy*; Desjardins, "Bauer and Beyond," and McCue, "Orthodoxy and Heresy."

demonstrably begins earlier, reaches its concrete state in the thought of Ferdinand Christian Baur (1792–1860). Among the very few that attempt to trace this trajectory, mention should be made of Robert W. Yarbrough's *Clash of Visions: Populism and Elitism in New Testament Theology*.[2] In this work, Yarbrough argues that most of the graduate-level education in the area of biblical studies (and related fields) has been heavily influenced by historical criticism (what he calls "elitist"), an approach that has created a dissonance between graduates from these academic institutions and most Christians in the church benches who adhere to a "populist" understanding of the Bible.[3] Elucidating further on the origins of the "elitist" reading of the Scriptures, Yarbrough comments:

> I have in mind the enterprise that bloomed in the German Enlightenment (with a prehistory long before then). This approach to the New Testament took its bearings especially from G. E. Lessing (1729–1781) and Immanuel Kant (1724–1804), and then F. C. Baur (1792–1860) and the Tübingen school, and later the history of religion school, and eventually the grand synthesis of New Testament presented by Rudolf Bultmann. From this movement have arisen scores of books entitled "theology of the New Testament" or the like, particularly in Germany, and studies contributing to a synthetic grasp of the whole of New Testament teaching, history, and sometimes both.[4]

This paragraph by Yarbrough is almost a textbook summation of this chapter. In other words, these developments that he sees as having taken place in the field of New Testament studies, and having their impetus in German Enlightenment, are also evident in the area of early Christian

---

2. Yarbrough, *Clash of Visions*.

3. Yarbrough defines the terms "elitist" and "populist" this way: "By elitist I refer to a tradition arising in the wake of the Reformation, but with ideological resemblance to much earlier movements like Gnosticism and pagan-like skeptics like Celsus, who rejected popular reading [of the Bible] . . . which has existed since the first century, and read the Bible in the light of contrasting, and often hostile convictions" (Yarbrough, *Clash of Visions*, 25). And concerning the term "populist" Yarbrough writes, "By populist in this book I mean primarily two things: (1) Populist Christianity refers to the movement whose reading of the Bible . . . has been under attack by academicians since at least the seventeenth century . . . A 'populist' reading of Scripture is one that continues to privilege Scripture [as opposed to the 'elitist' position] . . . (2) More positively, populist Christianity as I am defining it refers to groups affirming the view of God, the world, and the church's identity and mission more clearly derivable from the Bible and representative of historic Christianity" (Yarbrough, *Clash of Visions*, 22–23).

4. Yarbrough, *Clash of Visions*, 18.

history. Thus, in a similar manner, this chapter (and the entire book) will attempt to do to with early Christian history what Yarbrough does here with the Scriptures: trace the development of the historical-critical approaches, emphasizing the genealogical connections of the key thinkers.[5] As such, the chapter will demonstrate and explore how F. C. Baur and his contemporaries utilized Hegelianism in the study of the emergence and development of early Christianity, setting the pace for subsequent generations of critical scholars of the history of the early church.

A PREHISTORY OF CHRISTIAN FERDINAND BAUR: THE FORMATION OF THE CLOUDS

James C. Livingston introduces his brief discussion of the life, thought, and work of F. C. Baur by observing that "F. C. Baur is widely considered the most important theologian of the nineteenth century, at least until the work of Adolf von Harnack later in the century."[6] Livingston adds that Baur was a very prolific author during his lifetime. "His prodigious output," he writes, "was equivalent to the writing of a four-hundred page-book every year for forty years."[7] Indeed, Baurian scholarship is littered with these kinds of accolades. Even before Livingston, Claude Welch had considered Baur "the greatest historian of the church and theology in the nineteenth century (at least until Harnack), who first and most fully developed the idea of a 'historical theology' and in whom, it has been said, 'the truly historical investigation of primitive Christianity and the New Testament is fist established.'"[8] In addition, in his preface to the German edition of an anthology of essays on Baur entitled *Ferdinand Christian Baur and the History of Early Christianity*, Martin Bauspiess writes, "Ferdinand Christian Baur ... may be regarded as one of the most resolute scholars of the development of historical-critical research in the

---

5. There are many works, especially in the area of New Testament theology, that have responded to this "elitist" approach from more "populist" underpinnings. These include (but are not limited to): Ladd, *Theology of the New Testament*; Guthrie, *New Testament Theology*, Marshall, *New Testament Theology*, and Schreiner, *New Testament Theology*.

6. Livingston, *Modern Christian Thought: The Enlightenment*, 127.

7. Livingston, *Modern Christian Thought: The Enlightenment*, 128.

8. Welch, *Protestant Thought in the Nineteenth Century*, 155. See also Hodgson, *Ferdinand Christian Baur*; Hodgson, *Formation of Historical Theology*.

nineteenth century."[9] Finally, while this list of accolades accorded to Baur is not exhaustive, Christophe Chalamet's laudatory introductory remarks of this giant scholar crown them. "Ferdinand Christian Baur (1792–1860)," he writes, "is undoubtedly one of the giants of historical-criticism in theology."[10] He adds that some people "call him 'the father of historical theology' since, with him, for the first time, a New Testament theology was presented 'on the basis of a fully critical evaluation of the sources and reconstruction of early Christian history.'"[11] But who was Baur? What were his views that proved to be so groundbreaking in the area of historical criticism of both the Bible and early Christian history? The beginning point towards answering these questions is a brief examination of Baur's prehistory.

Although Baur is primarily known for his biblical scholarship (on the New Testament canon), he actually came up with one of the oldest alternatives to the classical theory of early church historiography. As it will be shown here below, Baur came up with the "Tübingen hypothesis" primarily to explain the rise of early Christianity. In a truncated manner, William Varner explains this hypothesis this way:

> Baur maintained that early Jesus-faith was characterized by a conflict among Jewish believers, some of whom desired to maintain ties to Judaism and so maintain Christianity as a *particularist* religion, and Gentile believers (along with some Hellenistic Jewish Christians) who desired to sever ties with Judaism in order to make the new faith a *universalist* religion. The conflict

---

9. Bauspiess, "Preface," vi.

10. Chalamet, *Challenge of History*, 123.

11. Chalamet, *Challenge of History*, 123. It should be noted that all these accolades do not necessarily indicate an agreement with Baur's thought here. Indeed, not all Baur scholars pamper him this way. For example, in a brief comparison of F. C. Baur and the more conservative New Testament scholar Adolf Schlatter, Yarbrough argues that once you remove miracles in the Bible (as Baur did and Schlatter did not), there is nothing left for pastors to say at funerals. Yarbrough sees this contrast ironically displayed in the grave markings of these men. He writes on a page with pictures of the tombstones of both: "It is worth noting the respective heavenly hopes attested to by F. C. Baur's grave marker when contrasted with the tombstone of an equally brilliant and prolific New Testament who viewed the biblical documents as early and authentic. The first tombstone, that of Baur, gives no suggestion of Christian identity or heavenly hope, unless it would be the deceased's title *Theologiae*. The second, that of Adolf Schlatter, calls the observer to core Christian themes and to the Scriptures. The Bible verse on the cross is from John 7:37 of the Luther translation: 'Wen da dürstet, der komme zu mir und trinke!' English Bible readers know it in this form: 'If anyone thirsts, let him come to me and drink'" (Yarbrough, *Clash of Visions*, 52).

was spearheaded by Peter, head of the Jewish-Christian faction, and by Paul, head of the Gentile/Hellenistic faction. In the end there was no clear winner, but what emerged was a historical compromise that melded into what became the early "catholic" church.[12]

While a fuller exploration of this thesis will be made as it relates to its impact in the development of critical early church historiography, the point being highlighted here is that such conceptions had been undertaken even before Baur.

In terms of this thesis (and especially as it applies to the NT), David Rensberger demonstrates that Baur was not the first one to postulate it. That is, even before Baur came to the picture, others had postulated a kind of "Jewish-Pauline" controversy and later compromise. "But Baur," he writes, "in one matter . . . was anticipated to a certain extent by the biblical critic and theologian Karl August Credner."[13] Rensberger explains that Credner saw early Christianity as seen in the thought of Justin Martyr as having already distanced itself from Paul and reverted back to Jewish Christianity. "It was Credner's opinion," he writes, "that Justin Martyr was under the influence of Jewish Christianity, and that one symptom of this was a distance from the Apostle Paul. Even Credner was not the first to posit this, having been preceded by F. A. Stroth in 1777, and by G. Rosenmüller and others."[14] In other words, according to Credner, Justin already shows evidences of having divorced himself from Pauline Christianity, pointing to "Justin's complete silence about Paul and Paul's letters as an indication of his covert inclination toward Jewish Christianity rather than the 'freiere Paulinische Lehre.'"[15] Thus, it seems that even before Baur came onto the scene, from both his contemporaries such as Credner and his predecessors such as Stroth, historical-critical approaches especially to the New Testament and early Christianity were being tested out.[16] However, by all estimations, it was Baur, who O. W. Heick and J. L. Neve describe as "one of the most eminent representations of the intellectual nobility of Germany in the university of the world,"[17]

12. Varner, "Baur to Bauer," 95.
13. Rensberger, "As the Apostle Teaches," 3.
14. Rensberger, "As the Apostle Teaches," 3.
15. Rensberger, "As the Apostle Teaches," 4.
16. For a complete exploration of these trajectories, see Neill and Wright, *Interpretation of the New Testament*.
17. Heick and Neve, *History of Christian Thought*, 2.124.

Christian Ferdinand Baur and His Contemporaries

who propelled historical-critical approach to its greatest heights in the areas of dogma, the history of Christianity in the first few centuries, as well as the history of the New Testament Canon.

F. C. Baur: His Life, Work, and Thought

One of the most interesting exercises is to trace how scholars treat F. C. Baur and his influence in the fields that he addressed in his lifetime. That is, while, on the one hand, some argue that his influence has waned and he should be relegated to the dustbin of history, others see him as having a continuing influence in current scholarly discussions. Concerning the former, for example, while recognizing the impact of the Tübingen hypothesis, Ehrman also comments that "no one subscribes to the precise views of Baur and the Tübingen school today."[18] As well, Varner reaches the same conclusion, writing; "Despite the towering erudition of Baur, there few today who follow his views."[19] On the other hand, a few others have insisted that the ghost of Baur is powerfully present in modern German theological scholarship. Neill and Wright, for example, observe that "One of the curious features in German theology is that no ghost is ever laid [to rest]. A century after his death Baur still walks abroad, and echoes of his ideas are found in all kinds of places."[20] As well, Yarbrough sees the recent appearance of a major anthology entitled *Ferdinand Christian Baur and the History of Early Christianity* (2014) as clear evidence that Baur still deserves our attention.[21] And, elsewhere, he treats Baur's continued influence under what he describes as the "Baur-Wrede-Bultmann" approach to the study of the New Testament.[22] This work sides with the latter concerning Baur's importance. Of course, it would be a mistake to argue that the New Testament scholars noted above who see Baur's influence as waning also see this happening to all the views that Baur held. Indeed, both Ehrman and Varner see his views especially on the book of Acts as relevant. "But the basic point," writes Ehrman, "is widely recognized that Acts, like the Gospels, is driven a theological agenda that

---

18. Ehrman, *Lost Christianities*, 172.
19. Varner, "Baur to Bauer," 96.
20. Neill and Wright, *Interpretation of the New Testament*, 62.
21. Yarbrough, *Clash of Visions*, 47.
22. Yarbrough, *Salvation Historical Fallacy*, 1–58.

sometimes affects its historical accuracy."[23] On his side, Varner comments that Baur's "shadow is still cast over the study of Christian history in its earliest period, however, particularly manifested in the continued skepticism toward the tendential bias of the book of Acts."[24] Clearly, therefore, Baur's influence continues. But who was he?

While a full excursion into his biography is impossible here, a few highlights are in order.[25] Baur "was born near Stuttgart, Germany, in 1792 and was educated at the Blaubeuren seminary and at Tübingen University."[26] Although he briefly taught at the same seminary (1817–26), it was his teaching at Tübingen University that occupied the rest of his life. However, before his ideas finally matured, Baur underwent an interesting historiographical voyage in his scholarship. Most of this academic voyage took place in his many years of teaching at the University of Tübingen. As Peter Hodgson notes, although Baur had studied at the lower theological seminary in Blaubeuren, it was after he entered the then-relatively conservative evangelical seminary at the University of Tübingen that his ideas began to develop.[27] During his time of studying, Baur's influence was generally from the conservatives. However, this was to significantly change when he returned to the school as a member of the faculty in 1817.[28] At Tübingen, his views, fueled by several influences, took a major turn from conservatism.

While, as many historians note, the greatest influence came from Schleiermacher, Schelling, and Hegel, there were also other thinkers who influenced him along the way. For example, according to Steven Goetz, one such early influence on Baur was Ernst Bengel, himself grandson of the most notable New Testament critic, Johann Albrecht Bengel.[29] Indeed, this influence began even earlier, when Baur was a student at Tübingen before returning as a faculty member. Goetz further evaluates Bengel's influence upon Baur during his four years of study, writing;

---

23. Ehrman, *Lost Christianities*, 172.

24. Varner, "Baur to Bauer," 96.

25. For a helpful biography of Baur, see Goetz, "Historical Consideration." See also Hodgson, *Formation of Historical Theology*; Hodgson, "Rediscovery of Ferdinand Christian Baur."

26. Livingston, *Modern Christian Thought: The Enlightenment*, 127.

27. Hodgson, *Ferdinand Christian Baur*, 3.

28. Hodgson, *Ferdinand Christian Baur*, 3.

29. Goetz, "Historical Consideration," 52.

> It was Bengel's open minded willingness to give consideration to speculative theological thought in his treatment of historical theology that first stimulated Baur's interest in philosophical theology, and although Bengel's lectures were not steeped in erudition, nevertheless, their suggestiveness, sensibility and tastefulness worked in Baur's mind to create a keen interest in historical theology and its problems.[30]

However, while Baur's interest in historical theology and its problems (really, historiography) was created through the lectures of Bengel, most of the lasting influence, as already noted, came from Fredrick von Schelling, Friedrich Schleiermacher, and Georg Wilhelm Friedrich Hegel.

Schelling's influence on the young Baur began to be noticed during his professorial years at the lower seminary at Blaubeuren. While it is hard to pinpoint a specific time period in Baur's life when he directly came across the ideas of Schelling (as well as those of Fichte), that Schelling had great impact on him, is clearly evident in his later writings. Again, although most of the information concerning the process of this influence is anecdotal, when all was said and done, the influence had clearly taken place. Goetz writes concerning the anecdotal nature of this influence:

> It was probably during his years at Tübingen that Baur first came into contact with the ideas of Fredrick von Schelling. The first hint that this was the case comes from a letter from Ferdinand's brother Friedrich August Baur written to Eduard Zeller which suggests that Baur studied both Fichte and especially Schelling while still a student at Tübingen. Although Baur himself has left no indication that he studied Schelling at so early a time, there is external evidence to at least make this plausible. This evidence is primarily based on the fact that a new professor joined the Tubingen theological faculty in 1811, A. K. A. Eschenmayer, whom Zeller describes as a "freund der schellingischen Naturphilosophie" [friend of Schelling's natural philosophy]. It is Zeller's contention that Baur would naturally have had at least some exposure to Schelling's philosophy through him. But as both Zeller and Hodgson are aware of, when Eschenmayer began lecturing in the summer of 1812, Baur had already completed the requisite two-year philosophical course and would not, therefore, have heard him in the course of his normal studies. There is therefore no hard evidence, to suppose that Baur was already moving out of his supernaturalistic theological stance

---

30. Goetz, "Historical Consideration," 52.

through the influence of Fichte and Schelling while at Tubingen. Later, of course, Schelling had a great impact on Baur's thought as is clearly evident in his writings.[31]

Although Schelling's thought cannot be fully evaluated here, it would suffice to point out that his influence upon Baur pertained to his perception of history as revelation itself. As Goetz comments further, "From Schelling, Baur derived a fundamental perception of history as revelation itself, a perception which effectively began to undermine his earlier supernatural view-point."[32] Overall, Schelling's main contribution to history pertained to the issue of the relationship between the "Idea" and its manifestation (thus, *idealism*).[33] For Baur, church history is the tracing of the actualization of the Idea in the movement of the church. "If it is right to speak of an Idea of the church, then that Idea, like any other," Baur wrote, "must possess within itself the living impulse to go out from itself and to become actualized in a series of manifestations that can be regarded as various aspects of the relation that exists generally between the Idea and its manifestation."[34] Baur fleshed Schelling's ideas as he came into contact with the thought of Hegel. However, a word needs to be said concerning Baur's interaction and criticism of his other influence, Friedrich Daniel Ernst Schleiermacher.

Schleiermacher (1768–1834), who is sometimes referred to as the father of theological liberalism, according to Chalamet, "undoubtedly ranks among the most significant theologians between the sixteenth-century Protestant Reformers and the towering figures of theology in the twentieth century."[35] To some extent a contemporary of Baur, Schleiermacher is further described by Livingston as "the most important Protestant theologian between John Calvin and Karl Barth."[36] Further, Livingston argues that Schleiermacher "carried out a 'Copernican revolution' in theology as consequential as Kant's in philosophy."[37] His most consequential works are *On Speeches: Addressed to Its Cultured Despisers*

---

31. Goetz, "Historical Consideration," 52–53.
32. Goetz, "Historical Consideration," 109–10.
33. For more information, see Schelling, *Vorlesungen Über Die Methode*.
34. Hodgson, *Ferdinand Christian Baur*, 242. For a good argument that German idealism owes its greatest impetus in the thought of Schelling and not Hegel, see Medley, "History Is Divine Art," 59–76.
35. Chalamet, *Challenge of History*, 93.
36. Livingston, *Modern Christian Thought: The Enlightenment*, 93.
37. Livingston, *Modern Christian Thought: The Enlightenment*, 93.

(1799), *Brief Outline of Theology as a Field of Study* (1811, 1830), and *Der christliche Glaube* (*Christian Faith*—1821–22). So, what aspects of Schleiermacher's thought did Baur find helpful? How did he interact with them?

Although Schleiermacher is best known for his definition of religion in terms of a "feeling" in an attempt to sew together what Immanuel Kant so severed with his demarcation of noumena and phenomena, he is also "the first scholar to give academic lectures on the life of Jesus, first in 1819 and then four more times in the ensuing years, at the University of Berlin . . . His lectures, however, were published in 1864, nearly thirty years after his death, amidst a flurry of books, some of them sensational, on the historical Jesus."[38] As he studied the Gospels and the life of Jesus through a historical-critical approach, Schleiermacher concluded that "we cannot achieve a connected presentation of the life of Jesus."[39] This and other conclusions would prove attractive to Baur.

Baur's interaction with Schleiermacher was interesting. Schleiermacher, who, as noted above, is known as the father of theological liberalism, understood the "essence" of religion to be feeling of the infinite and eternal. He chastised those who approached religion from a rationalistic perspective, arguing that such an approach betrays a shallow understanding of religion that is only focused on the "external and dispensable husk concealing the real essence of religion."[40] He writes, for example, in his *On Religion: Speeches to Its Cultured Despisers*:

> Why do you not regard the religious life itself, the first of those pious exaltations of the mind in which all other known activities are set aside or almost suppressed and the whole soul is dissolved in the immediate feeling of the Infinite and Eternal? In

---

38. Chalamet, *Challenge of History*, 93.

39. Chalamet, *Challenge of History*, 93. Chalamet further helpfully summarizes Schleiermacher's thought this way: "With his scholarship, Schleiermacher demonstrated that it is possible to combine deep, rigorous constructive theological reflection with a no-less rigorous and deep interest in historical criticism. It is an understatement to say that Schleiermacher's historical scholarship has not stood the test of time in the same way his dogmatic work has, and several critics have objected that his presentation of the life of Jesus is dogmatically and philosophically determined . . . But the significance conferred to historical and critical scholarship in his *Brief Outline*, in relationship to Scripture as well as the Christian tradition up to the present, is quite remarkable and still worth pondering today" (Chalamet, *Challenge of History*, 93). For Schleiermacher's ideas, see Schleiermacher, *On Religion*.

40. Livingston, *Modern Christian Thought: The Enlightenment*, 95.

such moments this disposition you pretend to despise reveals itself in primordial and visible form. He only who has studied and truly known man in these emotions can rediscover religion in those outward manifestations.[41]

In reducing religion to "feeling," Schleiermacher himself shows his affinity for German romanticism, a movement that sought to curtail the reducing of experience to mere rationalism. Rather, "Romantics were unwilling to reduce experience either to an abstract rationalism or narrow, scientific empiricism. Experience involved much that eluded both analytical reasoning and scientific experiment, including the power of imagination, feeling and intuition."[42] Further, "common to the Romantics was the feeling that behind Nature some Spirit or Vital Force was at work. This Spirit in Nature, call it God if you will, was not the Deist watchmaker God, dispassionately transcendent over creation."[43] It is this romanticism that Baur found attractive.

However, while Baur found this form of romanticism attractive, which views the essence of religion as feeling, he nevertheless felt that it was still incomplete, just as he had done with Schelling's idealism. "However," writes Goetz concerning Baur's interaction with the views of both Schelling and Schleiermacher, "Baur never read either of these philosophers uncritically, notwithstanding their tremendous influence upon him at his most formative stage of scholarly development."[44] Rather, "later, Baur looked on the work of these men as too subjective."[45] Thus, he had to turn elsewhere for a complete development of his historiography.

Baur turned to Hegel. Indeed, the influence of Hegel on Baur cannot be overstated.[46] While it is impossible to evaluate Hegel's thought fully here, a few comments are in order, especially those that are pertinent to the concern of this work. Particularly, Hegel's dialectic philosophy comes to mind here. According to Hegel's historiography;

---

41. Schleiermacher, *On Religion*, 15.

42. Livingston, *Modern Christian Thought: The Enlightenment*, 84.

43. Livingston, *Modern Christian Thought: The Enlightenment*, 85. See also Randall, *The Making of the Modern Mind*.

44. Goetz, "Historical Consideration," 110.

45. Goetz, "Historical Consideration," 110.

46. While Baur's reliance on Hegel is not a disputed issue in scholarship, surprisingly, Baur himself denied that he was Hegelian in any sense (see Baur, *Ausgewählte Werke in Einzelausgabe*, 313, quoted in Varner, "Baur to Bauer," 96n18.

> The principle of the movement of history must rather be understood as "the concrete universal, thinking Spirit [Geist], whose immanent moving principle is in the nature of thinking itself, and which strives toward freedom of its self-consciousness in the single individuals who are the living members of the organism of history."[47]

According to Hegel, as it was the case with Schleiermacher, this Spirit, which is broader than either "God" or "man," "describes that quality of conscious Being which God and man have in common, yet exemplify in different modes."[48] According to him, history is the outworking of this Eternal Spirit in nature. He writes, for example, in *The Philosophy of History*, concerning the nature of his historical investigation;

> It must be observed at the outset, that the phenomenon we investigate—Universal History—belongs to the realm of the *Spirit*. The term "World" includes both physical and the psychical Nature. Physical Nature also plays its part in the World's History, and attention will have to be paid to the fundamental natural relations thus involved. But Spirit, and the course of its development, is our substantial object. Our task does not require us to contemplate Nature as a Rational System in itself—though in its own proper domain it proves itself such—but simply in its relation to the *Spirit*.[49]

Therefore, it is out of this conception of history as the mirroring of the interworking of this Spirit that Hegel derived his dialectic philosophy of history. Indeed, it is this dialectic view of history that Baur borrowed.

From Hegel, "Baur derived a model in which both History and Idea, both Subjectivity and Objectivity, were considered in close relation without either taking precedence."[50] In other words, "Idea and History appeared in dialectical relationship to one another and together were considered as the means by which the development of the Spirit's self-consciousness becomes actual."[51] For Baur, therefore, Hegel's dialectical method was the best way to understand especially the early church. Thus, as Livingston notes, following Hegel, Baur saw "the process of historical development as the temporal working out of the Idea or the Divine Spirit

---

47. Hodgson, *Ferdinand Christian Baur*, 21–22.
48. Hodgson, *Ferdinand Christian Baur*, 22.
49. Hegel, *Philosophy of History*, 16.
50. Goetz, "Historical Consideration," 110.
51. Goetz, "Historical Consideration," 110.

to full expression or self-manifestation."[52] Baur further "saw this historical movement of Spirit, which is not simply the process of abstract thought, as developing in a Hegelian-like dialectic of opposing movements."[53] Baur then applied his reworked Hegelianism to his understanding of church history.

Using Hegelian dialect philosophy of history, Baur "interpreted both the development of early Catholicism—as the synthesis of Jewish and Gentile Christianity in the primitive Christian community—and the great doctrinal controversies of the early centuries in terms of such a dialectical process of opposing tendencies."[54] Put in other words, Baur understood early church history to have proceeded "dialectically, with a thesis (in this case, Jewish Christianity) encountering an antithesis (Gentile Christianity), resulting then in a synthesis (catholic Christianity)."[55] Applying this theory into the entire dogmatic development, Baur further elucidates:

> The whole movement of dogma proceeds between two mutually opposing points, which should be brought together in the union of objectivity and subjectivity. On the one hand stands dogma in its objective truth before Spirit, whose task is to assimilate it into its subjective consciousness and to become ever more certain of its content; on the other hand, the absolute truth of dogma can only correspond to the equally absolute certainty of the subject within himself. Between these two poles the entire movement of dogma takes place as the unending work of Spirit struggling with itself, aspiring toward a free self-consciousness in the absolute content of dogma. Every new configuration of dogma is a new attempt by Spirit to become more certain of truth, to take deeper and more comprehensive possession of the content of dogma.[56]

In other words, Baur sees this pattern as continuing throughout the history of the church.

---

52. Livingston, *Modern Christian Thought: The Enlightenment*, 128.

53. Livingston, *Modern Christian Thought: The Enlightenment*, 128.

54. Livingston, *Modern Christian Thought: The Enlightenment*, 128. Sometimes the phrases "Petrine Christianity" and "Pauline Christianity" are used to indicate Baur's conception of this "thesis" and "antithesis" phase of the history of the early church.

55. Ehrman, *Lost Christianities*, 171.

56. Hodgson, *Ferdinand Christian Baur*, 305–06.

In contrast to the Roman Catholic view of history, which Baur judged to be "static," he "believed that the development of Catholicism and subsequently Protestantism were but steps in the development of the synthetic conception of the history of dogma which, in his own day, was coming to realization."[57] Thus, he saw the earliest period of Christian history as a period that was "characterized by 'dogmatic assertions, doctrinal determinations, and propositions of faith, all propounded as incontestable truths.'"[58] Further development, however, especially in the scholastic period, resulted in the church being more reflective and "increasingly restive in its bondage to external object, i.e., dogma, and begins to seek a way of mediation between objective dogma and himself." The result of this restiveness, argues Baur, is Protestantism. For Baur, therefore, the history of dogma progressed thusly: "Subject (thesis), in the first period, gives birth to Object (antithesis) and finally Subject, confronted by Object, finds a way of mediation with it whereby both become synthetically related."[59] He concludes concerning the place of Protestant Reformation in this dialectical scheme of the philosophy of church history and doctrinal development:

> Thus, through the Reformation the subject obtained for the first time the consciousness of his freedom, or the freedom of his self-consciousness, in relation to dogma. Dogma no longer confronted him in its externality and with the externally imposed authority of ecclesiastical doctrine; rather, it derived its significance only from the subject's knowing himself to be internally at one with divine truth, which he recognized as the essential content of dogma.[60]

But, as noted above, Baur sees this thesis-antithesis-synthesis pattern continuing in the subsequent Catholic-Protestant historical reality. "Thus," he writes, "the new period of dogmatic development inaugurated by the Reformation is the period of antithesis between Catholicism and Protestantism in which the religious and dogmatic consciousness shows itself to be divided and split asunder."[61] This is Baur's Hegelian historiography of church history.

57. Goetz, "Historical Consideration," 118.
58. Goetz, "Historical Consideration," 118.
59. Goetz, "Historical Consideration," 119.
60. Hodgson, *Ferdinand Christian Baur*, 304.
61. Hodgson, *Ferdinand Christian Baur*, 304.

The influence of Baur's historiography in dealing with the New Testament and the early church documents cannot be overestimated. Despite his protestation,[62] Baur is clearly recognized as the founder of the "Tübingen school," a specific group focused on a critical approach to the study of the New Testament as well as early church history.[63] Horton Harris explains that the Tübingen school was comprised of eight members: F. C. Baur, Eduard Zeller, Albert Schwegler, Karl Christian Planck, Karl Reinhold Köstlin, Albrecht Ritschl, Adolf Hilgenfeld, and Gustav Volkmar.[64] And, in terms of the school's central tenets, Darin Land summarizes:

> The members of the School were those who (1) accepted a "purely historical" method of interpretation and (2) made an "essential contribution to the historical development of the School." One distinguishing feature of the School is that it was the first to apply the historical-critical method from a definite historical viewpoint to the whole New Testament.[65]

While the school underwent a number of changes over time, the interest of this work here is in its initial stage identified by Land as "'preparation and emergence,' [and was] marked especially by the controversy surrounding Strauss' *Life of Jesus* and the resulting disagreement between Baur and Strauss."[66] I believe that this was the most significant phase of

---

62. Köpf, "Ferdinand Christian Baur," 3. "Ferdinand Christian Baur," Köpf writes, "long resisted connecting the term 'Tübingen School' with his name, as opponents did in the middle of the fourth decade of the nineteenth century" (Köpf, "Ferdinand Christian Baur," 3). As Baur states it, "I assume that my method of historical criticism is well known. Recently I have received the dubious honor of being named the founder and master of a new critical school. This is an honor against which—even if I were to take it more seriously than it is intended—I can only protest" (Baur, *Paulus, Der Aposte*, 1., vi, quoted in Köpf, "Ferdinand Christian Baur," 3).

63. Founded in 1477, Tübingen University (today known as Eberhard Karls University of Tübingen) has, since 1536, maintained a Protestant faculty.

64. Harris, *Tübingen School*, xvii; v. See also Land, "Synthesis Searching." For an early exploration of the issue, see Mackay, *Tübingen School and Its Antecedents*.

65. Land, "Synthesis Searching," 31.

66. Land, "Synthesis Searching," 31. Land further elucidates concerning these phases: "Harris identified three periods during the life of the School. The years 1835–1841 comprise the period of 'preparation and emergence,' marked especially by the controversy surrounding Strauss' Life of Jesus and the resulting disagreement between Baur and Strauss. 'Formation and consolidation' distinguished the time from 1842–1846. During this period, leadership was provided by Zeller under the patronage of Baur, and the journal *Theologische Jahrbücher* began to be published. The years 1847–1860 resulted in 'decline and dissolution.' After 1847 the Tübingen school's

Christian Ferdinand Baur and His Contemporaries

the Tübingen school, and the one whose ghost continued to rear its head in successive historiographers of the early church.[67]

Ulrich Köpf introduces D. F. Strauss by explaining that "David Friedrich Strauss became a student of Ferdinand Christian Baur (sixteen years his senior) during his residence at the lower seminary in Blaubeuren from 21 October 1821 to 27 September 1825."[68] While there were many other influences at the seminary on the young Strauss, it seems like it was Baur's teaching that impacted him the most. As Köpf elaborates, Baur "taught Greek and Roman prose writings, and to that end, ancient history and mythology at Blaubeuren."[69] Further, Köpf explains that, along many other things, Strauss learned two things in particular from Baur. He writes:

> Along with much else, Strauss learned two things in particular from Baur's teaching that would prove important for his own later work. First, he mentions that Baur introduced "the problem of Niebuhrian historical criticism, using Livy." The basis for this was the work in which the Danish financier Barthold Georg Niebuhr (1776–1831) published in his Berlin lectures on Roman history. In these lectures he offered for the first time a critique of the historiography of early Rome that was not simply a rebuttal of the traditional account but rather had its goal a new, critically refined picture of the events. These lectures made Baur aware of the distinction between the mere critic and the historian, which later proved to be of fundamental importance for his relationship with Strauss.[70]

Further, Köpf elucidates another impact of Baur's teaching on the young Strauss:

> Second, according to the Blaubeuren "Diarium" Baur offered a regular course on mythology in 1924 and 1925, which Strauss attended prior to his graduation. In his biography of Märklin,

---

influence diminished with the gradual dispersal of its members. During the 1850s Baur, Ritschl, Hilgenfeld, and Volkmar continued to propagate the convictions of the Tübingen school, but their individual perspectives brought disagreement to the extent that Ritschl and Hilgenfeld increasingly dissociated themselves from the school. When Baur died in 1860, the Tübingen School virtually came to an end" (Land, "Synthesis Searching," 31–32).

67. For a reception of Baur in Britain, see Paget, "Reception of Baur in Britain."
68. Köpf, "Ferdinand Christian Baur," 5.
69. Köpf, "Ferdinand Christian Baur," 6.
70. Köpf, "Ferdinand Christian Baur," 6.

> Strauss reports that Baur introduced "us to the higher mythology through Herodotus," and the teacher had his students "as it were take part in a voyage of discovery." "On his mythological journey, which at that time Baur undertook albeit without a proper compass, he touched on many shores indeed—a voyage from which, in an orderly way, he subsequently brought home such rich enduring fruits for German scholarship.["71]

Thus, without doubt, Baur's lectures had a significant and enduring impact on his student, Strauss (even though they would later disagree).

Strauss's own introduction to the world of scholarship came though the publication, when he was only twenty-seven years old, of his groundbreaking two-part work entitled *Life of Jesus* (*Das Leben Jesu*), which was "published in June and November 1835."[72] In this work, Strauss argued that the miracles of Jesus were not authentic. This is because, even though they are reported in the Gospels, the Gospels themselves "cannot be accepted as authentic."[73] Rather, these stories of Jesus "must be legends which gradually came to be believed and which were woven about the head of the Master by the devoted disciples."[74] In the preface to his fourth edition, Strauss makes clear his program in the project when he writes:

> The new point of view, which must take the place of the above, is the mythical. This theory is not brought to bear on the evangelical history for the first time in the present work: it has long been applied to particular parts of that history, and is here only extended to its entire tenor. It is not by any means meant that the whole history of Jesus is to be represented as mythical, but only that every part of it is to be subjected to a critical examination, to ascertain whether it have not some admixture of the

---

71. Köpf, "Ferdinand Christian Baur," 7.

72. Chalamet, *Challenge of History*, 107. According to Eduard Zeller, Strauss had a brief encounter with Hegel. "In October 1831," he writes concerning this encounter, "Strauss went to Berlin, in order to become personally acquainted with the men to whom he felt he owed the most as regarded his scientific life, and to enjoy their instruction; and in so doing, above all others, not even excepting Schleiermacher, he had Hagel in view. Scarcely, however, had he introduced himself to the great philosopher and attended his first lectures, than, on November 14, Hegel was suddenly carried off by cholera. Strauss heard of this event, which so sadly crossed his plans, from Schleiermacher, when he was paying him his first visit, and, startled by it, he exclaimed, to the evident displeasure of the host, 'It was for his sake that I came here!'" (Zeller, *David Friedrich Strauss*, 33).

73. Heick and Neve, *History of Christian Thought*, 2.123.

74. Heick and Neve, *History of Christian Thought*, 2.123.

mythical. The exegesis of the ancient church set out from the double presupposition: first, that the gospels contained a history, and secondly, that this history was a supernatural one. Rationalism rejected the latter of these presuppositions, but only to cling the more tenaciously to the former, maintaining that these books present unadulterated, though only natural, history. Science cannot rest satisfied with this half-measure: the other presupposition also must be relinquished, and the inquiry must first be made whether in fact, and to what extent, the ground on which we stand in the gospels is historical. This is the natural course of things, and thus far the appearance of a work like the present is not only justifiable, but even necessary.[75]

Thus, it is clear that Strauss sought to free New Testament studies from the shackles of "antiquated supernaturalism and naturalism."[76] This was the most critical work to appear on the life of Jesus in the history of the church up to that point.[77]

---

75. Strauss, *Life of Jesus*, xxix.

76. Livingston, *Modern Christian Thought: The Enlightenment*, 216.

77. The only other scholar who had highlighted what he thought to be irreconcilable discrepancies in the life of Christ up to that point was the German deist Hermann Samuel Reimarus (1694–1768). Ehrman writes concerning Reimarus: "The basis evidence for this point of view [the view by Reimarus, that the disciples began a religion contrary to what Jesus intended] involves some of the major points that Reimarus himself made: There are differences among the Gospel accounts that cannot be reconciled: Did Jesus die the afternoon before the Passover meal was eaten, as in John (see 19:14), or the morning afterwards, as in Mark (see 14:12, 22; 15:25)? Did Joseph and Mary flee to Egypt after Jesus' birth as in Matthew (12:13–23), or did they return to Nazareth (2:39)? Was Jairus's daughter sick and dying when he came to ask Jesus for help as in Mark (6:23, 35), or had she already died, as in Matthew (9:18)? After Jesus' resurrection, did the disciples stay in Jerusalem until he had ascended into heaven, as in Luke (24:1–52), or did they straightaway go to Galilee, as in Matthew (28:1–20)?" (Ehrman, *Lost Christianities*, 169–70). Livingston summarizes concerning the skepticism of Reimarus this way: "The most prominent of the German Deists was Hermann Samuel Reimarus (1694–1768), a professor of oriental languages in Hamburg. Only three of his works appeared during his lifetime, the most important being an essay entitled 'The Leading Truths of Natural Religion,' his deistical replacement for what he considered a discredited form of Christianity. At his death he left a four-thousand-page manuscript on which he had labored for twenty years. The work remained unpublished until the philosopher G. E. Lessing obtained permission from Reimarus's daughter to issue it on the condition that the name not be divulged. The manuscript was originally entitled *Apology for the Rational Worshippers of God*, but Lessing published only seven portions of it as *Wolfenbüttel Fragments* claiming that he had found the anonymous fragments at Wolfenbüttel where he was serving as librarian" (Livingston, *Modern Christian Thought: The Enlightenment*, 30).

Strauss's work had its goal to cast suspicion on the foundational stories of the life of Jesus. However, as Livingston notes, according to Strauss, "the Gospel writers were generally not guilty of fraudulent intention."[78] Rather, their mythological representation of the life of Jesus was based on Jewish messianic (eschatological) expectations. "Perhaps it may be admitted that there is a possibility of unconscious fiction," he writes, "even when an individual author is assigned to it, provided that the mythical consists only in the filling up and adorning some historical event with imaginary circumstances."[79] He further elaborates:

> Whatever view may be taken of the heathen mythology, it is easy to show with regard to the New Testament, that there was the greatest antecedent probability of this very kind of fiction having arisen respecting Jesus without any fraudulent intention. The expectation of a Messiah had grown up amongst the Israelitish people long before the time of Jesus, and just then had ripened to full maturity. And from its beginning this expectation was not indefinite, but determined, and characterized by many important particulars. Moses was said to have promised his people a prophet like unto himself (Deut. xviii. 15), and this passage was in the time of Jesus applied to the Messiah (Acts iii. 22; vii. 37). Hence the rabbinical principle: as the first redeemer (Goel) so shall be the second; which principle was carried out into many particulars to be expected in the Messiah after his prototype Moses. Again, the Messiah was to come of the race of David, and as a second David take possession of his throne (Matt. xxii. 42; Luke i. 32; Acts ii. 30): and therefore in the time of Jesus it was expected that he, like David, should be born in the little village of Bethlehem (John vii. 42; Matt. ii. 5 f.) . . . In no case could it be easier for the person who first added any new feature to the description of Jesus, to believe himself its genuineness, since his argument would be: Such and such things must have happened to the Messiah; Jesus was the Messiah; therefore such and such things happened to him.[80]

Therefore, while some other critics like Schleiermacher, "advocated for a 'pact' between scientific inquiry and faith, Strauss all but destroyed such endeavors by describing large segments of the Gospel narratives as 'mythical;' that is, imaginative formulations typical of premodern

---

78. Livingston, *Modern Christian Thought: The Enlightenment*, 218.

79. Strauss, *Life of Jesus*, 83.

80. Strauss, *Life of Jesus*, 83–84.

cultures that had not yet reached the level of conceptualization of rational thought."[81] However, his definition of "myth" is a question that continues to be debated.[82] In Hegelian idealism, Strauss, therefore, found the basis

81. Chalamet, *Challenge of History*, 107. Because of the critical nature of this work, it propelled Strauss to the limelight. However, as well, as Livingston notes, it also "destroyed any opportunities for further advancement in either the university or Church. J. C. F. Steudal, the conservative president of the theological college, succeeded in having Strauss removed from his post as lecturer" (Livingston, *Modern Christian Thought: The Enlightenment*, 215). Again, as Heick and Neve explain, Strauss's "radicalism was the cause for his removal from theology into a position of classical subjects. Declining to do this work he accepted a call as professor to Zuerich [sic]. But protests from the church soon caused him to be pensioned after which he lived the life of a private scholar" (Heick and Neve, *History of Christian Thought*, 2123). Similarly, Köpf summarizes concerning the effect of this publication on the life of Strauss: "The immediate consequence of this book was that—before even examining the first volume, and solely on the grounds of a bookseller's notice in the 'Swabian Chronicle' of the Schwäbischer Merkur on 6 June 1835—the Imperial Council for Studies in Stuttgart brought charges against Strauss on 11 June. Despite a noncommittal and cautious vote of the Inspectorate of the Tübingen *Stift*, Strauss was removed from his tutorial appointment on 28 July . . . Suffice it to say that for Strauss this was the beginning of the end of his ecclesiastical and academic career" (Köpf, "Ferdinand Christian Baur," 12). Even his teacher, F. C. Baur, noticed the impact of this work, commenting: "One must oneself have lived through the period in which Strauss's book appeared in order to have any conception of the reaction which it caused. Seldom has a work of literature produced such a great sensation so quickly and so universally, and summoned the forces of war with great excitement to a battleground on which the most varied parties opposed each other and raised the ardour of the conflict to the most intense passion. The Straussian *Life of Jesus* was the glowing spark by which the already long-collected tinder burst into blazing fame" (Baur, *Geschichte Der Christlichen Kirche*, 363, quoted in Harris, *Tübingen School*, 27. For a synopsis of Strauss's life and works, see Morgan, "Strauss, David Friedrich").

82. Neill and Wright perceptively write concerning Strauss and myth: "Strauss never defined too clearly what he meant by the mythical, and many woes have descended on theology through this lack of precision. The word 'myth' is commonly used in one of three connexions. A myth may relate to the doings of gods and other more-than-human beings; in many cases we can see that the myth is a rude and poetic attempt to understand the world, in fact, a kind of 'philosophy before philosophy.' Secondly, the word is used of those majestic tales, such as the early stories in Genesis, in which a profoundly religious understanding of the human situation, such as can hardly be conveyed than through such a tale, is made known to us. In the third place, as in the case of the Oedipus sequence, the myth may be a projection outwards of the human sense of man's inner problems as he wrestles with a dark and perplexing destiny. In none of these cases has the myth any direct connexion with history; and it makes no difference to the significance of the myth whether there is any basis in history for the tale or not" (Neill and Wright, *Interpretation of the New Testament*, 14). They further warn that "Nothing could be more dangerous than to use the term 'myth' without the clearest possible delimitation of the sense in which it is being used.

for his mythical interpretation of the New Testament. "Hegelianism," writes Van Harvey, "enabled him to think historically, which is to say, to discover a mentality different from his own or his contemporaries' in the New Testament; hence, the category of myth and devastating criticism of the supernaturalists and rationalists."[83] However, his affinity with Hegel was much more complex. That is, while, on the one hand, he saw Hegelian idealism, as noted above, helpful, on the other hand, "his idealism seduced him into an interpretation of myth that does vitiate his work as an interpreter of the texts; hence his fantastic concluding observation on dogma."[84] Indeed, in his *Defense of My Life of Jesus against the Hegelians*, Strauss is clear that his work was intended to go way beyond his (brief) teacher, Hegel. He writes:

> My whole critique of the life of Jesus grew out of Hegel's thesis that religion and philosophy have the same content, the first in representational [*Volstellung*] and the second in conceptual [*Begriff*] form. Here is how Hegel's school understood their master's words: The historical credibility of the gospel accounts is demonstrated by the fact that they convey, in representational form, true philosophical ideas. The actuality of history is understood to be derived from the truth of ideas. The whole critical part of the *Life of Jesus* was directed against this position . . . From the truths of ideas, said I, nothing can be derived concerning historical reliability. The latter must be judged solely in the light of its own laws, in accordance with the rules of events and the nature of accounts.[85]

In other words, as opposed to Hegel, Strauss argued that "positive history" and "philosophy" do not have the same content. For him, "the judgement about historical facts must . . . be separate from a priori philosophical or theological claims."[86] In so doing, Strauss was able to "put

---

At the very outset, we encounter one of the imperfections of the method of Strauss. The 'mythical' is used as the key to unlock all the mysteries of the Gospels; but in point of fact the Gospels are a phenomenon far too complex to be unlocked by any single key, especially when that key is itself so simplified and lacking in subtlety" (Neill and Wright, *Interpretation of the New Testament*, 15).

83. Harvey, "D. F. Strauss's Life of Jesus," 92.

84. Harvey, "D. F. Strauss's Life of Jesus," 92.

85. Strauss, *Gesammelte Schriften Von David Friedrich Strauß*, 177, quoted in Frei, *Eclipse of Biblical Narrative*, 336.

86. Livingston, *Modern Christian Thought: The Enlightenment*, 220.

the historical warrants for Christian faith in an uncertain foundation,"[87] something with which all who come after him and take the historicity of Christianity seriously must contend.

Finally, while many key and legitimate criticisms have been levelled against Strauss's ideas and methodologies by successive generations of scholars, his import in our tracing of the genealogical trajectory from Baur to Ehrman lays in his conception of the science of history (historicism).[88] The issue here is that of the relationship between his-

---

87. Livingston, *Modern Christian Thought: The Enlightenment*, 220.

88. Concerning these criticisms, two deserve mention here. Neill and Wright, for example, write: "In the first place, he [Strauss] had not subjected his sources, the Gospels, to any careful literary and historical criticism before beginning to work upon them. He had, for instance, played off John against the Synoptic Gospels, and the Synoptic Gospels against John, without taking serious account of the historical, literary and theological characteristics which separate John from the other Gospels, an account of which must be taken seriously if the use of historical source is not to lead to confusion . . . Secondly, Strauss overlooked the most obvious fact of all—the existence of the Christian Church. Here is a tremendous movement in history, which started in Palestine in the first century AD, which spread rapidly through the ancient world, and the spiritual impulses of which have not died away after so many centuries. How is all this to be accounted for? What was the power that launched the movement? What kind of a stone could it be that, once thrown into the pool of human existence, could set in motion ripples that would go on spreading until the utmost rim of life of the world had been reached? When Strauss has finished his critical work, and given us Jesus as he understands him to have been, has sufficient account been given of what lies at the origins of a great world movement? As Strauss understands it, Jesus lived only in the faith of disciples, and this faith was strong enough to create the belief in his resurrection. But the kind of Jesus who is indicated in Strauss's pages was not the kind of a person to create that kind of faith. The causes, suggested by Strauss, do not measure up to the consequences; something in the evidence that is of the greatest significance must somehow have been overlooked" (Neill and Wright, *Interpretation of the New Testament*, 19). Similarly, Livingston argues that "Strauss's work, it was soon shown, had many serious faults. Like many innovators, he carried his discovery too far. The historical material in the New Testament is more extensive than Strauss was wont to admit, and his rather narrow concern with the question of 'What really happened' blinded him to other important historical questions such as the meaning of the mythical narratives" (Livingston, *Modern Christian Thought: The Enlightenment*, 220). Indeed, some of this criticism came from no other than his brief teacher and fellow critic, F. C. Baur. While not going into the details that led to the fallout between Baur and Strauss, it is clear that Baur saw Strauss as going far in his skeptical and mythical approach to NT history. After highlighting the exchanges between both of these scholars, Köpf comments: "Baur spoke out with clarity . . . on behalf of historical criticism, but Strauss could not have been satisfied with what he wrote. To be sure, Baur defended him against the charge of demonization brought by the *Evangelische Kirchenzeitung* and by Eschenmayer, and he acknowledged their friendship. But when it came to concrete issues, he spoke without notable sympathy for his student, indeed

tory and the question of doctrinal development of Christianity. This is essentially the question being pursued in this work. In his two-volume follow-up work to *Leben Jesus* entitled *Die christliche Glaubenslehre in ihrer geschichtlichen Entwicklung und im Kampfe mit der Wissenschaft dargestellt* (*Christian Doctrine, Presented in Its Development and Conflict with Modern Science*),[89] Strauss "tried to demonstrate that traditional Christian faith is untenable through a critical analysis of the history of theology."[90] He, in other words, argued that the study of Christian religion must be a historical study. As Svensson elucidates, "A scientific study of the Bible is, according to Strauss, historical-critical in nature. And by the historical-critical method, he meant a rational, disinterested, and objective investigation exclusively controlled by the specific laws of history."[91] And, while Strauss, as noted above, saw others as such as Schleiermacher as having attempted to study religion scientifically, he regretted that they had only gone "half-way."[92]

Having achieved his purpose of putting "the historical warrants for Christian faith on an uncertain foundation,"[93] Strauss opened the door for scholars to begin to separate the essence of Christianity from what would

---

distanced himself from him, and claimed for his own part to hold on to the historically given, albeit evaluated critically, whereas he spoke very clearly about how Strauss 'calls into question the entire objective foundation of Christianity.' This is the basis for a constantly reiterated distinction between his own critical work and that of his student" (Köpf, "Ferdinand Christian Baur," 21). For more information about the some of the trenchant criticisms that Baur raised upon Strauss's handling of the Gospels and extreme negativity towards some of the NT data, see Hodgson, *Formation of Historical Theology*, 73–84.

89. Strauss, *Christliche Glaubenslehre*.

90. Svensson, "Theology for the Bildungsbürgertum," 45.

91. Svensson, "Theology for the Bildungsbürgertum," 39.

92. Strauss complained about Schleiermacher's approach in his review of his lectures this way: "Schleiermacher's treatment of the life of Jesus, insofar as it promised at the outset to commence without dogmatic presuppositions, cannot keep its word; to be sure, it liberated itself from some of the fetters of church prejudice, but by no means did it liberate itself from all. And if previous theologians were like the companions of Ulysses who stopped their ears against the Sirens of criticism, then Schleiermacher indeed kept his ears open, but had himself tied with cables to the mast of the Christian faith in order to sail past the dangerous island unharmed. His conduct is only half-free, therefore also only half-scientific. The truly scientific conduct is to engage in criticism unfettered and with open ears, in which case it will turn out that the entire legend of the Sirens was but the whisperings of the old sorceress Circe" (Strauss, *Christ of Faith*, 36–37).

93. Livingston, *Modern Christian Thought: The Enlightenment*, 220.

be considered uncritical accretions either by the apostles, Jesus, or early Christians. For him, the true meditation "must be just as much separation and division. It can only be accomplished through a process of smelting or fermentation whereby the slag and the dregs are eliminated, or rather eliminate themselves."[94] Indeed, according to Strauss, the New Testament scholar and historian of doctrine must be able to separate the "kernel" of the gospel message from the "husk" of mythical accretions. As Welch summarizes, "with the emergence of a freer spirit and the renewal of *Wissenschaft* in the humanistic period, the dissolution begins, in which both inner contradictions and the conflicts with the increasingly powerful philosophy and science are exposed, and the inner kernel of truth is disclosed."[95] This task of surgical separation of the "kernel" and "husk" is extended to the entirety of the early church by scholars, beginning with Adolf von Harnack (1851–1930) whose historiography I have designated "Hellenistic." These are addressed in the next chapter.

CONCLUSION

This chapter has surveyed two of the most significant innovators of the historical-critical approach to both the NT and early Christianity: F. C. Baur and his student, D. F. Strauss. Both scholars, while having some differences in terms of the *extent* of the application of the historical-critical approach to the study of the NT and the beginnings of Christianity, argued for the utilization of present historiography in the study of the past. Baur highlighted his Hegelian historiography in his approach to the development of doctrine in early Christianity. He saw an earlier setting where Christianity was dominated by the teachings of the apostle Peter

---

94. Strauss, *Christian Doctrine*, 1.70–71, quoted in Welch, *Protestant Thought in the Nineteenth Century*, 153.

95. Welch, *Protestant Thought in the Nineteenth Century*, 153. Welch concludes his study of Strauss by summarizing the impact of his method this way: "The historical outcome, then, in the dissolution of each of the major doctrinal creations, is just the (at present at least) unbridgeable opposition of dogma and science, faith and knowledge, in both form and content . . . Although Strauss's *Glaubenslehre* was overshadowed by the publication of Feuerbach's *Essence of Christianity* [*Das Wes des Christentums*, 1841), its importance should not be underestimated. . . . Now, with Strauss, theology has a history in a new way. The serious study of the history of theology, and especially of the problem of the development of doctrine, must begin, and dogmatics must justify itself in relation to historico-critical investigation" (Welch, *Protestant Thought in the Nineteenth Century*, 153–54).

(the thesis state). This was later substituted by Paul's Christianity (the antithesis). When both of these clashed, they produced early Catholicism (synthesis). However, his student, Strauss, took this approach a step further, utilizing the idea of "myth" in his approach to the Gospels. In his analysis, when all is said and done, almost nothing remains concerning the way Jesus' teaching and works are reported in the Gospels. And, as noted, judgment of the success and failure of their historiographies is divided. Commenting on the precise failure of Strauss, Harvey perceptively observes:

> Strauss's failure ... is that he does not properly grasp the nature of the historian's task. This is visible in his radical separation of two related obligations: to reconstruct the past and to make it intelligible to the present. It is at this point that the relationship between his Hegelian presuppositions and his historical work can best be seen and criticized. Such a criticism, in turn, may serve to illumine the more general problem of New Testament interpretation ... It is at precisely this point that Strauss's work is disappointing. He fails to discern the question to which the New Testament documents were intended as an answer. Rather, he comes to the New Testament with a different and alien question, with the result that the most crucial materials are dismissed as irrelevant for historical purposes and the positive meaning of the text.[96]

However, despite these methodological issues, both Baur and Strauss initiated a novel historiography whose trajectory extends to the present. Thus, it seems fair, in my opinion, to state that while Baur sneaked in through the historiographical door that Hegel opened, Strauss sprang both doors open for his posterity to walk through. With twists and turns, this genealogical trajectory continues.

---

96. Harvey, "D. F. Strauss's Life of Jesus," 205.

CHAPTER 3

Adolf Von Harnack and His Posterity

"Hellenistic" Historiography

INTRODUCTION

AFTER AN EXPLORATION OF Hegelian historiography of the New Testament and early Christianity, our attention now shifts to what I have designated "Hellenistic" historiography of the historian of doctrine, Adolf von Harnack (1851–1930) and his successors. By "Hellenistic" historiography, I am referring to the approach to the understanding of early church history that was offered and defended by the Berlin Ritschlian scholar Harnack. In an attempt to offer an alternative to the "classical theory" as the long-held historiography of early Christianity, Harnack, in conformity with his liberal tradition, "found the true link between experience and reality in the realm of moral and spiritual values rather than in the formal categories of an idealistic mystic."[1] He, in other words, attempted to extricate what he conceived to be the "kernel" of the gospel from the "husk" of Hellenistic accretions.

The goal of this chapter is to explore this kind of historiography. It will begin by locating Harnack within his scholarly context and situate his thought within the ongoing contest for early church historiography. This will be followed by a presentation of his contemporaries and successors, such as Martin Werner (1887–1964) and Rudolf Bultmann (1884–1976).

---

1. Turner, *Pattern of Christian Truth*, 126.

This discussion will pave the way for the epoch-making historiography of Walter Bauer (1877–1960), itself the content of chapter four.

ADOLF VON HARNACK: SCHOLARLY CLIMATE AND HISTORIOGRAPHY

As soon as one opens any kind of literature dealing with Adolf Harnack, all kinds of accolades emerge. Chalamet introduces him by noting that in his own day, Harnack was "the world's foremost historian of Christianity."[2] Similarly, Livingston estimates him this way: "No person in Germany had a greater influence on Protestant Christianity than Harnack."[3] He adds that this was mainly a result of his prolific writing, "which included over sixteen hundred books, monographs, and articles."[4] Neil and Wright, as well, comment that for "nearly forty years, he [Harnack] bestrode that world like a colossus, as Schleiermacher and Ritschl had done before him, and as, in a rather different way, Karl Barth did the years between 1930 and 1950."[5] And, on his part, W. H. C. Frend simply comments that "By any measure von Harnack (he was ennobled by the Kaiser in March 1914) is one of the 'greats' of European historical scholarship."[6] So, who was this man? What was his scholarly context? What was his historiography?

Adolf von Harnack was born "in the Baltic German university town of Dorpat (now Tartu in Estonia) on 7 May 1851."[7] He was the son of a pietist Lutheran university professor of theology (homiletics and historical theology at Erlangen), Theodosius Harnack. From his early years, Harnack decided to pursue his own academic path, different from his siblings. "While Harnack's twin, Axel, and two younger brothers were all to flourish in the professions," Frend writes, "he made up his mind before he entered Dorpat University in 1869 that he wished to be a theologian."[8] Livingston further explains that Harnack "was educated in Dorpat and Erlangen and in 1872 entered the University of Leipzig, where he completed

---

2. Chalamet, *Challenge of History*, 159.
3. Livingston, *Modern Christian Thought: The Enlightenment*, 286.
4. Livingston, *Modern Christian Thought: The Enlightenment*, 286.
5. Neill and Wright, *Interpretation of the New Testament*, 140.
6. Frend, "Church Historians," 84. See also Glick, *Reality of Christianity*.
7. Frend, "Church Historians," 84.
8. Frend, "Church Historians," 84.

the doctorate in Church history in 1873."[9] After debuting as Privatdozent at Leipzig in 1873, he went on to hold professorships in Giessen and Marburg. While he was appointed chair at the University of Berlin in 1888, this was delayed for several years due to a serious controversy as a result of his work entitled *History of Dogma* (see below). This matter was only resolved "by the Emperor William II's decision overruling the Church officials."[10] This began his long and productive career, which included multiple other appointments. Livingston summarizes concerning these:

> It is difficult to believe that a man of such scholarly erudition and productivity could also be a man of action, yet Harnack held many time-consuming administrative positions during his career. In 1876 he founded the *Theologischen Literaturzeitung* and for many years was its only editor. He served as Rector of the University of Berlin, and his counsel was frequently sought in the Ministry of Education. In 1906 he was appointed Director General of the Royal Library and in 1911 to the position of President of the Kaiser Wilhelm Foundation, established for the creation of numerous scientific research institutes. He was raised to the rank of the hereditary nobility in 1914 by Kaiser Wilhelm II, to whom Harnack was a friend and confidant. In 1921 Harnack was offered the post of German Ambassador to the United States, but he declined the honor.[11]

Above everything else, however, Harnack is best known for his affinity with the Ritschlian school of Protestantism. This affinity began to concretize as soon as he moved to Berlin. Chalamet notes that soon after this move, "he [Harnack] belonged to a small group of bright young scholars who considered Albrecht Ritschl, whose main works were being published in the 1870s, as the thinker showing the way for Protestant theology—namely, a way influenced by Luther's own writings rather than strict adherence to the Lutheran symbolic . . . documents."[12] Harnack became the greatest historian of doctrine in the Ritschlian school.

While the focus of the discussion here is not on Albrecht Ritschl (1822–89), known as the founder of the Ritschlian school of theology (theological liberalism), it is in order to briefly remind the reader that Ritschlianism was a major theological movement that dominated

---

9. Livingston, *Modern Christian Thought: The Enlightenment*, 286.
10. Livingston, *Modern Christian Thought: The Enlightenment*, 286.
11. Livingston, *Modern Christian Thought: The Enlightenment*, 286–87.
12. Chalamet, *Challenge of History*, 159.

Germany from 1875 to World War I and America from the turn of the twentieth century to the 1930s. As Livingston summarizes:

> The school is named after Albrecht Ritschl, whose writings influenced a generation of theologian who, though independent in many respects, reflected certain common tendencies that are traceable principally to Ritschl himself. By and large, the Ritschlian theologians turned aside from classical metaphysics or the investigation of the "universal foundations of being," in large part because it failed to make the crucial differentiation between the realm of nature and the spiritual life [*geistige Leben*], the life of persons. Consequently, they [the Ritschlians] rejected the speculative theology of the rationalists and their "proofs" of the existence of God. The Ritschlians also distinguished between religion and dogma and often associated the latter with metaphysics. They did not reject dogma but, like Schleiermacher, saw it as derived from religious experience and as protecting religious truth. They were highly critical of what they considered to be the sterile dogmatism of Protestant "confessionalists" ["dead orthodoxy"] and called reappropriation of the vital, living religion of biblical faith and of the Protestant Reformers, especially Luther. In addition, the Ritschlians were suspicious not only of speculative and dogmatic Christianity but of mystical and individualistic expressions of piety which they detected both in medieval Catholicism and in later German Pietism, and even with Schleiermacher and his followers. By contrast, the Ritschlians understood Christianity as essentially an historical and practical or moral religion, with emphasis on the historical revelation of Jesus Christ and on the theme of the kingdom of God—as the community of spiritually free persons—as the regulative principle of a Christian theology. Because they gave special attention to these matters, many consider Ritschlianism to be the perfect expression of Protestant Liberal theology. The identification is accurate, although the position of the Ritschlians has often been caricatured by their conservative and Neo-Orthodox critics. Many Ritschlians were theologians and historians of great erudition, whose ideas were more subtle and complex than it is generally realized.[13]

However, while Livingston's last comment here may be a matter of debate, John Hannah is certainly correct in his observation that, "While Schleiermacher is said to have founded an epoch, Albrecht Ritschl

---

13. Livingston, *Modern Christian Thought: The Enlightenment*, 270–71.

(1822–89) established a school of thought."[14] Thus, as a school of thought whose main goal was to bridge the Kantian chasm between the noumena and phenomena (and, therefore, find a place for religion [Christianity] in a post-Kantian age), Ristchlianism focused on morality as the essence of religion.[15]

Ritschl, attempting to move religion from "dull indifference or bold recklessness or Stoic imperturbability,"[16] sees the essence of Christianity especially "joined to its moral component—'labor for the Kingdom of God' in the fulfillment of one's vocation."[17] While Ritschl emphasized that Christianity is not a matter of doctrine, but personal realization, scholars agree that his most important focus is the moral aspect of redemption—the kingdom of God. Many of Ritschl's interpreters argue that, for him, "*the* Kingdom of God is the regulative principle"[18] of his theology. Indeed, for Ritschl, "Christianity is not principally a good already gained for the individual but a social ideal yet to be realized."[19] Ritschl contends:

> Justification, reconciliation, the promise and the task of the Kingdom of God, dominate any view of Christianity that is complete. The outstanding ethical character of this religion comes out in the fact that the *summum bonum*—the Kingdom of God—is promised only as the ground of blessedness, while at the same time it is the task to which Christians are called. Now the teleological relation of justification to this aim may be understood either directly or indirectly.[20]

Thus, for Ritschl, the kingdom of God is "the highest good of the Christian community."[21] However, this is "insofar as 'it forms at the same time an ethical ideal, for whose attainment the members of the community bind themselves together through their reciprocal action.'"[22] This action is the ethic of love. That is, for Ritschl, the "ethical realization of

---

14. Hannah, *Our Legacy*, 99.

15. For more information on Ritschl's thought, see Ritschl, *Christian Doctrine of Justification*. See also Hefner, *Albrecht Ritschl: Three Essays*.

16. Livingston, *Modern Christian Thought: The Enlightenment*, 280.

17. Livingston, *Modern Christian Thought: The Enlightenment*, 280.

18. Livingston, *Modern Christian Thought: The Enlightenment*, 280.

19. Livingston, *Modern Christian Thought: The Enlightenment*, 280.

20. Ritschl, *Christian Doctrine of Justification*, 35.

21. Livingston, *Modern Christian Thought: The Enlightenment*, 280.

22. Livingston, *Modern Christian Thought: The Enlightenment*, 280.

the Kingdom is rooted in the motive of love of God and one's neighbor."[23] In reaching this conclusion, Ritschl "accomplished a moralizing of Christianity according to the Kantian tradition."[24] It is within this scholarly climate that Harnack's doctrinal history emerged.

In pursuit of this concept of "love" as the ideal of the kingdom of God, Ritschl rejected the idea of "divine simplicity" as held by many medieval theologians. For him, "Since love is only thinkable in terms of a relationship, it follows as a logical consequence, from Ritschl's perspective, that the perfect, simple, immutable, and impassible God of Thomas Aquinas and other representatives of classical theism is incapable of love."[25] Indeed, Ritschl's rejection of classical theism seems to be based on this understanding of God. According to him, not only does classical theism undermine the personal God (since divine simplicity does not allow for love to exist), "it undermines the very idea of God's existence."[26] This is precisely the point where Harnack picks up the discussion.

---

23. Livingston, *Modern Christian Thought: The Enlightenment*, 280.

24. Heick and Neve, *History of Christian Thought*, 2.149. Heick and Neve further comment concerning the results of this "Kantianized" Christianity of Ritschl: "With such an appraisal of the Reformation it is quite comprehensible that Ritschl desired a new Protestant reformation and wanted to accomplish it through his teachings. Thus, in spite of his Biblical *Ansatz*, Ritschl effected a marked alteration of historical Christianity into the form of an ethical Neo-Protestantism. Through his opposition to metaphysics, he effected the transfer of Christ into an ideal man who was made by divine providence to be a perfect revealer of God's love and the transfer of the Person of the Holy Spirit into the conception of an impersonal power emanating from God and dwelling in the Church" (Heick and Neve, *History of Christian Thought*, 2.151). Once Christ is reduced to the title of the "revealer" of God's love, it is only a short ideological distance to Bart Erhman's claim that the theory that Jesus is God emerged in the early church (similar to ancient Judaism and Greek mythology in his Ehrman, *How Jesus Became God*).

25. Svensson, "Theology for the Bildungsbürgertum," 184.

26. Svensson, "Theology for the Bildungsbürgertum," 184. Ritschl's rejection of the classical conception of God seems to largely bypass the biblical concept of the Trinity (itself a tenet of Christian classical theism). As Svensson helpfully clarifies in a footnote that, in my opinion, needs to be at the forefront: "Ritschl's critique of classical theism seems to presuppose that God must stand in a relationship to one or more personal beings outside of himself in order to be able to love. That, however, is an opinion that sharply contrasts with the discussion of the inter-trinitarian relations and the emphasis on the movement of eternal love within the Trinity in many accounts of the doctrine of the Trinity in patristic, medieval, and reformation theology, and also in the recent so-called trinitarian renaissance or revival" (Svensson, "Theology for the Bildungsbürgertum," 184n608. For helpful discussion on intratrinitarian love, see Holmes, *Quest for the Trinity*).

Ritschl's objection to classical theology was based on his understanding that the essence of the gospel had been distorted by Greek ideas. This argument was "adopted and made more profound by his disciple Adolf von Harnack, who developed it into a full-scale attack on patristic and medieval theology in a number of works, not least in the multi-volume *Lehrbuch der Dogmengeschichte* (1886–89; *History of Dogma*)."[27] As noted, Harnack had immense interest in the history of the early church. This is evident from his massive study and writings focusing on this time of the church. As Frend notes, Harnack's time at Dorpat between 1869 and 1872 "gained him a gold medal for a study of Marcion, his first essay, like his last major work, devoted to the second century non-orthodox follower of Paul."[28] Most of this interest was generated through his interaction with his teacher at the Lutheran university at Leipzig, Moritz von Engelhardt (d. 1881). Frend further explains concerning von Engelhardt's influence on Harnack; "Engelhardt was to be a permanent influence, despite his early death, pointing to the universality of Christianity and its ability to make the ethical ideals of the non-Christian world its own."[29] In other words, Engelhardt directed Harnack to the possibility of the application of Ristchlianism in the area of early church historiography.

It is no wonder that, when Turner introduces Harnack's historiography, he starts by emphasizing that the "reconstruction of the history of Christian doctrine offered by the great Berlin savant was decisively influenced by his general theological position."[30] That is, as a Ritschlian, Harnack "found the true link between experience and reality in the realm of moral and spiritual values rather than in the formal categories and barren concepts of all idealistic metaphysic."[31] For Harnack, consistent with Ritschl's views, "the essence of Christianity lay in its spiritual message, and attempts to translate its Gospel into metaphysical terms were little short of a betrayal of trust."[32] Concerning Harnack's conception of doctrinal development in the early church (which, of course, is regression), Frend summarizes:

27. Svensson, "Theology for the Bildungsbürgertum," 184.
28. Frend, "Church Historians," 85. See, for example, Harnack, *Marcion*.
29. Frend, "Church Historians," 85.
30. Turner, *Pattern of Christian Truth*, 16.
31. Turner, *Pattern of Christian Truth*, 16.
32. Turner, *Pattern of Christian Truth*, 16–17.

Harnack believed that Church dogma in its conception and development was "the product of the Greek spirit rooted in the Gospels." It grew out of the religious attitudes and philosophies of the Greeks and Romans, principally Platonism, applied to the different and foreign structure of the Gospels. To a degree this development was inevitable once the Church had outgrown its Jewish origins and the eschatological and apocalyptic hopes in which it had been born. In the first two centuries the Catholics had been content to spiritualise and conserve the Old Testament aided by concepts derived from contemporary Greek philosophy. Their Gnostic opponents, on the other hand, under the leadership of able thinkers such as Basilides, Valentinus and Heracleon aimed at doing away with the Old Testament and "in a swift advance, attempted to capture Christianity for Hellenic culture" and Hellenic culture for Christianity. Their systems represented in Harnack's time-honoured judgement "the acute secularising or Hellenising of Christianity." Marcion, on the other hand, was not a Gnostic but a theologian who "succeeded in placing the greatness and uniqueness of redemption through Christ in the clearest light, and in beholding this redemption in the person of Christ, but chiefly in his death upon the cross." Marcion, the climax of Harnack's first volume, was a teacher of the Gospel and an authentic interpreter of Paul.[33]

As noted above, Harnack fleshes out his historiography in his key writings. For example, in his monumental lectures entitled *Das Wesen des Christentums (The Essence of Christianity)*,[34] he expressed the gospel in these terms: "God the Father, Providence, the position of men as God's children, and the infinite value of the human soul."[35] Summarized, therefore, according to Harnack, the essence of the gospel, in classic Ritschlian formulation, is that it is the Fatherhood of God and the brotherhood of all men.

33. Frend, "Church Historians," 89.

34. Harnack, *Wesen Des Christentums*. This book is a series of lectures that were originally delivered at the University of Berlin in the winter semester of 1899–1900. It went through multiple editions within a very short period of time. In it, Harnack defines his understanding of the gospel, writing: "If, however, we take a general view of Jesus' teaching, we shall see that it may be grouped under three heads. They are each of such a nature as to contain the whole, and hence it can be exhibited in its entirety under any one of them. *Firstly, the kingdom of God and its coming. Secondly, God the Father and the infinite value of the human soul. Thirdly, the higher righteousness and the commandment of love*" (Harnack, *Wesen Des Christentums*, 51).

35. Harnack, *Wesen Des Christentums*, 68.

According to Harnack, therefore, early church history is the record of the deterioration and regress in terms of doctrinal development. For him, "Christian theology had united itself to a Hellenistic philosophy which led to perverse metaphysic reflection and dogmatic definition."[36] As noted above, Harnack saw this as a betrayal of the "pure" gospel. This is because, as the gospel interacted with Hellenism and especially Gnosticism, it transformed itself into a system of doctrines. As he writes, "*They* [the Gnostics] *were, in short, the Theologians of the first century.* They were the first to transform Christianity into a system of doctrines (dogmas)."[37] Thus, the Gnostics' systems, for him, "represent the acute secularizing or Hellenizing of Christianity."[38] This understanding serves as the foundation for Harnack's historiography.

Harnack's historiography needs further elucidation. For him, although the gospel "entered into the world not as a doctrine, but as a joyful message and as a power of the Spirit of God,"[39] this soon changed. Rather, the gospel "stripped off these forms with amazing rapidity, and united and amalgamated itself with Greek science, the Roman Empire and ancient culture, developing, as a counterpoise to this, renunciation of the world and striving after supernatural life, after deification."[40] For Harnack, therefore, "Doctrinal development in early Christianity . . . meant change in the gospel, its misdirection, its impairment."[41] In other words, in its interaction with the "Greek soil,"[42] the gospel lost its original joyousness, only to be recovered later by Martin Luther during the Protestant Reformation of the sixteenth century.[43] Harnack identified traces of this Hellenization of the faith to two key sources. According to Lowe, these are "1) the Apologetic movement of the first century in which the

---

36. Bingham, "Development and Diversity," 49.
37. Harnack, *History of Dogma*, 1.228.
38. Harnack, *History of Dogma*, 1.227.
39. Harnack, *History of Dogma*, 7.272.
40. Harnack, *History of Dogma*, 7.272.
41. Bingham, "Development and Diversity," 49.
42. For an elucidation of Harnack's idea of the "Greek soil," see Rowe, "Harnack and Hellenization." Rowe explains: "Dogma in Harnack's view is something more than Church teaching, or even an intellectual interpretation of this teaching; it is a form of the Christian faith. Dogma is that species of Christianity which represents 'a work of the Greek spirit on the soil of the Gospel'" (Rowe, "Harnack and Hellenization," 78). See also Clouse, "Hellenization of Christianity."
43. Harnack, *History of Dogma*, 7.273.

principle of Greek philosophy—*logos*—was brought into unity with the content of Christian teaching and 2) the struggles in the second century against Gnosticism which forced the Church to commit itself to intellectual—that is, philosophically respectable—methods of defense."[44] However, Harnack saw Augustine as the one who concretized this process during his lifetime. He comments: "by Augustine the traditional dogma was on the one hand strengthened, *i.e.*, the authoritative force of it, as the most important possession of the Church, was intensified, while on the other hand it was in many ways expanded and recast."[45] And, concerning the progression of this process, he contends:

> That dogma which, in its conception and construction, was a work of the *Hellenic* spirit on the soil of the Gospel . . . continued to exist; in thinking of dogma one thought of a supernatural world and history, a knowledge that was revealed by God, that was embodied in unalterable articles of doctrine, and that conditioned all Christian life; but into its structure there were interwoven by Augustine in a marvelous way the principles of Christian life-experience, of the experience which he had passed through as a son of the Catholic Church and as a disciple of Paul and the Platonists, while the Roman Church thereafter gave to dogma the force of a great divine system of law for the individual and for Christian society.[46]

Therefore, it is clear that Harnack saw this development as having started with Paul and the Platonists and progressed slowly. As Turner writes, if "Gnosticism represents an acute form of the invasion of Christianity by Hellenism, orthodoxy implied a more gradual process, a low-grade infection by the same germ."[47] And, as noted above, Harnack fleshes this out in his massive *History of Dogma*.

However, as a historian clearly interested in the factuality of the events in history, Harnack realizes that he has to address two issues that pose a threat to his understanding of doctrinal development in the early church as regress. On the one hand, "Harnack follows the antimetaphysical tendencies of Kant and Ritschl."[48] This means that he "fears the danger that in the Church's dogma religious knowledge would supplant faith,

---

44. Rowe, "Harnack and Hellenization," 78.
45. Harnack, *History of Dogma*, 7.3.
46. Harnack, *History of Dogma*, 7.3.
47. Turner, *Pattern of Christian Truth*, 19.
48. Heick and Neve, *History of Christian Thought*, 2.134.

and in his opinion, dogma, in all its forms, contradicts the very principles of Christianity."[49] However, on the other hand, Harnack "recognizes the fact that even with Jesus the Gospel already possessed a clearly defined content which could not be formulated otherwise than in definite conceptions, that is in dogmas."[50] In order to navigate this conundrum, Harnack ends up rejecting dogma that he sees as formulated by the early church specifically. That is, he had to "admit that the Reformation not only permitted the dogma to continue but even filled the ancient formulas with a new religious significance for the Church."[51] However, Harnack is conscious of the fact that what he is attempting to propose goes beyond all similar previous attempts. Perhaps a bit boastfully, he aptly declares in the *History of Dogma*: "The task of describing the genesis of ecclesiastical dogma which I have attempted to perform in the following pages, has hitherto been proposed by very few scholars, and, properly speaking, undertaken by one only."[52] Again, he rightly believes that all future historians from that point onwards must reference him. He writes, "I must therefore crave the indulgence of those acquainted with the subject for an attempt which no future historian of dogma can avoid."[53] Thus, Harnack sees himself as charting a new territory in Protestantism. Even Turner, who came up with the clearest exploration of the classical view of early church historiography, concedes concerning Harnack's theory, compared to others, "is marked by a refreshing and scholarly moderation."[54] For many, therefore, Harnack is the demarcation between old and new Protestantism.

Finally, concerning his vision for how to rectify this mistake, after discussing how Luther and other reformers tried but without much success to return the gospel to its original form of not doctrine, but, as noted a "joyful message and the power of the Spirit," Harnack makes the final call on what Christendom must do in order to restore it. He writes in his concluding passage of the *History of Dogma*:

> Christendom must constantly go on to learn, that even in religion the simplest is the most difficult, and everything that is

49. Heick and Neve, *History of Christian Thought*, 2.134.
50. Heick and Neve, *History of Christian Thought*, 2.134.
51. Heick and Neve, *History of Christian Thought*, 2.134.
52. Harnack, *History of Dogma*, 1.ix.
53. Harnack, *History of Dogma*, 1.ix.
54. Turner, *Pattern of Christian Truth*, 19.

a burden upon religion quenches its seriousness ("a Christian's man's business is not to talk grandly about dogmas but to be always doing arduous and great things in fellowship with God," Zwingli). Therefore the goal of all Christian work, even of all theological work, can only be this—to discern ever more distinctly the simplicity and the seriousness of the gospel, in order to become ever purer and stringer in *spirit*, and ever more loving and brotherly in *action*.[55]

In a nutshell, this is Harnack's early church historiography. He, in other words, provides a Ritschlian interpretation of the early church, an interpretation that, according to Neve, "became normative in wide circles."[56] These "wide circles" become more evident as the study progresses.

In conclusion, while Harnack's historiography will be evaluated as the study continues, it will suffice to note here, as Turner argues, in his "Hellenistic" historiography, Harnack, while joining others who have interpreted the history of the church this way,[57] distinctively roots it in his Kantian-Hegelian-Ritschlian interpretation of Christianity. In so doing, however, he exaggerates the results of the marriage between Christianity and Hellenism. Turner correctly observes that the marriage between these two "did not leave either partner unaffected, but the evidence for radical modification of the Greek spirit by its new subject-matter is at least as strong as that which points towards the secularization of Christianity by the terms in which it came to be expressed."[58] In other words, this view of "one-way" street of impact only upon the gospel by "Greek soil" that Harnack argues for is not as clearly supported by the historical reality. Nevertheless, when Ristchlianism became the mainline version of Christianity for most of eighteenth, nineteenth, and twentieth centuries, Harnackianism was its imbedded historiography. Early church historians

---

55. Harnack, *History of Dogma*, 7.274.

56. Heick and Neve, *History of Christian Thought*, 154.

57. Concerning these comparisons, Turner explains: "Harnack constructs an interesting comparison between the development of Christian theology and the corresponding evolution of secular philosophy. The four stages of Christian theology—the Apologists, the Alexandrians, the Cappadocians, and the Pseudo-Dionysius—correspond to the elaboration of ancient philosophy through Seneca and Marcus Aurelius, Plutarch, Epictetus and Numenius, Plotinus and Porphyry, and finally, Iamblichus and Proclus. But such a comparison can [at best] only be rough and approximate" (Turner, *Pattern of Christian Truth*, 19–20).

58. Turner, *Pattern of Christian Truth*, 21.

during and after Harnack's lifetime have had to interact with his historiography in one way or another. While some rejected his accounting of the corruption of the pure gospel of Jesus as it interacted with Greek thought, others saw this as a viable early church historiography. However, what was common in these historians is the grand realization that it is impossible to ignore Harnack in constructing early church historiography. A few examples will suffice here.

Martin Werner and Rudolf Bultmann

Our trajectory in the presentation and analysis of the quest for early church historiography from F. C. Baur to B. Ehrman now turns to two scholars who interact with the Hanarckian tradition, Martin Werner (1887–1964) and Rudolf Bultmann (1884–1976). While the former is not as well-known as the latter in scholarly circles, he is no less significant especially in the area of early church historiography. They will be treated in this order here.

One of the most neglected yet influential early church historians is Martin Werner, who Turner describes as "brilliant" and "learned . . . professor of theology at Berne."[59] Werner was heavily influenced by his mentor, New Testament scholar and jungle doctor Albert Schweitzer. According to F. W. Gingrich, Werner belongs to the school of New Testament interpretation "known as *konseqent-eschatologisch (consistent* or *thorough-going eschatological)* . . . founded by Johannes Weiss (1892) and Albert Schweitzer (1901)."[60] In his introduction to his *The Formation of Christian Dogma*, Werner writes:

> If search be made in the literature of New Testament study during the last fifty years for a comprehensive, yet unifying, insight into the history of Primitive Christianity, such as will serve as the point of departure for history of doctrine, no other construction will be found which so notably achieves this, and at the same time with such attention to detail, as that which has come to be known as the "Consistent-Eschatological" interpretation. There are, of course, many essays in interpretation which are concerned with the solution of certain specific problems, but no such undertaking gives more attentive care and consideration to

---

59. Turner, *Pattern of Christian Truth*, 20.

60. Gingrich, "Review of *the Formation of Christian Dogma*." See Schweitzer, *The Mysticism of Paul*.

details, with equal concentration on the issue as a whole, than this "Consistent-Eschatological" approach.[61]

Therefore, Werner, instead of seeing the original (pure) gospel in the kingdom ideals as historians of the Ristchlian tradition like Harnack had done, sees it in the entirely eschatological message that Jesus preached. And, as noted, this understanding was in affinity with the views of both his mentor and teacher, Schweitzer, as well as that of Weiss. The reader may recall here that, in his *Quest*, Schweitzer had argued that Jesus' entire preaching and life was dominated by eschatological conceptions.[62] Again, as noted above, in what has come to be classified as "consequent" or "consistent" eschatology, Schweitzer "maintained that eschatological conceptions dominated not only Jesus' preaching, but his entire life."[63] And, while Weiss had focused on Jesus' preaching on eschatology as the essence of his message, Schweitzer saw it as the culmination of his life and ministry. For Schweitzer, however, Jesus was mistaken in his eschatological expectations by believing that the parousia would come with the preaching of the kingdom of God by the disciples that he sends according to Matthew 10. When the parousia did not take place, the so-called "postponement of eschatology" began.[64]

Following Schweitzer (and Baur), Werner argued that the "inner presuppositions of primitive Christianity which served as impulses for early doctrine"[65] were Jesus' catastrophic eschatology, something that Werner saw as being later deemphasized. Turner comments that, according to Werner, as "the hope of proximate Parousia waned, the Church was forced to undertake a complete re-orientation of her life and thought which Werner describes as *Enteschatologisierug* or 'De-eschatologizing.'"[66] For Werner, consistent with his historiography, therefore, later orthodoxy is "virtually an ersatz production with little or no real continuity with the faith of the New Testament."[67] And, in a conceptual agreement with Harnack, In this case, the progress of early Christianity was actually not

---

61. Werner, *Formation of Christian Dogmas*, 9. For the German edition on which this translation is based, see Werner, *Entstehung Des Christlichen Dogmas*.

62. Schweitzer, *Quest of the Historical Jesus*.

63. Hoekema, *Bible and the Future*, 309.

64. Hoekema, *Bible and the Future*, 291.

65. Bingham, "Development and Diversity," 50.

66. Turner, *Pattern of Christian Truth*, 20.

67. Turner, *Pattern of Christian Truth*, 20.

progress but regress. According to Werner, this change of de-eschatologizing Jesus' message "led to primitive Christianity's transformation into Hellenized dogmatism; the new eschatology of a more personal, realized type was not the 'consequence of [Christianity's] Hellenization,' but rather 'the cause of it.'"[68] As Bingham further summarizes;

> Thus, Martin Werner offered another way to understand development. For Werner, only the consistent eschatology of Albert Schweitzer (to whom he dedicated his book) accurately portrayed the viewpoint of primitive Christianity. The history of the development of Christian dogma, from his perspective, is the history of a departure from the eschatological expectation of authentic Christianity and the theological and Christological elements inherent within it. In doctrinal development, the primitive gospel is de-eschatologized and transformed into the dogmas of Catholic and, eventually, Protestant orthodoxy.[69]

Thus, even though some like Turner see Werner's starting point as differing "widely from that of Harnack," I would argue that the results are conceptually the same: doctrinal development in the early church evidences a regress from its pristine nature to something more corrupt, the contributing factors notwithstanding. And, consistent with other historiographies surveyed here, I agree with Turner that this reconstruction of early church history "cannot be accepted at its face-value." Evidently, its "root difficulty lies in the fact that it involves a radical recasting not only of the theology and experience of the early church but also of the New Testament itself." This recasting tends to produce more of a caricature than a correct explanation of developments of the church in her earliest history.

68. Bingham, "Development and Diversity," 50.

69. Bingham, "Development and Diversity," 50. Turner further elucidates concerning Werner's theory: "At the most optimistic valuation his theory needs to be scaled down to more modest proportions before it can even be seriously considered. The most awkward single fact which Werner tries vainly to take into account is that the early Church, so far from abandoning eschatology, even included it in her Catholic Creeds . . . The real problem, however, to which he calls our attention in its sharpest possible form is virtually identical with that which Harnack had already raised, whether the differences between the New Testament religion and the theology and life of the early church are in the main matters of transposition or translation or whether they involve the substitution of something qualitatively different—what Werner calls 'a Hellenistic-syncretistic Mystery religion laden with the decadence of postclassical religiosity strutting about in Christian dress'" (Turner, *Pattern of Christian Truth*, 22). In essence, it is a historiographical battle!

Rudolf Bultmann is a household name in biblical exegesis and systematic theology. Like Harnack, Bultmann's name is glazed with accolades from all kinds of sources. For example, introducing him, Chalamet notes that although there were other scholars who would be considered both exegetes and systematic theologians, Bultmann "was arguably among the most significant of them."[70] Reflecting on his existentialism as well, Neve comments that Bultmann is "the greatest exegete of the Barthians."[71] Turner, as well, introduces Bultmann by describing him as "the greatest and perhaps the most controversial theological figures of our time."[72] Finally (although the list is not exhaustive), Livingston and Fiorenza describe Bultmann as the only historian who "bridged the gulf between historical and philosophical theology as no other theologian had succeeded in doing in this century."[73] So, who was Bultmann and what role does he play in our quest here?

Bultmann was born in Wiefelstede, Lower Saxony, Germany. Like many other German thinkers of his day, Bultmann was "the son of an Evangelical Lutheran pastor."[74] He schooled at Tübingen University, Berlin, and Marburg. As expected, in his schooling, most of his professors were of Ritschlian school of thought, such as Harnack and Herrmann. However, as Livingston explains, Bultmann also studied under the biblical scholars such as "Gunkel, Jülicher and Johannes Weiss."[75] After his studies, Bultmann taught at Marburg in 1912. However, it was during his teaching at Breslau between 1916 and 1920 when he wrote his influential work entitled *Die Geschichte der synoptischen Tradition*.[76] In this work, it was clear that Bultmann was trying to situate himself between Ritschlian liberalism and Barth's dialectical theology. As Turner explains in terms of this comparison, "if Harnack was a declared Ritschlian, Bultmann is a thoroughgoing Existentialist."[77] He adds that there is "no connexion

---

70. Chalamet, *Challenge of History*, 203.
71. Heick and Neve, *History of Christian Thought*, 180.
72. Turner, *Pattern of Christian Truth*, 23.
73. Livingston et al., *Modern Christian Thought: The Twentieth Century*, 154.
74. Livingston et al., *Modern Christian Thought: The Twentieth Century*, 154.
75. Livingston et al., *Modern Christian Thought: The Twentieth Century*, 154.
76. Livingston et al., *Modern Christian Thought: The Twentieth Century*, 154. See also Bultmann, *Geschichte Der Synoptischen Tradition*.
77. Turner, *Pattern of Christian Truth*, 23.

between *Enteschatologisierung* of Werner and the *Entmythologisierung* of Bulmann."⁷⁸ Bultmann tries to locate himself in this midst, writing:

> It seemed to me that this new theological movement [dialectical theology], as distinguished from the "liberal" theology out of which I had come, it was rightly recognized that the Christian faith is not a phenomenon of the history of religion, that it does not rest on a "religious a priori" (Troeltsch), and that therefore theology does not have to look upon it as a phenomenon of religious or cultural history. It seemed to me that the new theology had correctly seen that Christian faith is the answer to the Word of the transcendent God that encounters man and that theology has to deal with this word and the man who is encountered by it. This judgment, however, has never led me to a simple condemnation of "liberal" theology; on the contrary, I have endeavoured to carry further the tradition of historical-critical research as it was practiced by the "liberal" theology and to make theological knowledge the more fruitful as a result.⁷⁹

Thus, Bultmann was very clear that his approach would be neither the one taken by the liberal theology nor that of the history of religion school.⁸⁰ But how different was his approach (if so), especially in his early church historiography, itself the subject of our inquiry here?

---

78. Turner, *Pattern of Christian Truth*, 23.

79. Kegley, *The Theology of Rudolph Bultmann*, xxiv.

80. Bultmann argued that the Ritschlians were shell-shocked by the conclusions of both Schweitzer's and Weiss's findings concerning the historical Jesus. This is illustrated by his recollected reaction of the Ritschlian Julius Kaftan after Weiss published his findings concerning the eschatological nature of Jesus' message, writing: "When I began to study theology, theologians as well as laymen were excited and frightened by the theories of Johannes Weiss. I remember that Julius Kaftan, my teacher in dogmatics in Berlin, said: 'If Johannes Weiss is right and the conception of the kingdom of God is an eschatological one, then it is impossible to make use of this conception in dogmatics'" (Bultmann, *Jesus Christ and Mythology*, 13.) For a critique of the view that Ristchlianism was seriously damaged by the apocalyptic critique of Weiss and Schweitzer, see Wyman, "Kingdom of God in Germany." It would be impossible, however, to deny that this criticism had some meaningful impact on Ritschlianism. As Svensson so perceptively observes, "If the apocalyptic critique never gave rise to the kind of despair usually associated with it, it seems, nevertheless, undeniable that many Ritschlians of the first generation experienced this interpretation of Jesus as a fundamental challenge. And in any case, as also Wyman hints at, it must be conceded that Weiss and Schweitzer from a systematic perspective dealt a blow at the heart of Ritschl's theology" (Svensson, "Theology for the Bildungsbürgertum," 114n368).

So far, it is clear that most of Bultmann's scholarship, was in the area of New Testament studies. "While Harnack was a scholar of equal eminence in the fields of New Testament theology and Church history," writes Turner, "and Werner makes his principal contribution to the history of Christian doctrine, Bultmann is primarily a New Testament theologian."[81] But, as Turner further notes, Bultmann almost accidentally landed himself into the question of early church historiography.[82] However, as a New Testament scholar, it was almost inevitable for Bultmann to talk about early church history.

Conceptually, Bultmann's historiography embraces the evolutionary view advocated by F. C. Baur. But, contrary to Baur, who saw this process as beginning in the differing gospel understandings of Peter and Paul, Bultmann "finds the beginning of the evolution within the New Testament itself."[83] According to him, the New Testament unveils four main strata of history this way: "the teaching of Jesus Himself, the Messianism of the primitive Christian community, the Kerugma of the Hellenistic Church, and the infiltration of Gnostic themes."[84] For Bultmann, however, the most significant of these strata is the aspect of gnostic themes and their impact on the gospel. He introduces these in this manner:

> In the Hellenistic world it was a historical necessity that the gospel should be translated into a terminology with which that world was familiar—this gospel of the one true God and of Jesus the Messiah-Son-of-Man with its eschatological message of imminent judgment and salvation, all of which had at first been embodied in the concepts of the Old Testament-Jewish tradition. How the Messiah-Son-of-Man, whose parousia was expected, became the cultically-worshipped Kyros has been shown . . . To express convincingly to Hellenistic ears his eschatological meaning and also the whole eschatological message and the eschatological dualism involved in it . . . Gnosticism and its myth offered a stock of terms that were intelligible to great numbers of people . . . Here our task is to set forth connectedly the extent to which the understanding of the Christian message in Hellenistic Christianity was unfolded by means of Gnostic terminology.[85]

81. Turner, *Pattern of Christian Truth*, 23.
82. Turner, *Pattern of Christian Truth*, 23.
83. Turner, *Pattern of Christian Truth*, 23.
84. Turner, *Pattern of Christian Truth*, 23.
85. Bultmann, *Theology of the New Testament*, 164. See how Bultmann develops

Bultmann's understanding here is in line with that of Harnack. Similar to Harnack, Bultmann "recognizes the impact of the thought-forms of the Hellenistic [gnostic] age upon the nascent Church."[86] However, slightly contrary to both Harnack and Werner, Bultmann does not see this development as necessarily a bad thing. He argued that it was a necessary development as necessary. According to him, this was a historical necessity, as noted above. For him, since Gnosticism antedates Christianity, it "could provide a ready-made stock of ideas already intelligible to many available for the interpretation of Christianity."[87] On the other hand, and in agreement with both Werner and Harnack, Bultmann still saw the results of the interaction especially between Christianity and Gnosticism as furthering the dualistic tension already in place. For example, in his *Primitive Christianity in Its Contemporary Setting*, Bultmann writes:

> Thus Hellenistic Christianity is no unitary phenomenon, but, taken by and large, a remarkable product of syncretism. It is full of tendencies and contradictions, some of which were to be condemned later on by orthodox Christianity as heretical. Hence also the struggles between the various tendencies, of which the Pauline Epistles give such vivid impression.[88]

Indeed, as noted above, for him, this Rubicon "was crossed early in within the New Testament period."[89] In this case, Bultmann differs with both Harnack and Werner in terms of what they all perceive as the beginning point for the "Hellenization" of Christianity as well as the cause(s) and results of this Hellenization. But they agree in their historiography: doctrinal development in the early church amounted not to progress, but, instead, regress.[90]

---

this concept in the following pages. See also Bultmann, *Das Urchristentum*.

86. Turner, *Pattern of Christian Truth*, 23.

87. Turner, *Pattern of Christian Truth*, 24.

88. Bultmann, *Primitive Christianity*, 177–78.

89. Turner, *Pattern of Christian Truth*, 24.

90. Turner further outlines Bultmann's understanding of this development: "Without loosing its essential continuity the Church, originally an eschatological Jewish community which could pass for just another sect within Judaism, assumed different forms as it confronted the Hellenistic world. From this derives its cult-piety and its indebtedness to the popular philosophy of the day. The old stream flows on, but it is reinforced by two tendencies. Beside the Jewish conception of the Two Ages there appears the Gnostic dualism of Light and Darkness" (Turner, *Pattern of Christian Truth*, 24).

While, again, Bultmann's understanding of the New Testament is not our main focus here, his methodology is applicable. Bultmann speaks of NT Christology in terms of kerygma. Steeped in the existentialist philosophy, Bultmann's conception of kerygma is in opposition to what he conceives as "the reduction of God to a series of propositions which can be rationally apprehended, an 'it' with which we can play as we will."[91] Neil and Wright further elaborate:

> Bultmann is conditioned by a violent hostility to any tendency to reduce the Gospel to history. In contrast to a number of scholars, who would be prepared completely to volatilize the narrative elements in the Gospels, Bultmann would be the last to deny that "something happened" . . . he holds that we know very little of what happened; but the *Kerygma*, the message of Jesus Christ, is concerned with something that actually happened in time. His hostility is directed not against those who hold that there is a historical basis for Christian faith, but against those who imagine that the truth of the Christian Gospel can be demonstrated by the verification of historical evidences. Nothing in this field can be *demonstrated*. The acceptance of the Gospel is a matter of faith and nothing else.[92]

However, Bultmann sees this kerygma, the gospel of Jesus Christ, as having been hidden to the modern reader because of the prescientific *mythos* in which it is presented in the New Testament. Calling it a "stumbling block," Bultmann argues that it "must be removed so that the New Testament message can be heard for what it really is." He understands the New Testament drama of redemption as being pictured in the terms of "an elaborate cosmological and eschatological mythos." He writes in *Kerygma and Myth*:

> The cosmology of the New Testament is essentially mythical in character. The world is viewed as a three storied structure, with the earth in the centre, the heaven above, and the underworld beneath. Heaven is the abode of God and of celestial beings—the angels. The underworld is hell, the place of torment. Even the earth is more than the scene of natural, everyday events, of the trivial round and common task. It is the scene of the supernatural activity of God and his angels on the one hand, and of Satan and his daemons on the other. These supernatural forces

---

91. Neill and Wright, *Interpretation of the New Testament*, 248.
92. Neill and Wright, *Interpretation of the New Testament*, 248.

intervene in the course of nature and in all that men think and will and do. Miracles are by no means rare. Man is not in control of his own life. Evil spirits may take possession of him. Satan may inspire him with evil thoughts. Alternatively, God may inspire his thought and guide his purposes. He may grant him heavenly visions. He may allow him to hear his word of succour or demand. He may give him the supernatural power of his Spirit. History does not follow a smooth unbroken course; it is set in motion and controlled by these supernatural powers. This aeon is held in bondage by Satan, sin, and death (for "powers" is precisely what they are), and hastens towards its end. That end will come very soon and will take the form of a cosmic catastrophe. It will be inaugurated by the "woes" of the last time. Then the Judge will come from heaven, the dead will rise, the last judgement will take place, and men will enter into eternal salvation or damnation.[93]

Bultmann saw the concept of mythology as being present in Jewish and gnostic apocalypticism. Thus, according to him, the only way any modern reader can be able to read the New Testament is to *demythologize* it. Indeed, according to him, this process started with the apostle Paul. He sees it as being done "most decisively" by John.[94] However, what Bultmann means by "demythologization" has been debated. As Brent Hege observes, "The term "demythologizing" (*Entmythologisierung*) is, by Bultmann's own admission, problematic."[95] Essentially, the term, as

---

93. Bultmann, "New Testament and Mythology," 1–2. Elsewhere, contrasting ancient and modern worldviews, Bultmann writes: "Now that the forces and the laws of nature have been discovered, we can no longer believe in *spirits, whether good or evil.* We know that the stars are physical bodies whose motions are controlled by the laws of the universe and not daemonic beings which enslave mankind to their service. Any influence they may have over human life must be explicable in terms of the ordinary laws of nature; It cannot in any way be attributed to their malevolence. Sickness and the cure of disease are likewise attributable to natural causation; they are not the result of daemonic activity or of evil spells. The *miracles of the New Testament* have ceased to be miraculous, and to defend their historicity by recourse to nervous disorders or hypnotic effects only serves to underline the fact . . . It is impossible to use electric light and the wireless and to avail ourselves of modem medical and surgical discoveries, and at the same time to believe in the New Testament world of spirits and miracles. We may think we can manage it in our own lives, but to expect others to do so is to make the Christian faith unintelligible and unacceptable to the modem world" (Bultmann, "New Testament and Mythology," 4).

94. Livingston et al., *Modern Christian Thought: The Twentieth Century*, 157. See also Bultmann, *Jesus Christ and Mythology*, 31–33.

95. Hege, *Rudolf Bultmann on Myth*, 46. See also Bersee, "Miracles in the Age of

Bultmann used it, means the process of interpreting the objectified myths of the New Testament. For Bultmann, the process of interpreting the New Testament "involves demythologizing the event ('act of God') of Jesus Christ *insofar as that event is presented in mythical terms*."[96] Hege succinctly clarifies concerning the term "demythologization" as Bultmann conceives it:

> This term implies the elimination of myth, as if myth were a disposable husk containing a kernel of truth, which is how myth was often understood in the nineteenth century. For Bultmann myths are to be interpreted but not eliminated, because the form cannot be eliminated without also endangering the content. Instead, the kerygma is always contained and expressed in a particular cultural form, but the kerygma itself can and must be translated into the cultural forms of those to whom it is addressed. For the New Testament writers, that cultural form was the mythical world-picture of the first century. For modern people a very different cultural form is operative, which is why the New Testament kerygma must be demythologized, or translated, from an alien cultural form into a familiar cultural form.[97]

An example of this process, for Bultmann, is how he "demythologizes" the event of the cross resurrection of Jesus Christ, essentially skirting the entire debate of the "historical Jesus" versus the "Jesus of faith." For him, "to believe in the cross of Christ does not mean to concern ourselves with the mystical process wrought us outside and our world with an objective event turned by God to our advantage."[98] Rather, we need "to make the cross of Christ our own, to undergo crucifixion with him"[99] For him the "cross in its redemptive aspect is not an isolated incident which befell a mythical personage, but an event whose meaning has 'cosmic' importance. Its decisive, revolutionary significance is bought out by the

---

Science."

96. Livingston et al., *Modern Christian Thought: The Twentieth Century*, 159.

97. Hege, *Rudolf Bultmann on Myth*, 46. Hege further helpfully clarifies that while the term is widely associated with Bultmann, "Bultmann did not coin the term. It was first used in a 1914 review of Herrmann's Ethik by Hermann Strathmann, but Bultmann most likely borrowed it from Hans Jonas's study of Augustine published in 1930" (Hege, *Rudolf Bultmann on Myth*, 46n23). See also Congdon, *The Mission of Demythologizing*.

98. Bultmann, *Kerygma and Myth*, 36.

99. Bultmann, *Kerygma and Myth*, 36.

eschatological framework in which it is set."¹⁰⁰ Bultmann, therefore, in the process of demythologizing the cross, argues that "the most significant thing about the cross is not that it happened once but that when it did happen, 'it created a new and permanent situation in history.'"¹⁰¹ That is how he demythologizes the cross of Christ.

Finally, Bultmann similarly demythologizes the resurrection. Conjoining it with the cross, Bultmann "frankly denies the resurrection as an empirical fact in the realm of human history."¹⁰² According to him, *"faith in the resurrection is really the same thing as faith in the saving efficacy of the cross."*¹⁰³ In other words, he sees both the crucifixion and the resurrection as the same thing, with the separation having only been done in the apostles' faith in the risen Christ, "which became the basis of the apostolic preaching."¹⁰⁴ He marshals a number of Pauline quotations to argue his case (remember, for him, Paul was the first demythologizer of the New Testament). He writes:

> Once again, in everyday life the Christians participate not only in the death of Christ but also in his resurrection. In this resurrection life they enjoy a freedom, albeit a struggling freedom, from sin (Rom. 6. 11ff). They are able to "cast off the works of darkness," so that the approaching day when the darkness shall vanish is already experienced here and now. "Let us walk honestly as in the day" (Rom. 3. 12f.): "we are not of the night, nor of the darkness . . . Let us, since we are of the day, be sober . . ." (I Thess. 5. 5–8). St Paul seeks to share not only the sufferings of Christ but also "the power of his resurrection."¹⁰⁵

These two examples, therefore, demonstrate how Bultmann goes about the process of demythologizing the New Testament. Indeed, he see this as an ongoing process, arguing that "the meaning of history lies always in the present, and when the present is conceived as the eschatological present by Christian faith the meaning in history is realized."¹⁰⁶ His historiography, therefore, is centered on an ongoing process of separating the kernel from the husk.

100. Bultmann, *Kerygma and Myth*, 36.
101. Livingston et al., *Modern Christian Thought: The Twentieth Century*, 160.
102. Livingston et al., *Modern Christian Thought: The Twentieth Century*, 160.
103. Bultmann, *Kerygma and Myth*, 41.
104. Livingston et al., *Modern Christian Thought: The Twentieth Century*, 160.
105. Bultmann, *Kerygma and Myth*, 40.
106. Bultmann, *History and Eschatology*, 155.

At this point, these questions must be asked: what do we make of Bultmann's early church historiography based on his mythologizing methodological approach? How does his approach relate to the scholars addressed so far in this chapter: Harnack and Werner? Indeed, how does his approach relate to the entire quest for early church historiography? Although these and other questions will be addressed in the succeeding chapters, a few comments will suffice here as the chapter concludes.

CONCLUSION

This chapter has surveyed three early church historians: Adolf Harnack, Martin Werner, and Rudolf Bultmann. I have labelled their early church historiographies "Hellenistic" because all of them see the early church as having been impacted, somehow, by an aspect of Hellenism. As noted, for Harnack, his historiography focuses on what he sees as the corrupting impact upon the gospel by the effects of its Hellenization. In other words, this interaction produced the negative results of depotentializing the pure gospel of Jesus Christ: the love of God upon all humanity and the love for one another. He described this process as secularization, a process that took place as soon as the gospel interacted with Greek soil. For him, therefore, early church historiography is about doctrinal regress, not progress. However, as noted, historically speaking, the question of the relationship between Greek philosophy and early Christianity is a bit more complex than the Harnackian portrayal here. Later chapters will address this.

Martin Werner, on his side, understood development in the early church in terms of *Enteschatologisierung* (de-eschatologizing). For him, as doctrine developed in the early church, she lost her eschatological emphasis, degenerating into "a hierarchically ordered and hierugically oriented society."[107] In other words, when all is said and done, what remains of a de-eschatologized Christianity is nothing better than the gnostic heresy.

Finally, the chapter explored the historiography of the German New Testament scholar Rudolf Bultmann. On his part, Bultmann, an existentialist theologian, understood the New Testament as a *mythos* that needs to be demythologized. This mythology is especially as a result of its admixture with aspects of Gnosticism (a version of Hellenization).

---

107. Turner, *Pattern of Christian Truth*, 22.

While in some respects Bultmann sees this as a necessary development (with the art of demythologization having been started by the apostle Paul and perfected by the apostle John), as a positive development, in other aspects (and in conformity with Harnack), he also sees it as a bad development. For him, when all is said and done, the only seeming difference between Bultmann's and Harnack's historiography is the starting point of this Hellenization.

Turner mentions a few more salient points concerning these historiographies. First, in spite of their seeming differences, all of them, in sharp contrast to the classical view, "agree in stressing the diversity and even fluidity of early Christian thought."[108] Second, all "agree in finding a marked difference between the developed Christianity of the fourth century and the primitive life and thought of the Church."[109] Third, all "accept as the root-principle of this 'sea-change' experienced by early Christianity the admixture of the original Hebrew and Christian stock with alien elements."[110] Finally, and most significantly, these historiographies are trying to answer the question of whether "this whole development can be adequately understood as a translation of the Christian realities into a Greek setting, a transposition of key with the consequent distortion of some harmonies, or whether it represents so strong an infiltration into the truth of the Gospel."[111] Thus, the question becomes whether "the resultant victorious faith was a mere shadow or even (put in the most extreme form) a travesty of its former self."[112] Frankly, the ensuing quest for early church history is an attempt to answer these questions.

One last issue needs to be highlighted as a transition point to the next category of early church historiographers in the following chapter. This pertains to Bultmann's conception of the influence of gnostic myth on early Christianity. Particularly, he brings the Mandean idea concept of "redeemed Redeemer" at the forefront as an idea that heavily influences especially the Fourth Gospel. Bultmann writes concerning this myth:

> The basic elements in the Gnostic myth of redemption, the concrete features of which can vary in detail, are as follows: A heavenly being is sent down from the world of light to the

---

108. Turner, *Pattern of Christian Truth*, 25.
109. Turner, *Pattern of Christian Truth*, 25.
110. Turner, *Pattern of Christian Truth*, 25.
111. Turner, *Pattern of Christian Truth*, 26.
112. Turner, *Pattern of Christian Truth*, 26.

earth, which has fallen under the sway of the demonic powers, in order to liberate the sparks of light, which have their origin in the world of light, but owing to a fall in primeval times, have been compelled to inhabit human bodies. This emissary takes a human form, and carries out the works entrusted to him by the Father; as a result he is not cut off from the Father. He reveals himself in his utterances ("I am the shepherd," etc.) and so brings about the separation of the seeing from the blind to whom he appears as a stranger. His own harken to him, and he awakes in them the memory of their home of light, teaches them to recognise their own true nature, and teaches them also the way of return to their home, to which he, as a redeemed Redeemer, rises again.[113]

Among the many questions that this assertion raises, the issue of the definition of Gnosticism as well as its nature and origins (including when it started) are pertinent. That is, in order for it to be able to affect Christianity so early, Gnosticism must antedate it.[114] While these questions will be addressed in the succeeding chapters, Bultmann's assumption that Gnosticism predates Christianity seems clearly related to what has come to be known as the "Bauer thesis." This is the subject of the next chapter.

---

113. Bultmann, *Religion in Geschichte Und Gegenwart*, iii col. 84, quoted in Neill and Wright, *Interpretation of the New Testament*, 180. As Neill and Wright further explain, "The curious and important phrase 'the redeemed Redeemer' refers to one element in the Mandean form of the myth—the Redeemer himself falls victim to the powers of evil in the lower world, and has to be delivered by further action from the side of the powers of light" (Neill and Wright, *Interpretation of the New Testament*, 180).

114. Occasionally, the idea of the myth of *salvator salvandus* in early Christianity comes up in scholarship. For a recent treatment of this idea, see Schlier, *Religionsgeschichtliche Untersuchungen*. For a rebuttal, see Mellink, *Death as Eschaton*.

CHAPTER 4

WALTER BAUER AND THE "PRIORITY OF HERESY" HISTORIOGRAPHY

The Emergence of the "Bauer Thesis"

INTRODUCTION

THE JOURNEY OF TRACING the quest for early church historiography from F. C. Baur to Bart Ehrman reaches a critical juncture with what has been described as the "prevailing paradigm with regard to the nature of early Christianity in popular American culture today."[1] This is what is popularly known as the "Bauer thesis" (sometimes referred to as the "Bauer-Ehrman thesis"[2]). Concerning this thesis, Köstenberger and Kruger perceptively observe that even "people who have never heard the name 'Walter Bauer' have been impacted by this scholar's view of Jesus and the nature of early Christian beliefs."[3] They see one of the main reasons for this as the present climate, which they see as "a fertile soil."[4]

While the second part of this thesis will be addressed in the ensuing chapters, the focus of this chapter is the "Bauer thesis" as well as its initial dissemination. It will explore the origins, statement, and interaction of this thesis which, according to Bingham, amounted to a "drastic change"[5]

---

1. Köstenberger and Kruger, *Heresy of Orthodoxy*, 23.
2. Köstenberger and Kruger, *Heresy of Orthodoxy*, 23.
3. Köstenberger and Kruger, *Heresy of Orthodoxy*, 23.
4. Köstenberger and Kruger, *Heresy of Orthodoxy*, 23.
5. Bingham, "Development and Diversity," 50. "A drastic change," writes Bingham,

in the conception of early church historiography. However, as Varner so helpfully clarifies:

> It is important to recognize that the theory of Christian origins expounded by Walter Bauer did not emerge in an intellectual vacuum. European scholars of early Christianity had been profoundly affected by the ideas of Ferdinand Christian Baur (d. 1860) and what came to be known as his "Tübingen Hypothesis" [see above]. While the topic of Jewish Christianity was not directly addressed by Walter Bauer, it lay at the very heart of Ferdinand Baur hypothesis. In the opinion of the present writer, the Bauer Hypothesis is in some ways the natural implication of the earlier Baur Hypothesis, simply extended beyond the immediate worlds of Peter and Paul.[6]

I cannot agree with Varner here more. This is precisely the argument of the present work. And, while Varner sees the Baur hypothesis as culminating in the Bauer hypothesis, the present work argues that the same thesis, finally, flowers in the historiography of Bart Ehrman.

The chapter begins by offering a brief biography of Walter Bauer (1877–1960), German "theologian, lexicographer and scholar of early church history."[7] This will be followed by a presentation of the "Bauer thesis," followed by its early dissemination and response. In the process, some key early proponents and respondents of this thesis will be highlighted. This will pave the way for the presentation and analysis of Ehrman's early church historiography, the *terminus ad quem* of this part of the work.

WALTER BAUER: A BRIEF SUMMARY OF HIS LIFE AND THOUGHT

Walter Felix Bauer was born in Königsberg, the eastern city of Prussia, on August 8, 1877. According to Jerry Flora, this was the city "in which Immanuel Kant spent his life."[8] His father was a professor at the University of Marburg, and the young Bauer "studied theology in the universities

---

"occurred in the fourth decade of the twentieth century [with] Walter Bauer's paradigm-shaping book *Orthodoxy and Heresy in Earliest Christianity* (ET 1971)" (Bingham, "Development and Diversity," 50).

6. Varner, "Baur to Bauer," 95.
7. Köstenberger and Kruger, *Heresy of Orthodoxy*, 24.
8. Flora, "Critical Analysis of Walter Bauer's Theory," 23.

of Marburg, Strasburg, and Berlin."[9] Marburg was one of the most influential universities. As Flora explains, founded in 1527, "Marburg was the first university to be established without papal privileges."[10] Speaking about its size, he adds that, in 1905, "it had 1576 students and a library of 140,000 volumes."[11] The other universities that Bauer attended were of a similar or larger size.

It is at Marburg where Bauer studied under Adolf Jülicher (1857–1938) who "taught New Testament and church history there from 1888 to 1923."[12] In addition, he studied under Johannes Weiss (1863–1914), "professor of New Testament from 1895 to 1908."[13] Other professors that were influential to Bauer as he waded through the academia were a student of Harnack, Wilhelm Hermann, as well as Hermann Cohen and Paul Watorp.[14] Bauer then proceeded to the University of Berlin to study under Otto Pfleiderer as well as under Adolf Harnack, whose "magnetic brilliance attracted pupils there from 1888 to 1921."[15] Pfleiderer, who operated within the Hegelian tradition, is especially known as the one through whom "the way was paved to the Historico-Religious School."[16] This school, which will be discussed later, was a school of thought where "theologians now began to lay special stress upon the development of Christianity as seen in the light of its historical and geographical environment."[17] As it will be demonstrated, this approach would prove to be one of the most influential aspects towards the conception of the "Bauer thesis."

9. Köstenberger and Kruger, *Heresy of Orthodoxy*, 24.
10. Flora, "Critical Analysis of Walter Bauer's Theory," 23n14.
11. Flora, "Critical Analysis of Walter Bauer's Theory," 23n14.
12. Flora, "Critical Analysis of Walter Bauer's Theory," 23.
13. Flora, "Critical Analysis of Walter Bauer's Theory," 23.
14. Flora, "Critical Analysis of Walter Bauer's Theory," 23–24.
15. Flora, "Critical Analysis of Walter Bauer's Theory," 24. As every historian of nineteenth-century Christian thought knows, many of the influential thinkers were associated with the University of Berlin. These include Schleiermacher, Hegel, Leopold von Ranke, Barthold Georg Niebuhr, Christian Matthias, Theodor Mommsen, Karl Lachmann, and Hermann Gunkel, with each lecturing in their respective disciplines such as philosophy, history, philology, theology, New Testament, and Old Testament.
16. Heick and Neve, *History of Christian Thought*, 126. Some of the key works of Pfleiderer, who studied under Baur, are: *Paulinism*; *Lectures on the Influence of the Apostle Paul*; *Primitive Christianity*; *Philosophy of Religion*.
17. Heick and Neve, *History of Christian Thought*, 155.

In addition to these thinkers, Bauer also came under the influence of H. J. Holtzmann during his years at Strassburg. Holtzmann, according to Flora, "lectured there [Strassburg] from 1874 to 1904."[18] He adds that Holtzmann, "along with Harnack, marked Germany's supremacy in the historical study of early Christianity between 1860 and 1900."[19] Thus, by the time his studies were done at Strassburg, Bauer was now ready to chart his way in the area of early Christianity.

Most significantly, this took shape when Bauer started teaching at Marburg as a Privatdozent (indicating fully trained professor but paid directly by students). He then moved to Breslau as professor extraordinarius (without chair) from 1903 to 1916. Finally, in 1916, he moved to Göttingen "(Ordinarius from 1919), where he followed Wilhelm Bousset."[20] It is at Göttingen where his writing career flourished for decades. Flora notes that his publications included books, contributions in collective works, as well as reviews. "His Marburg dissertation," he writes, "appeared in 1902, followed in quick succession by works on Syrian Christianity, the Johannine corpus, the New Testament apocrypha, the Catholic epistles, New Testament theology, the Fourth Gospel and nearly twenty major book reviews—all within the first decade of his professional career."[21] However, as Köstenberger and Kruger note, "Bauer is best known for his magisterial *Greek-English Lexicon of the New Testament and Other Early Christian Literature*."[22] Now in its third edition, this is one of the most highly respected Greek dictionaries.[23]

---

18. Flora, "Critical Analysis of Walter Bauer's Theory," 24.

19. Flora, "Critical Analysis of Walter Bauer's Theory," 24. See also Salvatorelli, "From Locke to Reitzenstein."

20. Flora, "Critical Analysis of Walter Bauer's Theory," 25. There are some slight discrepancies, however, in the dating of Bauer's presence in some of these institutions. Flora helpfully explains, concerning these discrepancies and how to resolve them: "The standard reference sources contain a problem in the dates of Bauer's early teaching career. RGG2 [*Die Religion in Geschichte und Gegenwart*, vol. 2], I, 798, places him at Marburg from 1903 to 1913 and at Breslau 1913–1916; RGG3 [*Die Religion in Geschichte und Gegenwart*, vol. 3], I, 925, places him at Marburg in 1903 and at Breslau from 1903 to 1915. W. G. Kümmel, who wrote the latter entry, agrees with the dating of the former in his Das Neue Testament, p. 574. The problem [therefore] may be typographical rather than editorial" (Flora, "Critical Analysis of Walter Bauer's Theory," 25n19).

21. Flora, "Critical Analysis of Walter Bauer's Theory," 25–26.

22. Köstenberger and Kruger, *Heresy of Orthodoxy*, 24. See Bauer and Arndt, *Greek-English Lexicon of the New Testament*, usually abbreviated as BDAG in scholarship.

23. For more information concerning his scholarly and other labors, see Flora,

However, while Bauer is well-known for this dictionary, "his most significant scholarly contribution came with his [less well-known] work *Orthodoxy and Heresy in Earliest Christianity*.[24] First published in 1934, this work is the basis of what has come to be termed the "Bauer thesis" of the history of earliest Christianity. Hardly noticed at the time of its writing (and virtually the end of Bauer's historical research), Bauer's hypothesis would, eventually, captivate the interest of many early church historians. But, again, the thesis did not appear in a historiographical vacuum. As already demonstrated, there was a lot of groundwork that had been laid by preceding historians of early Christianity. As Köstenberger and Kruger contend:

> Although Bauer provided a historical reconstruction of early Christianity that differed radically from his scholarly predecessors, others had put the necessary historical and philosophical building blocks into place from which Bauer could construct his thesis. Not only had the Enlightenment weakened the notion of the supernatural origins of the Christian message, but the history of religions school had propagated a comparative religious approach to the study of early Christianity, and the eminent

---

"Critical Analysis of Walter Bauer's Theory," 26–31. Flora argues that, as opposed to Pfleiderer, Bauer belonged more to the literary criticism (*literarkritische*) school rather than the history of religions school (*die religionsgeschichtliche Schule*). The literary criticism school "coincided to considerable extent with the followers of Ritschl, standing in the middle between biblicism and the radical history of the history of religions approach" (Flora, "Critical Analysis of Walter Bauer's Theory," 30).

24. Bauer, *Orthodoxy and Heresy*. For the original German edition, see Bauer, *Rechtgläubigkeit Und Ketzerei Im Ältesten Christentum Beiträge*. Concerning the long journey towards the translation of this work into English, Daniel J. Harrington offers this helpful explanation: "Because of the political conditions prevailing in Germany during the late 1930s and the very technical style in which the book was written, the German original did not receive the attention that it deserved. After 1934 Bauer turned from church history and devoted his energies to preparing his monumental Greek lexicon of the NT and other early Christian writings. But the corrections and annotations entered prior to his death in 1960 in his personal copy of the original publication were included in Georg Strecker's 1964 edition. Strecker also provided an appendix on the problem of Jewish Christianity and a survey of reactions to Bauer's thesis in general. In 1971 the English translation made by members of the Philadelphia Seminar on Christian Origins was published under the general editorship of Robert A. Kraft and Gerhard Krodel. In the English version Strecker's discussion of the reception of the book was revised and expanded by Kraft, and the resulting appendix published on pp. 286–316 constitutes a valuable feature of the English edition" (Harrington, "Reception of Walter Bauer's Orthodoxy," 290). See also Betz, "Orthodoxy and Heresy in Primitive Christianity."

church historian Adolf von Harnack had engaged in a pioneering study of heresy in general and the Gnostic movement in particular. Perhaps most importantly, F. C. Baur of the Tübingen School had postulated an initial conflict between Pauline and Petrine Christianity that subsequently merged into orthodoxy.[25]

Thus, as it has already been demonstrated, the seeds of what finally emerged as the radical "Bauer thesis" had already been planted. So, what was Bauer's historiography, and what was so radical about it?

In this work, Bauer simply reversed the classical theory of doctrinal development in early Christianity. In a very simplified form, according to Köstenberger and Kruger, "Bauer reversed this notion [the classical theory] by proposing that heresy—that is, a variety of beliefs each of which would legitimately claim to be authentically 'Christian'—preceded the notion of orthodoxy as a standard set of Christian doctrinal beliefs."[26] Indeed, according to Frederick Norris, the Bauer thesis is much more elaborate than this often-simplified presentation. It is, in other words, a two-part thesis, which Norris presents as follows: "1) In most areas of the Mediterranean basin—particularly Edessa, Egypt, Asia Minor, Antioch, Macedonia, and Crete—heresy was either earlier than and/or stronger than orthodoxy."[27] However, before proceeding to the second part of the thesis, some nuancing needs to be added here. For Bauer, even though this was generally the case for most geographical regions mentioned, Egypt's case was slightly different. According to him, in Egypt, "a clear differentiation between orthodoxy and heresy was still wanting into the third century."[28] Norris offers the second part of Bauer's thesis this way: "2) From the beginning of the second century the Roman community was singularly the dominant influence in the formation of orthodoxy."[29] In contrast to other Christian centers already mentioned, for Bauer, Rome "was from the very beginning the center and chief source of power for the 'orthodox' movement within Christianity."[30] Thus, in summary, Bauer, particularly in response to the "classical view" of the development of early church history, "formulated two theses: (1) 'heresy,' for most of

---

25. Köstenberger and Kruger, *Heresy of Orthodoxy*, 25.
26. Köstenberger and Kruger, *Heresy of Orthodoxy*, 24.
27. Norris, "Ignatius, Polycarp," 23.
28. Bingham, "Diversity and Development," 50.
29. Norris, "Ignatius, Polycarp," 23.
30. Bauer, *Orthodoxy and Heresy*, 229.

the Mediterranean Christian communities, was earlier and more dominant than 'orthodoxy'; and (2) the later victorious development of 'orthodoxy' was largely due to the influence of Rome."[31] Before assessing the initial reception of the "Bauer thesis," however, one may be wondering at this stage: from where did Bauer come up with the evidence in order to arrive at these conclusions? To this, the quest briefly turns.

Bauer goes through the process of reading especially the works of the second-century church father Ignatius of Antioch, as well as other pieces of evidence concerning the working out of heresy and orthodoxy in earliest Christianity, in a highly reconstructed manner. For example, according to him, the supporters of Ignatius and Polycarp of Smyrna must have been a minority in Asia Minor. As Norris explains, according to Bauer, "Ignatius' frantic concern for his allies is best explained against the background of a minority whose very existence is threatened."[32] He adds that, according to Bauer, "the argumentation which he [Ignatius] put forward for monarchial episcopacy is typical of minority groups."[33] Speaking specifically about what he sees as Ignatius' demands for the need of a monoepiscopacy in many of the Christian communities to which he addressed his letters, Bauer further explains:

> Demands like these are typical of minorities which, through their own strong man who is clothed with special aura and equipped with unusual power, endeavor to obtain that overriding importance which they are unable to gain by virtue of the number of their members. But if they can supply one who is in absolute control of the whole group, then the possibility emerges either of bringing those who differ to heel within the group, or else, if there is no alternative, of crowding them out.[34]

It is because of this attempt to assert authority by Ignatius that Bauer sees him using such an emphasis on the position of one bishop, who governs the other ecclesiastical bodies of councils, and "is like God or Christ in whose place he stands."[35] For Bauer, therefore, such emphases, including the theory that even his friend, bishop Polycarp of Smyrna, "wanted to leave troubled Smyrna and himself travel as a delegate to

---

31. Bingham, "Diversity and Development," 52.
32. Norris, "Ignatius, Polycarp," 24.
33. Norris, "Ignatius, Polycarp," 24.
34. Bauer, *Orthodoxy and Heresy*, 62.
35. Bauer, *Orthodoxy and Heresy*, 61.

Antioch,"³⁶ indicates a situation whereby his followers, the "orthodox," were the minority.

The case of the situation in Edessa deserves some special treatment. This is because, in addition to the fact that this is the first piece of evidence that Bauer adduces to support his thesis, it is also where most of his historical reconstruction takes place. In his reconstruction, Bauer begins by recalling "an apocryphal correspondence between our Lord and Abgar V (the Black) [which] is preserved both by Eusebius, who claims to have made his translation direct from Syriac, and in the Syriac *Doctrine of Addai*."³⁷ Through the process of a highly conjectured interpretation of these and other related documents, such as the *Edessene Chronicle*, Bauer "ascribes the origin of Church-life in Edessa to Marcionite influence."³⁸ While an assessment will be offered here below on how Bauer adduces and evaluates evidence for the support of his conclusions, it would suffice to point out, once again, that his historiography involves a significant amount of conjecture. As Turner summarily comments, of "the early history of the Church in Edessa, we know nothing and can conjecture a little more."³⁹ He offers this summary from F. C. Burkitt, who is considered more accurate in reconstruction of the events of the early Edessan church:

> He [Bauer] first calls attention to a passage from St. Justin in which the generic name of Christian is not refused to heretics, just as all philosophical schools, however discordant, lay claim to the same generic title. The point is put in a way which would appeal to a cultivated Roman official perusing the *Apology*, but is not impossible in the second century. By the time of Constantine a similar suggestion that the Church should be content with a philosophical *concordia discors* with Arius is greeted with contumely. That the Marcionites were called Christians at Edessa is expressly stated in a gloss to a late Syriac chronicle which explains it as a custom. The *Edessene Chronicle* mentions Marcion (described, however, as a deserter from the Church), Bardesanes and Mani before turning its attention to more orthodox figures . . . [Further,] Bauer suggests without evidence that Bardesanes not only used, but introduced at Edessa, the *Diatessaron of Tatian*.⁴⁰

36. Norris, "Ignatius, Polycarp," 24.
37. Turner, *Pattern of Christian Truth*, 40.
38. Turner, *Pattern of Christian Truth*, 42.
39. Turner, *Pattern of Christian Truth*, 41.
40. Turner, *Pattern of Christian Truth*, 42–43. See also Burkitt, "Tatian's

Before offering a brief response to Bauer's reconstruction of Edessan church history, it helps to point out that Bauer followed the same style of historical reconstruction with respect to the other main geographical region: Alexandria.

For Bauer, the situation in Alexandria was no different from that of Edessa. As Turner comments, "Bauer believes that at Alexandria no less than Edessa heresy was earlier in the field than orthodoxy, and points to Demetrius as the first to establish a Catholic pattern in his see."[41] Indeed, according to Bauer, this was the situation not only in Alexandria, but also in the entirety of Egypt. "This in Egypt," he writes, "at the beginning of the second century—how long before that we cannot say—there were gentile Christians alongside Jewish Christians, with both movements resting on syncretistic-gnostic foundations."[42] The case for Egypt even seems far more compelling because of the preponderance of such gnostic writings as the *Apocryphon of John* and the *Book of Jeu*. In addition, circulating from earliest times of Christianity in Egypt, were such apocryphal Gospels as *The Gospel According to the Hebrews, The Gospel According to the Egyptians,* and *The Gospel of Peter.*

However, even with this preponderance of "evidence," a few comments are in order pertaining to the situation in Egypt, as Bauer understands it. While, as noted, "Bauer deduces from the form of the titles that the two Gospels represent the official documents of two streams of Egyptian Christianity, a Gnosticizing majority and a Judaizing minority both within the Church,"[43] other moderate explanations have been offered. Turner, again, summarizes:

> A more moderate explanation of the semi-official titles of these Apocryphal Gospels is offered by Evelyn White in his edition of the Oxyrhynchus Logia. While Bauer ascribes them to Christians of Jewish and Gentile origin, he restricts them to two groups within Jewish Christianity itself, the one representing the more traditional type, the other emanating from Hellenized, almost assimilationist, Jewish Christian circles.[44]

Diatessaron."

41. Turner, *Pattern of Christian Truth*, 47.
42. Bauer, *Orthodoxy and Heresy*, 53.
43. Turner, *Pattern of Christian Truth*, 51.
44. Turner, *Pattern of Christian Truth*, 51. See also White, *The Sayings of Jesus*.

In other words, Bauer's theory is not the only (or even the most viable) explanation to account for the presence and titles of these apocryphal Gospels. Indeed, with further documents having been discovered since the publication of Bauer's thesis, interest has shifted to the place of the Fourth Gospel in early Christian Egypt as seen in these Gospels. These pieces of evidence suggest that, instead of heresy preceding orthodoxy in Egypt as argued by Bauer, more likely the earlier and larger influence came from the Fourth Gospel, a Gospel that both orthodoxy (as seen in the works of Irenaeus) and Gnosticism (especially of the Valentinian version) sought to exegete. As Turner, again, observes, "We might stress the orthodox character of the Gospel, of which after all St. Irenaeus is a more satisfactory exegete than the Valentinians, and deduce from this that early Alexandrine orthodoxy was more orthodox than Bauer suspects."[45] Thus, as he rightly concludes, "The [Fourth] Gospel is certainly orthodox enough, and its early and ready acceptance at Alexandria implies a genuine feeling for orthodoxy on the part of the Alexandrine Church."[46] This understanding runs contrary to Bauer's stated thesis on the state of affairs in early Christian Alexandria. Thus, while Turner sees a pattern where, in both Edessa and Alexandria, orthodoxy seems to pick up later, the larger problem is that "neither [Edessa nor Alexandria] serves to establish Bauer's further theses without a radical rehandling which the evidence refuses to support."[47] Again, before offering a few remarks in response, a note about the reception and place of Bauer's historiography is in order.

Virtually all scholars of early church historiography agree that Bauer's thesis was epoch-making. Jeroslav Pelikan, for example, simply notes, "Bauer's thesis has shaped an entire generation of scholars since its first appearance in 1934."[48] Similarly, Arland J. Hultgren comments: "Bauer's work is provocative, controversial, and influential. Its influence continues to exert itself in ways both explicit and implicit in New Testament

---

45. Turner, *Pattern of Christian Truth*, 57.

46. Turner, *Pattern of Christian Truth*, 57.

47. Turner, *Pattern of Christian Truth*, 59. As Turner comments, "In both, we find the full pattern of orthodoxy develop somewhat late. In both, teachers of blemished theological reputation leapt into an early prominence" (Turner, *Pattern of Christian Truth*, 59). The problem, of course, is to make these isolated cases into a wholly generalized scenario. They are, in other words, being asked to bear more weight than their abilities allow them.

48. Pelikan, *The Christian Tradition*, 365.

scholarship and studies in early church history."[49] Bingham comments that it "is difficult to exaggerate the importance of the Bauer thesis for either NT or patristic studies in the twentieth and twenty-first centuries."[50] Finally (of course, this list is not exhaustive), Bart Ehrman contends, "*Orthodoxy and Heresy in Earliest Christianity* (1934) was arguably the most important book in the history of early Christianity to appear in the twentieth century."[51] It is especially with Ehrman's historiography that the Bauer thesis has been firmly established and popularized in many areas of early church history studies today. This is the subject for the next chapter. Before that, however, it is necessary to trace some of the earliest interactions with this epoch-making thesis.[52]

As previously noted, there seems to have been a slow process in the appropriation of the Bauer thesis. There are several factors that serve to explain this rather slow reception. First, as noted above, the process of translating the work to English was a lengthy one. However, it seems that a better explanation for especially the earlier lack of attention to the theory is attributable to Bauer's own actions. Immediately after publishing the book, Bauer turned his attention to lexicography, a discipline that was to occupy him for the rest of his life. As Flora comments, "Undoubtedly his theory would have received more notice if he had continued to refer to it in later writings."[53] Indeed, Bauer "commented privately that

49. Hultgren, *Rise of Normative Christianity*, 9.
50. Bingham, "Diversity and Development," 52.
51. Ehrman, *Lost Christianities*, 173. For more information concerning the critical responses to the Bauer thesis, in addition to Strecker's "Appendix 2" in Bauer, *Orthodoxy and Heresy in Earliest Christianity*, 286–316 ("The Reception of the Book," by George Strecker, revised and augmented by Robert A. Kraft), see also Bingham, "Development and Diversity," 50–60; Desjardins, "Bauer and Beyond," 65–82; Dunn, *Unity and Diversity*, 3–5; Flora, "Critical Analysis of Walter Bauer's Theory"; Hultgren, *Rise of Normative Christianity*, 9–13; Johnson, "Unsolved Questions," 181–93; McCue, "Orthodoxy and Heresy," 118–30; Myllykoski, "Wild Beasts and Rabid Dogs," 342–77; Norris, "Ignatius, Polycarp," 24–44; Norris, "Asia Minor before Ignatius," 365–77; Harrington, "Reception of Walter Bauer's Orthodoxy," 289–98; Robinson, *Bauer Thesis Examined*; Schoedel, "Polycarp of Smyrna," 272–358; Svigel, "Second Century Incarnational Christology," 8–10; Thomassen, "Orthodoxy and Heresy," 241–56; Trebilco, "Christian Communities," 17–44; Turner, *Patern of Christian Truth*, 39–80; and Yamauchi, "Gnosticism and Early Christianity," 29–61.
52. There have been many scholarly interactions with the Bauer thesis. The goal here is to offer a brief trajectory of the main historical interactions with the thesis. For more detailed treatment especially of the critical responses to the "Bauer thesis," see Paul A. Hartog, "From Völker to This Volume."
53. Flora, "Critical Analysis of Walter Bauer's Theory," 34.

he regretted it [his thesis] had received so little attention."⁵⁴ The truth of the matter is that "he never returned to it in print although he actively engaged in research for another twenty-six years."⁵⁵ He simply moved on, and, therefore, his theory received not much attention in the meanwhile.

However, there were some early notices of the theory. As discussed in the previous chapter, one of the earliest proponents of the Bauer thesis was Rudolf Bultmann (1884–1976). Bultmann was professor of New Testament studies at the University of Marburg from 1921 to 1951.⁵⁶ As discussed in chapter 3, Bultmann's historiography was based on the concept of demythologizing the New Testament. The chapter also hinted at Bultmann's affinity to Bauer's thesis as well. Indeed, as it will be demonstrated here, it is "Bultmann and his pupils who are to a large extent responsible for the current interest in the theory of the Göttingen professor."⁵⁷ So, how did Bultmann and his pupils appropriate the "Bauer thesis"?

Specifically, Bultmann was interested in the thinking of both Paul and John in the New Testament. In a historiography reminiscent of that of Bauer, Bultmann "asserted that the distinguishing mark in the earliest Christianity was not orthodoxy but faith."⁵⁸ In other words, for him, "Orthodoxy arose out of controversies within the Christian congregations in which faith came to be interpreted as right belief or the right kind of belief."⁵⁹ Further, as Köstenberger and Kruger remind us, since Bultmann divorced faith from history, "keeping with his anti-supernatural historical-critical methodology . . . believed historical events such as the resurrection were inferior in importance to one's existential faith in Jesus."⁶⁰

---

54. Flora, "Critical Analysis of Walter Bauer's Theory," 34.

55. Flora, "Critical Analysis of Walter Bauer's Theory," 34. See also Fascher, "Walter Bauer Als Kommentator."

56. Köstenberger and Kruger, *Heresy of Orthodoxy*, 27. As Flora further explains, "Bultmann was Privatdozent at Marburg from 1912 until 1916 when he accepted a call to Breslau, apparently to succeed Bauer. While at Breslau, Bultmann wrote his History of the Synoptic Tradition, which appeared in 1921, the year he went back to Marburg after a year at Giessen. He had moved to Giessen in 1920 as successor to Bousset, who had gone there in 1916 from Göttingen" (Flora, "Critical Analysis of Walter Bauer's Theory," 25n18).

57. Flora, "Critical Analysis of Walter Bauer's Theory," 161. Of course, Flora's completed his dissertation in 1972, when Bultmann was still alive.

58. Flora, "Critical Analysis of Walter Bauer's Theory," 161.

59. Flora, "Critical Analysis of Walter Bauer's Theory," 161.

60. Köstenberger and Kruger, *Heresy of Orthodoxy*, 27–28.

Therefore, for Bultmann, "historical orthodoxy was largely irrelevant."[61] Of course, he found support for this view in the "Bauer thesis." He writes concerning the rise of the New Testament canon in the early church:

> The diversity of theological interests and ideas is at first great. A norm or an authoritative court of appeal for doctrine is still lacking, and the proponents of directions of thought which were later rejected as heretical consider themselves completely Christian—such as Christian Gnosticism . . . In the beginning, *faith* is the term which distinguishes Christian Congregation from Jews and the heathen, not *orthodoxy* (right doctrine). The latter along with its correlate, *heresy*, arises out of the differences which develop within the Christian congregations. In the nature of the case this takes place very early; even Paul already curses the Judaizers who offer a "different gospel" in wanting to impose the yoke of the Law upon converted Gentiles (Gal. 1:6–9). He likewise polemizes against those in Corinth who deny the resurrection (I Cor. 15) and against the gnosticizing preachers who proclaim "another Jesus" (II Cor. 11:4).[62]

Thus, for Bultmann, language that indicated the difference between "orthodoxy" and "heresy" was internal—used only in Christian congregations in the early church.

Indeed, Bultmann makes it very clear that his views on the subject are entirely reliant on Bauer's thesis. He, again, writes a couple pages later:

> W. Bauer has shown that that doctrine which in the end won out in the ancient Church as the "right" or "orthodox" doctrine stands at the end of a development or, rather, is the result of a conflict among the various shades of doctrine, and that heresy was not, as the ecclesiastical tradition holds, an apostasy, a degeneration, but was already present at the beginning—or, rather, that by the triumph of a certain teaching as the "right doctrine" divergent teachings were condemned as heresy. Bauer also showed it to be probable that in this conflict the Roman congregation played a decisive role. Later, but independently of Bauer, M. Werner defended a similar thesis, regarding heresy as a symptom of the great crisis of the post-apostolic period, which, according to him, consisted of the fact that in consequence of the delay of the parousia a chaos of teachings arose.[63]

---

61. Köstenberger and Kruger, *Heresy of Orthodoxy*, 28.
62. Bultmann, *Theology of the New Testament*, 2.135.
63. Bultmann, *Theology of the New Testament*, 2.137.

Finally, in a thorough adoption of the "Bauer thesis" in its two-part theses, Bultmann concludes:

> The essential fact is that in determining what is to be regarded as authoritative apostolic tradition for the Church, the office of bishop and the weight of written tradition worked together. In the end the authority of the bishop-office decided the matter: for the Greek Church, the thirty-ninth paschal letter of Athanasius (367 AD) conclusively set the extant of the New Testament at twenty-seven writings, and in the West this decision achieved recognition through Pope Innocent I (405 AD).[64]

As it can be seen, Bultmann basically treats the question of doctrinal development in the early church as that of the development of the New Testament canon. "Unity of doctrine," he concludes, "was assured by the canon and not by some normative system of dogmatics. But this means that this unity is *only a relative one*. For in point of fact, the canon reflects a multiplicity of conceptions of Christian faith or of its content."[65] For him, therefore, rather than a determined body of truth (however rudimentary), "orthodoxy" emerged as internal controversies were addressed in various early church congregations.

The other early proponent of the "Bauer thesis" who is briefly discussed here is Hans Conzelmann (1915–89). Conzelmann was Bultmann's pupil. He studied at the Universities of Tübingen and Marburg and came under the influence of Bultmann. He served as professor of New Testament at Göttingen University. Among his many publications, his historiography comes across in both his *Die Mitte der Zeit* (ET: *The Theology of St. Luke*)[66] and his *An Outline of the Theology of the New*

---

64. Bultmann, *Theology of the New Testament*, 2.141.

65. Bultmann, *Theology of the New Testament*, 2.141.

66. Conzelmann, *Die Mitte Der Zeit*. According to Neill and Wright, the German original was published "under the title, *Die Mitte Der Zeit* (The Mid-point of Time), alluding to what, in Conzelmann's view, is Luke's main point about the story of Jesus" (Neill and Wright, *Interpretation of the New Testament*, 283n4). However, while Neill and Wright see some beneficial contribution of Conzelmann's work, they also see some exegetical issues. They write: "Conzelmann's study is extremely careful and thorough, but at times he seems to impose his theories on the facts instead of letting the facts determine the theories. For instance, he lays great stress on the idea that for Luke the period of the ministry of Jesus is the time of present salvation, in which the great adversary has for the time being lost his power. In support of this view, he makes use of the statement at the end of the story of the temptation, 'the devil . . . departed from him for a season', which he interprets as meaning that the devil left him till the appointed time, that is, the time of the passion. But in point of fact the Greek words

*Testament.*⁶⁷ In his conception of early church historiography, Conzelmann follows Bultmann. As Scott Shauf comments, "Conzelmann took over the notion of what it means to speak of the theology of the New Testament writings from Rudolf Bultmann."⁶⁸ Bultmann's conception of early church history has already been explained "as the unfolding of the self-understanding awakened by the kerygma."⁶⁹ Conzelmann shows affinity to Bultmann but also seems to incorporate other developments.

Scholars also see Conzelmann as going a little bit beyond Bultmann in his historiography. "For example," writes Flora, "the kerygmas of the primitive Palestinian and Hellenistic communities are not sharply distinguished [in Conzelmann]; the Synoptic proclamation occupies a prominent place; and what Bultmann considered the final development toward the ancient church is placed by Conzelmann between Paul and John."⁷⁰ Shauf writes, concerning Conzelmann's implicit criticism of Bultmann: "While Bultmann spoke of 'theology' in the New Testament as only appropriately referring to Paul and John, for Conzelmann it is precisely in Luke that we see the kerygma becoming 'the subjection of reflection.'"⁷¹ He argues that:

> According to Bultmann's concept of theology, one cannot speak of theology as early as the synoptic gospels. Theology only comes with the conceptual elaboration of the kerygma by Paul and John. But this approach does not do justice to the historical facts. The kerygma is expounded not only by a conceptual exposition but also through historical narration. Moreover, each of the synoptists puts forward a developed overall theological conception.⁷²

Thus, Conzelmann sees the development of kerygma as starting as early as in Luke and not just in John and Paul as Bultmann conceives it.

However, he agrees with Bultmann in viewing Bauer's contribution to early church historiography as that of showing the picture of the early

---

ἄχρι καιροῦ [Luke 4:13] mean simply 'for a short period' and cannot be made to mean anything else; the argument based on a mistranslation of them falls to the ground" (Neill and Wright, *Interpretation of the New Testament*, 284).

67. Conzelmann, *An Outline*.
68. Shauf, *Theology as History*, 6.
69. Bultmann, *Theology of the New Testament*, 2.240.
70. Flora, "Critical Analysis of Walter Bauer's Theory," 162n14.
71. Shauf, *Theology as History* 7.
72. Conzelmann, *An Outline*, 98, quoted in Shauf, *Theology as History*, 7–8.

church as only presented by "the victorious trend controversies."[73] He writes, concerning the question of the "emergence of false doctrine":

> We have here a process, the wide extension of which was first recognized by Walter Bauer. The old picture of church history . . . still keeps influencing our conception: the first period of the untainted church followed by the invasion of heresy [the classical theory]—from outside—and this coincided with the cooling off of the first love. But there was still a possibility of overcoming heresy, because the powers of salvation and faith remained as effective as ever. The church, in the true faith, kept out of heresy by a heroic battle. Bauer, however, shows that this picture of history is that of the victorious trend.[74]

Conzelmann, further showing his full agreement with the "Bauer thesis," argues that, "in fact, it was by no means easy to tell true teaching from false, right from the beginning. What was later excluded as heresy first had a life in the church as a way of understanding the faith."[75] He further illustrates his point here, using the example of Gnosticism. He writes:

> There is a common tendency to regard gnostic ideas as an alien body, which forced a way into the church from outside. But they were there from the beginning (Paul). "Christianity" is a particular construction in its environment, a syncretistic religion. The gnostics formed themselves into groups because they believed that they understood the nature of faith more profoundly, indeed, that they were the only ones who understood it. They, too, refer to the apostolic tradition, which thus becomes ambiguous.[76]

In other words, according to him, what we have in the early church is not a clear demarcation between orthodoxy and heresy. Rather, there are competing interpretations of the apostolic tradition. Indeed, as noted above, for him, what came to be recognized as "orthodoxy" is the new conception of the "faith" that emerged from these struggles. He reasons:

> A question will indicate the new element in the situation. Why does Gnosticism now become intolerable? What boundary was

---

73. Flora, "Critical Analysis of Walter Bauer's Theory," 163.
74. Conzelmann, *An Outline*, 301.
75. Conzelmann, *An Outline*, 301.
76. Conzelmann, *An Outline*, 301.

overstepped? How was this boundary [between orthodoxy and heresy] defined? How was the category of heresy arrived at in the first place? Its introduction means that a change has also taken place on the other side [the "orthodoxy" side]. In the view of "orthodoxy" that it alone represents the original, unaltered faith, we can in reality recognize a new structure, a new relationship to the object of faith. It is clear from the style of the polemic against heresy and the doctrine that is expressed in it.[77]

Thus, he sees the "Bauer thesis" providing the foundation for his early church historiography.

Consequently, according to Conzelmann, the beginnings of this process of the extension of faith into a dogma begins in the book of 1 John. According to him, this is where "the confession of faith leads to a decision for or against certain groups in the church and to a critical defense against false doctrine."[78] Conzelmann elaborates:

In 1 John . . . different Christian groups confront each other, each claiming the truth for itself. Now it is necessary which truth is the "right" one. This process of reflection gives birth to a significant expression: John 6:69 runs: "And we have believed, and have come to know, that you are the Holy One of God." 1 John 2.3, on the other hand, says: "And by this we may be sure that we know him . . ." how? ". . . if we keep his commandments." The controversy is complicated by the fact that the opposition, too, appeals to the confession "Jesus is the Son of God." So this formula is no longer sufficient distinction. As a result, there is a need not only for the confession, but also for its proper interpretation: (a) ἐν τούτῳ γινώσκετε τὸ Πνεῦμα τοῦ Θεοῦ. (b) πᾶν πνεῦμα ὃ ὁμολογεῖ Ἰησοῦν Χριστὸν ἐν σαρκὶ ἐληλυθότα ἐκ τοῦ θεοῦ ἐστιν (I John 4.2).[79]

Conzelmann, therefore, sees the author of 1 John as providing the phrase ἐν σαρκὶ ("in the flesh") as the correct interpretation of the previous formula: "Jesus is the Son of God." For him, at this stage, therefore, "Anyone who disputes this statement not only rejects a part of the faith, but rejects the faith, because it is indivisible."[80] At this point, Conzelmann sees dogma as now having developed. The question of how and when the

---

77. Conzelmann, *An Outline*, 301.
78. Flora, "Critical Analysis of Walter Bauer's Theory," 164.
79. Conzelmann, *An Outline*, 302.
80. Conzelmann, *An Outline*, 302.

early church determined orthodoxy from heresy will be pursued in a later chapter.

Finally, Conzelmann sees Bauer's achievement as showing that, rather than a situation where heresy was a perversion of orthodoxy, for the early church, what we have in the heresiologists is a presentation of history from a "victor's" viewpoint. For him, versions of "Christianities" competed with each other in the early church. Showing close affinity to the "Bauer thesis," he contends that the winning side labelled the losing side as "heretical." But he sees the process as having started earlier. He sees it as showing evident progress in the dogmatic assertions of 1 John. But he does not seem to argue in such a refined version of the thesis, viz., in many geographical regions of the early church, "heresy" preceded "orthodoxy," and was, indeed, the majority view, as Bauer argues.

Before looking at two significant students of Bultmann who introduced the "Bauer thesis" to the American continent (Helmut Koester and James Robinson), two other names need to be brought up in connection with the early reception of the "Bauer thesis." These are, first, Ernst Käsemann (1906–98) and Arnold Ehrhardt (1903–63).

Käsemann was himself a student of Rudolf Bultmann. He was born in Westphalia in 1906. As Fergus explains concerning his education, his graduate studies, "in the leisurely and protracted German manner, were coming to a close in 1933, the year in which Hitler was voted into power and his dissertation on the concepts of the body and the body of Christ in St. Paul was published."[81] Eventually, Käsemann became a member of the Confessing Church, "the organized opposition to the influence of National Socialism among German Protestants."[82] After serving a number of

---

81. Kerr, "Theology of Ernst Käsemann—I," 100.

82. Kerr, "Theology of Ernst Käsemann—I," 100. It is interesting to note that, hoping for law and order, Käsemann first cast his vote for Hitler and "joined the 'DC' (*Deutsche Christen*='German Christians'), the right-wing Hitlerite movement within German Protestantism" (Harrisville, "Life and Work of Ernst Käsemann," 295). But, as Harrisville further explains, he then became "mistrustful of Hitler after the Führer intervened on behalf of a criminal storm-trooper, and witnessing the growth of the 'German Christians' in his parish, Käsemann denounced their head, Reichsbischof Müller, as a traitor to the evangelical church, for which he was himself denounced as a traitor and recommended for assignment to a concentration camp. Toward the end of September 1933, Käsemann joined the *Pfarrernotbund* ('Pastors' Emergency Union') founded by Pastor Martin Niemöller in Berlin-Dahlem. Later, in 1934, on the Day of Repentance and Prayer, together with colleagues and members of the newly formed 'Confessing Church' (*Bekennende Kirche*) Käsemann dismissed the 'German Christians' of the Rotthausen parish from church service, replacing them with new

years as a young *pfarrer* (pastor) in Westphalia, he returned to the academy. He first served as professor of New Testament studies at Mainz, then Göttingen before moving to Tübingen in 1959, where he taught until his retirement in 1971.[83] While he is well-known for his contribution in the area of New Testament, it is his conception of the history of the early church that concerns us here.

In scholarship, Käsemann's name is almost synonymous with the second quest for the historical Jesus. Indeed, it seems like it is here where

---

representatives" (Harrisville, "Life and Work of Ernst Käsemann," 295–96). He was eventually briefly imprisoned by the Gestapo (for twenty-five days, during which he completed his studies in the book of Hebrews, later publishing it as "The Wandering People of God" ["*Das Wandernde Gottesvolk*"]) (Harrisville, "Life and Work of Ernst Käsemann," 297). Finally, in addition to being drafted into the military and serving in various places including Greece and Bosnia-Herzegovina, Käsemann also, tragically, lost two of his children (his eldest son, Dietrich, died of diphtheria in 1945 and his youngest daughter, Elizabeth, who was doing sociology work in Argentina, was tortured and murdered during the dirty war on May 24, 1977) (Kerr, "Theology of Ernst Käsemann," 298–99).

83. By all estimates, his years in the pastorate seem to have been successful. In a letter to Paul Zahl, who wrote his dissertation on the theology of Käsemann, Käsemann complained that one of Zahl's dissertation examiners had misrepresented his years in the preaching ministry, writing on September 8, 1995: "One of your examiners refers to my own 'weakness' in making myself understood, especially in respect to my preaching. On that point I wish to protest energetically. When I was a professor, I tore up hundreds of sermons that I had worked on in earlier times when I served in the parish. I preached in those days at least four times a month. Seldom then did I preach to congregations that did not fill the church, which sat 1200. Seldom did I address a Bible study that did not have fewer than 200 participants. Critical services during the time of the Confessing Church were taken by myself. Once at a 'Church-Day' ('Kirchentag') we had to shut the doors of the hall after 7000 listeners crowded in. Later, over a 20-year period, my colloquia were the best attended, after Barth's, in Germany. In the early days (i.e., when EK was pastor in Gelsenkirchen-author), the academics had to come to the miners and steelworkers! The Gestapo was always there, taking notes when I was in the pulpit. All this is not to boast. It is simply to say that my so-called 'difficulty in making myself understood' seems to have resulted in my having opponents among the Nazis, among the Pietists, among colleagues and among laity. Rumour has always accompanied me, whether it was Nazis who saw in me a 'betrayer of the people' or whether it was Pietists who saw in me a concealed atheist. Had I not become a follower of St. Paul or had I suppressed the scandal of the Gospel, I would probably have become bored. Professors have their crosses to bear, too. In any event I was asked constantly to give beyond what I could. I could not see my way to living a right middle-class life in a world that had never felt the hangman's noose. Anyway I have almost turned 90. My portrait shouldn't be over-painted" (Zahl, "A Tribute to Ernst Käsemann." See also Zahl, "A New Source for Understanding German Theology").

he starts to differ with his teacher, Bultmann. Käsemann began to be suspicious of idealism as he saw how it had been incorporated to politics, especially in the political ideals of Johann Gottlieb Fichte (1762—1814). "In 1808," writes Harrisville, "sandwiched between Kant and Hegel, Fichte called his countrymen, not yet a nation, to a love for fatherland that not merely aimed at a flourishing of the eternal and divine in the world, but in which the divine life itself would reappear."[84] Fichte tied his political theory here with the de-historicizing tendency of historical (Christological) idealism. For him, "since the 'absolutely immediate existence of God' had become flesh in Jesus of Nazareth, the eternal had now taken on flesh in each one."[85] Thus, for him, this de-historization was the basis for the call to a "higher love." Of course, as Harrisville correctly observes, while this was his basis for calling the "nation" of Germany to embrace the "hull of the eternal," "Fichte would have been horrified at the suggestion that his idealism furnished fuel for Hitler's Third Reich, but, however obliquely, it belonged with those occasions which made up that horror of context for Käsemann's life and work."[86] How did this skepticism play into Käsemann's historiography in the tradition of Bultmann's and Bauer's?

As already noted, according to Flora, Käsemann was, of all the pupils of Bultmann, "the one who has been the most independent and provocative."[87] His suspicions of Bultmann's complete de-historization of Jesus had its impetus in a seminar while completing his master's degree at Marburg. There, for Käsemann, "Bultmann's anthropology with its roots in idealistic Protestantism became problematic."[88] Harrisville further summarizes, concerning these suspicions and the episode:

> When in seminar the master used his existential perspective to spoil usage of the term "humanity" as abstract, Käsemann retorted "almost insolently" that reference to the "individual" was just as abstract. The struggle took on concreteness with Käsemann's suspicions respecting Bultmann's expositions of

---

84. Harrisville, "Life and Work of Ernst Käsemann," 300. See especially Fichte, "Reden an Die Deutsche Nation, Achte Rede."
85. Harrisville, "Life and Work of Ernst Käsemann," 300.
86. Harrisville, "Life and Work of Ernst Käsemann," 300.
87. Flora, "Critical Analysis of Walter Bauer's Theory," 164.
88. Harrisville, "Life and Work of Ernst Käsemann," 301.

Johannine and Pauline texts, and erupted in public in a contest over the "quest" for the historical Jesus.[89]

Thus, more than Bultmann's "kerygmatic" approach, Käsemann saw in the "quest," to its credit, the church's "unwillingness to abandon, Fichtean-like, 'the real person, for whom hunger and thirst, passion and anxiety, love and death are whole events, embedding him in the cosmos.'"[90] This was especially so with the second "quest," to whose name Käsemann's is permanently attached. In addition, Käsemann's historiography is intrinsically tied to his exploration of the question of the "historical Jesus."

Käsemann interjected himself spectacularly into the quest for the historical Jesus through a lecture in 1953 in which he "ventured . . . to suggest that in fact more could be known about Jesus than had been realized."[91] This, of course, was after Albert Schweitzer, together with others such as Bultmann and Martin Kähler, had rendered the first "quest" a failure because it produced a "figure designed by rationalism, endowed with life by liberalism, and clothed by modern theology in an historical garb."[92] Then the new (second) "quest" was born.

---

89. Harrisville, "Life and Work of Ernst Käsemann," 301.

90. Harrisville, "Life and Work of Ernst Käsemann," 301.

91. Porter, "Dead End," 17. Porter argues that the narrative of the three-or-so "quests" for the historical Jesus are a misnomer for various reasons. "This intriguing yet fictitious narrative," he writes, "does not account for a variety of factors. These factors include: (1) questing after Jesus began soon after his death, as early Church disputes clearly reflect; (2) a number of original or first questers (many not German) were able to use critical methods and not separate the Jesus of history from the Christ of faith as has often been contended; (3) the writing of lives of Jesus did not halt with clarion call of Schweitzer, since others had anticipated his critique and even figured into his analysis (e.g., Weiss and Wrede); (4) developments in form in redaction criticisms promoted the development of criteria for determining authenticity which cut across such temporal categories; (5) in the eyes of many Jesus scholars, the third quest has not sufficiently distinguished itself, in terms of its emphasis upon either the Jewish background of Jesus or other factors, to merit distinction as a new quest; (6) other scholars have begun to recognize the continuity of the quest, from its earliest days (whether one looks to the early Church, the Renaissance or the eighteenth century) to the present, even during the twentieth century. The standard narrative does not even adequately explain German biblical scholarship of the time, since numerous Germans continued to write lives of Jesus in the first half of the twentieth century" (Porter, "Dead End," 18–19).

92. Schweitzer, *Quest of the Historical Jesus*, 398. This is how Schweitzer summarized the findings of the first "quest" of the Historical Jesus: "The Jesus of Nazareth who came forward publicly as the Messiah, who preached the ethic of the Kingdom of

As already noted, Käsemann delivered his address on October 20, 1953, entitled "The Problem of the Historical Jesus," later published as *Essays on New Testament Themes*.[93] In contrast to the argument of form critics to the effect that the early church was not interested in history (that is, "that the glorified *Kyrios Christos* had practically swallowed up the Man of Nazareth, and that the events of the earthly life of Jesus had but little interest for those Gentile believers who lived in the period after the resurrection"[94]), Käsemann wondered why the early church would, for example, ever come to write the Gospels. He writes:

> If the earliest Christians identified the humiliated with the glorified Lord, at the same time they proclaimed that it was possible for them, in their delineation of his history, to abstract from their faith. On the other hand, they also proclaimed that they were not willing to let a myth take the place of history, or to substitute a heavenly being for the man of Nazareth. So they were contending practically on the one hand against an "enthusiastic" docetism, and on the other against an historicizing doctrine of *Kenosis*. Quite clearly they held the opinion that the earthly Jesus can be understood only in the light of Easter, and of his dignity as the Lord of the Church, but, conversely, that Easter cannot be adequately understood, unless account is taken of the early Jesus. The Gospel is always engaged in this warfare on two fronts.[95]

For him, therefore, the gospel is itself "firmly bound to the one who both before and after Easter revealed himself to his own as the Lord, inasmuch as he brought them into the presence of the God who is not far off, and so into the liberty and the responsibility of faith."[96] In other words, Käsemann calls attention to the attempt by Bultmann and others to undermine the historicity of Jesus. However, he was selective on how to interpret the Gospels' presentation of Jesus. "For Käsemann," write Harrisville and Sundberg, "those portions of Synoptic tradition that the

God, who founded the Kingdom of Heaven upon earth, and died to give His work its final consecration, never had any existence" (Schweitzer, *Quest of the Historical Jesus*, 398).

93. Käsemann, *Essays on New Testament*. See also Käsemann, "Problem Des Historischen Jesus."

94. Neill and Wright, *Interpretation of the New Testament*, 289.

95. Käsemann, *Essays on New Testament*, 25, quoted in Neill and Wright, *Interpretation of the New Testament*, 289–90.

96. Neill and Wright, *Interpretation of the New Testament*, 290.

historian is required to recognize as authentic are concentrated in the first, second, and fourth antitheses as the Sermon on the Mount (Matt. 5:21–22, 27–28, 33ff)."[97] He, thus, sees these selective sayings as "unmistakably authentic, partly because they stand in such sharp contrast to anything that could be expected in the Jewish surroundings of the time of Jesus, partly because the earliest Christians, though they so faithfully kept those sayings on record in the traditions."[98] And, as historians of the "quest for the historical Jesus" know, Käsemann's approach was immediately picked up by some other students of Bultmann (as well as other scholars) such as Günther Bornkamm, Ernst Fuchs, Gerhard Ebeling, Herbert Brown, and James M. Robinson, among others.[99] Their approach comprises of what is known as the "second quest." But the question still remains: What is Käsemann's historiography, and how does it relate to the "Bauer thesis?"

Käsemann's historiography comes through in his paper that he presented to the Fourth World Conference on Faith and Order in 1963 entitled "Unity and Diversity in New Testament Ecclesiology."[100] As he argued in this paper, the "New Testament does not present us with an *ecclesiologia perennis* but offers us instead certain ecclesiological archetypes."[101] In other words, according to him, the New Testament "offers certain basic ecclesiological types in the primitive Jerusalem community, the Hellenists, Paul, post-Pauline developments and the Fourth Gospel."[102] In this approach, he shows affinity not only to W. Bauer but even to F. C. Baur's historiography as well. Flora summarizes Käsemann's early church historiography:

> No unbroken unity exists in the New Testament; it witnesses to the same patterns as the situation today, viz., differences, dilemmas, and antitheses. How, then, could early Christianity proclaim [to be] the one church? Käsemann replies that the unity of the church has been, and remains, primarily an eschatological

---

97. Harrisville and Sundberg, *Bible in Modern Culture*, 238.

98. Neill and Wright, *Interpretation of the New Testament*, 290.

99. See Durst, *Handbuch Der Bibelhermeneutiken*. For Bornkamm, see Bornkamm, *Jesus of Nazareth*. See also Barbour, "Theologians of Our Time."

100. Käsemann, *New Testament Questions*, 252–59.

101. Käsemann, *New Testament Questions*, 252.

102. Flora, "Critical Analysis of Walter Bauer's Theory," 164–65. For his understanding of the Fourth Gospel, see Käsemann, *Jesu Letzer* (ET: *The Testament of Jesus*).

datum to be received as a gift. There are ecclesiologies but no one ecclesiology.[103]

Thus, it is clear that Käsemann, here, shows affinity to Bauer's understanding of the picture of early Christianity as widespread diversity. In other words, his conception of "ecclesiologies" for the early church applies to all areas of doctrine.

Finally, combining both F. C. Baur's and W. Bauer's historiographies, Käsemann understands Paul to be the forerunner of what eventually became early catholicism. Käsemann begins by defining the phrase "early catholicism." According to him, "early catholicism" means "that transition from earliest Christianity to the so-called ancient Church, which is completed with the disappearance of the imminent expectation [of the return of Christ]."[104] However, in agreement with both F. C. Baur and W. Bauer, Käsemann sees this (doctrinal) development not happening uniformly in all geographical regions of the early church. "This by no means," he writes, "occurs everywhere at the same time or with the same symptoms and consequences, but nevertheless in the various streams there is a characteristic movement toward that great Church which understands itself as the *Una Sancta Apostolica*."[105] Thus, according to him, "Not only does historical investigation reveal the variability of the earliest kerygma; it also demonstrates the extraordinary wealth of theological positions in the primitive church; a phenomenon which extends beyond the horizon of the canon."[106] For him, therefore, rather than seeing some of the competing movements as "heretical" (classical theory), he sees them as aspects of theological diversities commensurate to the ecclesiologies evident in the early church.[107] As Flora explains, for Käsemann,

---

103. Flora, "Critical Analysis of Walter Bauer's Theory," 165.

104. Käsemann, *New Testament Questions*, 237. See also Matlock, *Unveiling the Apocalyptic Paul*, 186–246.

105. Käsemann, *New Testament Questions*. It is clear that Käsemann adored F. C. Baur. "On the wall in Ernst Käsemann's living room study," write Harrisville and Sundberg, "hung a copy of the University of Tübingen's portrait of Baur, a gift to the New Testament scholar upon his retirement. Once outside Baur's direct influence, the one-time pupil of Bultmann finally came to write of Baur as the true 'progenitor' of a criticism at the root, a criticism conceived not merely as a scientific method but as a presupposition for the life of the spirit. One summer day he pointed to that portrait on his study wall and said, 'greater even than Bultmann'" (Harrisville and Sundberg, *Bible in Modern Culture*, 122).

106. Flora, "Critical Analysis of Walter Bauer's Theory," 167.

107. For example, in his study of John 17, "Käsemann writes that the Johannine

"Bauer's historical description must give way to theological decision."[108] While Käsemann does not indicate his dependence on Bauer, it is evident that there is reliance on the "Bauer thesis" by him.[109]

In conclusion, Käsemann's demonstrable dependence on Bauer led him to go beyond the demythologizing historiography of his teacher, Rudolf Bultmann. In so doing, his early church historiography emphasizes diversities of not only ecclesiologies in the early church but, as well, theologies. For him, even the canon itself is not unified. As he proclaimed in his 1962 controversial address to the Commission on Faith and Order of the World Council of Churches in Montreal, Canada, "The Bible is not a unified book, that of the four Gospels none dared say what was the authentic voice, though for 1800 years the Gospel of John was assumed to be such."[110] For him, this was a good thing because "historical criticism had proved its right to exist by removing from the canon its binding character and freeing for a sight of what lay at the heart of the biblical message: The righteousness of God in the justification of the godless as 'canon within the canon.'"[111] This is Bauerism taken one step back in history: the New Testament church. Thus, since "the twenty-seven books of the New Testament did not establish the unity of the church but rather a variety of confessions, the biblical canon, though inseparable from, could not be identified with the gospel."[112] This concept of "varieties of Christianities" in the early church continues to be a major theory in many early church historiographies.[113]

---

writings have to be interpreted as antithetical to early catholicism, while at the same time influenced by gnosticism. In fact, the author of the Johannine Gospel and letters belonged to a conventicle that, although later hereticized by the Great Church, was by 'human error and the providence of God' allowed into the canon.' This author, a presbyter of docetic persuasion, nonetheless waged war on behalf of the 'Word become flesh'" (Harrisville and Sundberg, *Bible in Modern Culture*, 255).

108. Flora, "Critical Analysis of Walter Bauer's Theory," 167–68.

109. Flora speculates that this dependence is mediated through Käsemann's teacher, Bultmann (Flora, "Critical Analysis of Walter Bauer's Theory," 168).

110. Harrisville, "Life and Work of Ernst Käsemann," 308.

111. Harrisville, "Life and Work of Ernst Käsemann," 308.

112. Harrisville, "Life and Work of Ernst Käsemann," 308.

113. There is a lot more that can be said about Käsemann, but we must move on. It is clear, for example, that he reinvented the entire "quest" for the historical Jesus, ushering in the "second quest," a quest which, according to Porter, "finally blossomed in the 1980s into what has come to be called the third quest for the historical Jesus, distinguished by the further recognition that we know more about the time when Jesus lived, especially his Jewish background, than we had thought, and that we can

Before looking at the American students of Bultmann, who imported the "Bauer thesis" to America, it is in order to deal with the other early exponent of the "Bauer thesis," Arnold Ehrhardt (1903–63), who served as lecturer in ecclesiastical history at the University of Manchester. In his study of the origins and formulation of the Apostles' Creed and the concept of creedal language in the New Testament, he "applied Bauer's understanding of diversity in the early church."[114] In a lengthy article, Ehrhardt demarcates his inquiry into a three-set question, writing:

> It is only in these our days that the question is being asked why Ambrose and his contemporaries produced such a legendary foundation for their belief in the true Apostolicity of the Apostles' Creed. The question is really a threefold one. We have to ask first, how far back can we trace the literary form of Creed, a short formula intended to embody all that is absolutely essential for a Christian to believe in order that he might be saved. The second part of the question is, what authority was attached to these formulas in pre-Nicene time, and in particular whether they were being used as a touch-stone of orthodoxy, and as a means for the excommunication of unbelievers. The third and last part of the question is, whether or not it may be assumed that, even if no particular subscription to any formulated Creed is likely to have been exacted in the Apostolic and sub-Apostolic period there was yet at least a unanimity, a clear agreement, with regard to the content of the Christian Faith amongst those who spread and those who held it. These three may appear as

come to some firm understandings of key events in Jesus' life around which we can construct with levels of certainty other key events and understandings" (Porter, "Dead End," 17–18). As well, Neill and Wright concerning Käsemann's reputation, writing: "Käsemann's reputation stands deservedly high in the theological world. He is a man of great perceptiveness, patient diligence, and startling integrity, always ready to strike out beyond his past conclusions to new adventures of thought, and above all, like Bultmann, deeply concerned that the Gospel should be preached as a divine challenge to which the response of men is demanded" (Neill and Wright, *The Interpretation of the New Testament*, 289). Finally, it also seems like Käsemann was a man of great wittiness. Harrisville's description of this event after Käsemann's retirement, among other similar ones, speaks to this: "Following his retirement in 1971, those colleagues invited him to their *Arbeitsgemeinschaft*, a monthly meeting of members of the university's Catholic and Protestant faculties, and which featured monthly presentation of scholarly papers and responses. According to Käsemann, the invitation contained the proviso that he remain silent throughout. At the suggestion that he had misunderstood the invitation, he responded robustly that he had not, punctuating his insistence with a healthy rap on the nearest available surface" (Harrisville, "Life and Work of Ernst Käsemann," 312).

114. Köstenberger and Kruger, *Heresy of Orthodoxy*, 28.

logically separate and independent questions; but historical reality is never logically tidy, and it is therefore necessary to keep them together in mind when we enquire into Christianity before the Apostles' Creed.[115]

Ehrhardt interacts with these questions at great length in this article. He filters them into two related issues: whether the pre-Pauline creedal formula of 1 Cor 15:1–11, probably originating from Jerusalem, is the same document as the later Apostles' Creed, and, second (and most significant according to him), "whether the Primitive Church was unanimous in accepting them."[116] Not less emphatic is his response to both of these questions. He writes:

> To the first question no safe answer can be given. All that can be said is that the existence of more than one collection of such formulae cannot be excluded. For instance, the presumably Roman "credal formula" used by St. Paul in Rom. I.3 f., need not be of Jerusalem origin, whilst the mention of James' visitation by the risen Lord makes such an origin probable for i. Cor. XV. 1 f. The answer to the second question, however, has to be in the negative. It is evident from i. Cor. XV. 1 that the Apostle's technical name for the credal formula subsequently quoted was εὐαγγέλιον.[117]

While the question of the origin and dissemination of creedal formulae in the New Testament and the early church will be dealt with in a later chapter, it is clear that he sees no unanimity in the acceptance of the key creedal formulae in the early church. For him, and in accordance with the "Bauer thesis," the fact that Paul would threaten "anathema" to anyone who would profess "another Gospel"—ἕτερον εὐαγγέλιον—is an indication that there was no unanimity in the reception of the pre-Pauline formulae in the NT churches.[118]

Concerning his dependence on Bauer, Ehrhardt is quite overt. After arguing that it is in the two lesser Johannine epistles where we see "the first beginnings of excommunication for holding false doctrines, which was worked by the refusal of hospitality, and thus too the first signs for a

---

115. Ehrhardt, "Christianity before the Apostles' Creed," 75.
116. Ehrhardt, "Christianity before the Apostles' Creed," 77.
117. Ehrhardt, "Christianity before the Apostles' Creed," 77.
118. Ehrhardt, "Christianity before the Apostles' Creed," 78–79. See Gal 1:8, 10, 17; Rom 11:13, 16; 1 Cor 15:1–11, 2 Cor 11:5, 12:11.

consciousness of the need for an authoritative Creed,"[119] Ehrhardt credits Bauer for providing him with the basis to make such an assertion. "For the possibility of making such a survey with comparative ease," he further writes, "and indeed for the first attempt at analyzing Christianity before the Apostles' Creed without any doctrinal or denominational bias, we are indebted to that great New Testament scholar, the late Dr. Walter Bauer, whose Greek Dictionary of the New Testament alone will secure for him a place among the greatest."[120] After interacting with Bauer (who he agrees with for the most part), Ehrhardt concludes that "it appears in fact that the boundaries between Catholicism and Gnosticism at any rate were too fluid in Asia Minor during the second century to warrant any attempt at the conception of such a formula."[121] He credits the emergence of the NT canon with preventing further doctrinal developments (such as the views of Montanism and the "Cataphrygians") from taking root.

In conclusion, Ehrhardt, especially in his lengthy article discussed here, concludes that "the contents of the Apostles' Creed and the New Testament's creedal formulas differed, arguing that the diversity of early Christianity supported this contention."[122] His conclusions are based on his full agreement with the "Bauer thesis," and, therefore, becoming one of the key defenders of the thesis.

Attention now shifts to Bultmann's students who imported the "Bauer thesis" to the United States. As already indicated, these are Helmut Koester and James M. Robinson. As previously noted, in Germany, Rudolf Bultmann picked up and further developed the Bauer thesis. However, for the most part, the English-speaking world was in the darkness for as long as the book remained untranslated. However, as Bingham notes, some of Bultmann's students in America introduced the thesis to the continent, albeit with modifications. Specifically, James Robinson and Helmut Koester "introduced their own thesis influenced partly by Bauer under the title *Trajectories through Early Christianity*."[123] And, as the next chapter will demonstrate, the thesis has now gone mainstream.

James McConkey Robinson (1924–2016), whose name is eternally tied to the Nag Hammadi codices, explains in his "Theological

119. Ehrhardt, "Christianity before the Apostles' Creed," 92.
120. Ehrhardt, "Christianity before the Apostles' Creed," 92.
121. Ehrhardt, "Christianity before the Apostles' Creed," 108.
122. Köstenberger and Kruger, *Heresy of Orthodoxy*, 28–29.
123. Bingham, "Development and Diversity," 53. See Robinson and Koester, *Trajectories*.

Autobiography" that he was born and raised in "'the very sheltered existence of faculty housing.'"[124] This was at "The Columbia Theological Seminary in the suburban area in Atlanta, Georgia, where his father was 'an orthodox Calvinist' and a professor of church history for over 40 years.'"[125] His earliest life influence came from his father, William Childs Robinson (1897–1982), longtime conservative professor of church history and apologetics at Columbia Theological Seminary.[126] According to Robinson's student, Ky-Chun So, his father spent his sabbatical period just before World War II "studying under Karl Barth at the University of Basel, Switzerland."[127] According to So, this is when Barth debated Brunner on the issue of human ability to hear God's word. "Brunner argued," writes So, "that humans have an innate capacity to hear God's word, which Barth had repudiated as 'works righteousness,' in his famous pamphlet entitled simply 'Nein!'"[128] So impressed was Robinson's father that he decided to send his two sons to Basel in 1947 so that they could study under Barth.

However, as fate would have it, with the war still ranging, "German students studying in Basel smuggled into Marburg New Testament theology of Rudolf Bultmann; existentialism and demythologizing."[129] The result was "that Robinson had moved from Basel to Germany for the winter semester of 1950–1951 to attend Bultmann's class in Marburg just before he retired."[130] Finally, the turn on the young Robinson was complete: he "moved from the Barthian stream to the Bultmannian to be the most exciting Bultmannian."[131] However, it seems like he was first "post-Bultmannian" before he actually became a "Bultmannian."[132] His friend and coauthor of *Trajectories*, Helmut Koester, explains how this process took place this way:

---

124. Robinson, "Theological Autobiography," 3, quoted in So, "James M. Robinson's Impacts," 25.

125. So, "James M. Robinson's Impacts," 25.

126. See Calhoun, *Pleading for a Reformation Vision*.

127. So, "James M. Robinson's Impacts," 26. So further notes that he was Robinson's PhD student at Claremont Graduate University in California.

128. So, "James M. Robinson's Impacts," 26.

129. So, "James M. Robinson's Impacts," 26.

130. So, "James M. Robinson's Impacts," 26.

131. So, "James M. Robinson's Impacts," 26.

132. So, "James M. Robinson's Impacts," 26.

> The years after my release from the POW camp brought me to the study of theology at Marburg, where I developed from a devoted pietist into a real Bultmannian (without the detour via post-Bultmannianism). But then Robinson was in Basel being indoctrinated by Karl Barth. And when Robinson finally saw the light and came to Marburg, I had just left for my first assignment as an associate minister in the Lutheran Church of Hannover, where I spent little time pastoring and a lot of teaching Hebrew to theology students, who aspired to become missionaries.[133]

As Koester explains, he and Robinson went on to have the first "encounter" in 1958 when Koester was asked to review Robinson's *Das Geschichtsverständnis des Markus-Evangeliums*, which he gave "very high praise."[134] As noted above, both scholars would later collaborate to write the *Trajectories*.

After years (and spending some time with his house-father, Oscar Cullmann, at Alumneum in Basel), Robinson returned to Princeton Theological Seminary to complete his doctorate in New Testament Studies. He completed it in 1955. His dissertation was entitled "The Problem of History in Mark." According to Koester, in this work, Robinson "dealt with the problem of the famous 'Messianic Secret' that William Wrede had thrown like a firebrand into the world of New Testament scholarship in the beginning of the century."[135] Wrede's book, entitled *Das Messiasgeheimnis* (*The Secret of the Messiah*), was published in 1901.[136] As Neil and Wright summarize, in it, Wrede argued that

> The life of Jesus was not messianic, and Jesus himself never made any claim to be the Messiah. It was only the resurrection that convinced the disciples that Jesus was the Messiah. Having come into this conviction, they then realized that he had been the Messiah all along; they therefore proceeded to read back Messiahship into the life of Jesus. But, if Jesus was actually the Messiah all the time, how did it come about that the disciples were unaware of the fact throughout the ministry? How did it come that the Jews went so far as to crucify the one who was

---

133. Koester, "Intellectual Biography," xiii.

134. Koester, "Intellectual Biography," xiii. It is interesting to note that Koester also did a review of Willi Marxen's *Evangelist Markus. Studien zur Redaktionsgeschichte des Evangeliums*, which he says he "did not like at all" (Koester, "Intellectual Biography," xiii). See Marxen, *Evangelist Markus*.

135. Koester, "Intellectual Biography," xiv.

136. Wrede, *Messiasgeheimnis*.

actually their promised deliverer? To account for this, the tradition, or perhaps it was the author of Mark's Gospel himself, ingeniously invented the idea of the Messianic Secret—they did not realize that he was the Messiah because Jesus himself carefully concealed the fact from them; to the end they were unaware of it. The story of Peter's confession, his great utterance "Thou art the Christ," is a reading back into the time of the ministry of what was in reality a post-resurrection appearance of the risen Christ, and of the recognition by Peter of his messianic character.[137]

With this conclusion, Wrede's work was devastating to the confidence in the Gospels and the New Testament in general. As Koester states, it "destroyed the confidence at its roots by showing that exactly the framework of the oldest gospel, namely, the Gospel of Mark, was a theological construct and had little relationship to the historical course of Jesus' ministry."[138] Thus, the "question of the historical Jesus was thrown out of balance."[139] Robinson's work, however, brought it back to track after the hiatus that resulted from WWII. As he argued in *A New Quest of the Historical Jesus*, Robinson saw himself as launching "a quite different kind of quest based upon new premises, procedures and objectives."[140] It is the quest that has been pursued in the "Jesus Seminar," of which Robinson has been a key player.

Finally, although more can be said of the thought of this late professor of religion at Claremont Graduate University, it would suffice here to say that in addition to, together with Koester, Robert Funk, and George McRae, reformed the Society for Biblical Literature to where it is today, but, as Koester argues, Robinson helped many younger scholars to get started in their careers by working with them. The evidence of his ability to work with others and help them advance in their scholarly careers, according to Koester, was the "success of the publication of the Nag Hammadi documents, as compared to the agonies of the publication of the Dead Sea scrolls."[141] He did this through the work of members of the Institute for Antiquity and Christianity, an institute which he founded at

---

137. Neill and Wright, *Interpretation of the New Testament*, 267.
138. Koester, "Intellectual Biography," xv. See Robinson, *Geschichtsverständnis*.
139. Koester, "Intellectual Biography," xv.
140. Robinson, *A New Quest*, 9–10.
141. Koester, "Intellectual Biography," xv.

Claremont Graduate University. As So notes, Robinson's success in the Nag Hammadi Library progressed this way:

> He possessed good photographs of all the Nag Hammadi codices, and to this extent was in a position to break the monopoly. But then he had no publication rights. He was lucky to have access to the texts at the Coptic Museum in Cairo because he was working for the Arab Republic of Egypt and UNESCO as a Representative of the U.S.A. and was the Permanent Secretary of the International Committee for the Nag Hammadi Codices (1970–1984). Using the contract at UNESCO, Robinson was able to bypass the exhibition of obscurantism, and eventually the monopoly of the Nag Hammadi documents was completely broken.[142]

Indeed, all of these photographs are still available on the institute's website. Since his work on the Sayings Gospel (Q) has already been noted, attention now shifts to the main concern of this project: his coauthored work with Koester, *Trajectories*.

Much of what has been said about Robinson is also true of the German-born American scholar, Koester. Both of them proudly let us know that they "studied under Rudolf Bultmann."[143] Specifically, Koester, for many years the towering New Testament professor at Harvard Divinity School, had Bultmann as his doctoral dissertation chair. His dissertation was entitled *Synoptische Überlieferung bei den Apostolischen Vätern* (*Synoptic Tradition in the Apostolic Fathers*).[144] Among many other significant

---

142. So, "James M. Robinson's Impacts," 33–34. See Robinson, *Nag Hammadi Library*. See also Robinson, *Nag Hammadi Library: Translated and Introduction*. As So further explains, after his Nag Hammadi projects were done, Robinson returned to his work on the Sayings Gospel Q at age of sixty (So, "James M. Robinson's Impacts," 34). He further explains that "according to Robinson, the Q archetype behind Matthew and Luke is based on a written Greek text for this saying; here we surely have the oldest attestation for written sayings of Jesus, even older than the copy of Q shared by Matthew and Luke 24. Furthermore the Q people, that is to say, the few who still identified themselves with Jesus in Galilee, have largely been lost from sight, as has always been the case since Luke almost completely bypassed Galilee in Acts, e.g. Acts 1:8: 'You shall be my witnesses in Jerusalem and in all Judea and Samaria and to the end of the earth.' A Galilean church is only mentioned once in passing, in a generalized statement (Acts 9:21): 'So the church throughout all Judea and Galilee and Samaria had peace and was built up'" (So, "James M. Robinson's Impacts," 35–36). See Robinson, Hoffmann, and Kloppenborg, *Critical Edition of Q*. For more information on Robinson's Nag Hammadi scholarship, see Hedrick, "Liberator of the Nag Hammadi Codices."

143. Robinson, "Introduction: The Dismantling."

144. See Koester, *Synoptische Überlieferung*.

contributions to New Testament and early church scholarship, Koester, together with other scholars such as Robert W. Funk, James M. Robinson, and George W. MacRae, was to spearhead the project that would later become the *Hermeneia* commentary series.[145]

In his introduction to *Trajectories*, Robinson notes that he and Koester, students of Bultmann, "are involved in the current indigenization of the Bultmann tradition on American soil."[146] So, right from its beginning, the nature of the project was clear. However, while Robinson and Koester take a cue from Bauer via Bultmann, arguing, as noted above, that their work is intended to indigenize Bultmann on American soil, their own historiography "differs somewhat from that of their teacher."[147] Rather, their focus is to reconfigure the traditional terms used to categorize early church (and any other) historiography. Again, introducing the work, Robinson starts by noting that there is now a crisis in New Testament studies that has resulted from the static nature of the categories used. He writes, concerning this crisis:

> The current crisis at the basis of New Testament scholarship moves through the whole spectrum of its presupposition and categories, from such empirical items as the correlated categories "Palestinian" and "Hellenistic" (presupposing a nonexistent correspondence between geographical and cultural boundaries) to the most abstract presuppositions of scholarship, its metaphysical (or antimetaphysical) assumptions.[148]

He continues, establishing the need for the work:

> One of the basic instances of the latter has to do with the very concept of the "background" of the New Testament itself; indeed, the title of the present volume, *Trajectories through Early Christianity*, suggests a dismantling and reassembling of perhaps the most embracing and foundational category of all: the traditional static, substantival essence/accidence-oriented metaphysics which gave our inherited categories their most basic form. It suggests the need to replace that metaphysics with a dynamic, historic, existence/process-oriented new metaphysics,

---

145. Koester served as its first chair of the New Testament Editorial Board. For more information on his life and work, see Smith III and Sellew, *Fabric of Early Christianity*.

146. Robinson, "Introduction: The Dismantling," 1.

147. Bingham, "Development and Diversity," 53.

148. Robinson, "Introduction: The Dismantling," 8.

in terms of which a whole table of restructured categories may be envisaged.[149]

Thus, their proposal is set against the backdrop of what they conceive to be static historiographies of the New Testament and, by extension, that of the early church. In other words, as Köstenberger and Kruger note, "In this influential appropriation of Bauer's thesis, Koester and Robinson argued that 'obsolete' categories within categories within New Testament scholarship, such as 'canonical' or 'non-canonical,' 'orthodox' or 'heretical,' were inadequate." Koester had argued for the same position earlier.[150]

To overcome these static categories, Robinson and Koester posit a historiography that argues for the concept of "trajectories." This approach, according to them, is more reflective of the reality of what happened in earliest Christianity. According to them, rather, "events, persons, and texts can only be understood 'in terms of the trajectories in which they are caught up,' and these trajectories involve 'a plurality of spinning worlds, with conflicting gravitational fields.'"[151] It is here where the authors agree and disagree with Bauer. After noting that his work is "epochal," they also are quick to observe that the work merely presented one trajectory, and, actually, a bifurcating one. "It drew attention to a bifurcating trajectory," writes Robinson, "out of the fluid, primitive Christianity there gradually emerged a polarized antithesis between secondary developments, known to us as orthodoxy and heresy, as the initial plurality gave way to the dominance of the Roman view."[152] Thus, according to them, although helpful, Bauer's thesis still caught up in the problematic static categorization of these early trajectories. However, Robinson and Koester have more in agreement with Bauer than disagreement. As Köstenberger and Kruger further explain, similar to Bauer, for these scholars, the assumption is that "earliest Christianity did not espouse orthodox beliefs from which later heresies divulged [the classical theory]."[153] They add that in this belief, "these authors argued that earliest Christianity was

---

149. Robinson, "Introduction: The Dismantling," 8–9.

150. See Koester, "Apocryphal and Canonical Gospels." For his similar approach to the New Testament, see Koester, "Gospel Traditions in the Apostolic Fathers."

151. Bingham, "Development and Diversity," 54.

152. Robinson, "Introduction: The Dismantling," 16.

153. Köstenberger and Kruger, *Heresy of Orthodoxy*, 29.

characterized by diversity and that the phenomenon of orthodoxy emerged only later."[154] This is classic Bauerism.

However, more than any other proponent of the "Bauer thesis," Robinson and Koester are careful not to be understood as posting random trajectories that have no control whatsoever. For example, Robinson attempts this correction: "To be sure, the term *trajectory* may *suggest* too much determinative control at the point of departure, the angle at which the movement was launched, the torque of the initial thrust."[155] However, they see the control as the reality, speaking of many Christianities, but only of one *reality*.[156] According to them, therefore, "this singular reality is the ultimate cause or essence which determines all that becomes visible in history."[157] This point needs to be pressed further.

Even with these caveats, Bingham is right in arguing that the historiography of Robinson and Koester is actually the application of classic historicism to early church history. He states that this historicism

> reads history as a scene which displays the diversity of human existence in a dizzying variety of forms. As a critique of the Enlightenment, classical historicism assumes that there is no human nature, there is only history. Furthermore, it assumes that history is not a flowing stream of continuity, but a series of spaces contiguous, but discontinuous; that all knowledge and experiences are historically conditioned; that there are no natural laws, only those which arise within particular historical contexts; that truth is a function of historical situatedness; and yet, that there is at least some notion of continuity between diverse historical occurrences.[158]

This historicism is based on the authors' commitment to the historiography of the "history of religions school" (*Religionsgeschichtliche Schule*). With this understanding, Bingham further summarizes concerning not only Robinson and Koester but also the historiography of the history of religions school, itself a classic historicist historiography: "Here

---

154. Köstenberger and Kruger, *Heresy of Orthodoxy*, 29.
155. Robinson, "Introduction: The Dismantling," 14.
156. Bingham, "Development and Diversity," 55.
157. Bingham, "Development and Diversity," 55.
158. Bingham, "Development and Diversity," 57. For recent studies in historicism, see Castleman, Lockett, and Presley, *Explorations in Interdisciplinary*. See also Meinecke, *Historism: The Rise of a New Historical Outlook*. For the "history of religions" school, see Rudolph, *Historical Fundamentals*, and Rudolph, *Gnosis*.

one finds the cosmological metaphor of Robinson: development in early Christianity must be understood as a dynamic taking place amidst 'spinning worlds' and 'conflicting gravitational fields.'"[159] It is not the implicit germ becoming explicit, although some have argued that Robinson's view of trajectories is heavily deterministic with his assumption that history is "always composed of sequential developments which lead to terminal points."[160] However it is conceived, therefore, Robinson and Koester's early church historiography is averse to any category that they consider "static." Indeed, it detests the idea of "background" in the conception of the early church. Indeed, in the grand scheme of early church historiography, these scholars' view, in a way, continues the thread argued in this work. As Harrisville and Sundberg conclude on the legacy of F. C. Baur,

> the prevailing opinion that from the outset of the Christian community was beset by conflicts over theology and practice—a view developed more by Walter Bauer (1904–60) than anyone else in the twentieth century, a study that still later gave stimulus to Robinson's and Koester's argument for the cultural and religious pluralism of the Hellenistic and Roman era—that opinion had Ferdinand Christian Baur for its father.[161]

Thus, this genealogical thread started with Baur. This is the quintessence of this work. But it was Robinson and Koester, students of Bultmann, who introduced this thesis onto American soil.[162]

---

159. Bingham, "Development and Diversity," 58.

160. Bingham, "Development and Diversity," 58. The historiography of Rudolph and other proponents of the history of religions school is a bit eclectic in its approach to early church. Bingham summarizes: "Rudolph is happy to place all models, from Bauer to Bultmann to Robinson and Koester, under the influence of the history of religions school on account of their emphasis on understanding early Christianity within the context of its environment. Here it has been freed from a historiography which was theologically and canonically restrained. Even Bauer takes a few words to clue the reader into his allegiance to such a historiography. Each model continues Hermann Gunkel's emphasis on the syncretistic nature of Christianity, yet they understand the dynamic of development differently. The first sees it as the integration and coexistence of the nascent and the Gnostic. The second sees it as the late introduction and ultimate victory of orthodoxy. The third understands it as a pattern of historically situated interpretations of a primitive religious figure, Jesus. Gone in the second and third is the concept of an original, primitive, nascent orthodoxy" (Bingham, "Development and Diversity," 58–59).

161. Harrisville and Sundberg, *Bible in Modern Culture*, 115–16.

162. The application of the "Bauer thesis" to the New Testament is beyond this work. For this specific aspect, see Dunn, *Unity and Diversity*.

Walter Bauer and the "Priority of Heresy" Historiography 109

Before turning attention to the full dissemination and popularization of the "Bauer thesis" beyond academia in the next chapter, it is in order here to briefly outline some of its main opponents in history. The question of its key proponents has already been addressed. Thus, the focus here would be on some of its earlier critical reviews.[163]

As already noted, some of the earliest criticism came from the noted Anglican scholar H. E. W. Turner in his Bampton Lectures, published as *The Pattern of Christian Truth* in 1954. However, as Paul Hartog highlights, the very first major criticism of the "Bauer thesis" came from Walther Völker in an essay review published in the *Zeitschrift für Kirchengeschichte* in 1935.[164] According to this German church historian, Bauer was not unaware of the fact that "proof cannot be conclusively drawn because of the fragmentary nature of our source material."[165] Völker does not mince words in his criticism of Bauer, writing:

> Consequently on occasion he himself considerably limits his conclusions, as when he points out that this book "is forced to rely heavily on conjectures" (224), or when he invokes a "perhaps," or a "probably" (105, 90, 45, 47: "I indulge in conjectures with reluctance"). He binds himself to strict standards whenever it is necessary to refute the views of other researchers. He points to the "extremely fragmentary nature of our knowledge" (221), he forswears claims of certainty, he demands evidence (51, A. 1)—however, all this does not prevent Bauer from recording the following sentence: "in order to acquire a true-to-life picture from indications in the sources, some degree of imagination should be necessary" (115).[166]

Thus, according to Völker, "Unfortunately the author has made rich use of his imagination, and the result is that in many passages his evidence cannot stand up in the face of careful scrutiny."[167] His conclusion is even more forceful. He writes:

> The author arrives at these astonishing conclusions by repeated use of the argument from silence, by bold combinations of

---

163. This is just a summary. For detailed discussions, see Strecker, "Appendix 2: The Reception of the Book."

164. Völker, "Walter Bauer's Rechtgläubigkeit," 628–31. For a recent English translation, see Völker, "Walter Bauer's *Rechtgläubigkeit*."

165. Völker, "Walter Bauer's *Rechtgläubigkei*," 400.

166. Völker, "Walter Bauer's *Rechtgläubigkei*," 400.

167. Völker, "Walter Bauer's *Rechtgläubigkei*," 400.

unrelated passages, by unprovable conjectures which themselves are reused as a precarious foundation for further conjectures, by inferences drawn from later periods, and finally by the arrangement of all isolated facts into the schema orthodoxy/heresy, whereby the variegated historical events are robbed of the full richness of their causes and motivations.[168]

However, his concluding prophesy would, obviously, not come to pass. "I cannot believe," he writes in his concluding remarks, "that such a reconstruction of history has any prospect of becoming accepted in the Protestant approach to church history (to say nothing of the Catholic). It is only the most extreme swing of the pendulum of a view that ultimately traces back to G. Arnold's estimation of the heretics."[169] As Hartog observes, contrary to Völker's prediction, "Bauer's framework has taken up permanent residence, within both academia and the popular

---

168. Völker, "Walter Bauer's *Rechtgläubigkei*," 404. McCue reaches the same conclusion. He writes: "Throughout the book Bauer argues extensively from silence. This is always a difficult argument, since one must be able to establish that the silence is significant and not just accidental, that there ought to be something there which is missing. An argument from silence, to be persuasive, must present us with an absence that needs explaining and that can only be explained in a particular way. But quite often, Bauer simply uses silence as a space within which to create history out of whole cloth" (McCue, "Bauer's Rechtgläubigkeit Und Ketzerei," 31. Similarly, Hultgren reaches the same conclusion, arguing that Bauer's thesis, especially as it concerns Edessan Christianity, is "too simplistic, and there are several considerations based on evidence, however slight, that speak strongly against it" (Hultgren, *Rise of Normative Christianity*, 11.)

169. Völker, "Walter Bauer's *Rechtgläubigkeit*," 404–05. It is important to note that Völker's criticism of the book was not the only one to appear that early. According to Köstenberger and Kruger, there were more than twenty-four book reviews appearing in six different languages in the years following the book's publication (Köstenberger and Kruger, *Heresy of Orthodoxy*, 33). While they note that many were appreciative of Bauer's thesis, several views were raised by these critics. These are: (1) that "Bauer's conclusions were unduly conjectural in light of the limited nature of the available evidence and in some cases arguments from silence altogether," (2) that "Bauer unduly neglected the New Testament evidence and anachronistically used second-century data to describe the nature of 'earliest' (first-century) Christianity. Bauer's neglect of the earliest available evidence is especially ironic since the title of the book suggested that the subject of his investigation was the *earliest* form of Christianity," (3) that Bauer "grossly oversimplified the first-century picture, which was considerably more complex than Bauer's portrayal suggested. For example, orthodoxy would have been present in more locations than Bauer acknowledged," and (4) that Bauer "neglected existing theological standards in the early church" (Köstenberger and Kruger, *Heresy of Orthodoxy*, 33). Many of these issues will be addressed in the final chapter of this work.

imagination."[170] Of course, mere acceptance of Bauerism does not *ipso facto* make it true. The latter aspect of the "Bauer thesis" will be taken up in the next chapter.

Next, as already discussed, came Turner's major criticism of the "Bauer thesis" in 1954. However, since the work has already been interacted with significantly, it will only suffice here to note his conclusion. Contrary to the diverse nature of doctrine that Bauer sees as the situation in the early church, Turner emphasized that the early church evidences some "fixed elements." Köstenberger and Kruger summarize these thusly:

> First, the core of early Christianity included what Turner called "religious facts": a "realistic experience of the Eucharist": belief in God as Father-Creator; belief in Jesus as the historical Redeemer; and belief in the divinity of Christ. Second, Turner maintained that the early Christians recognized the centrality of biblical revelation. However one delineates the New Testament canon and views its closure, the early church viewed it (at least in part) as revelatory. Third, the early believers possessed a creed and a rule of faith. Turner here refers to the "stylized summaries of *credenda* which are of frequent occurrence in the first two Christian centuries to the earliest creedal forms themselves." Such creeds include the earliest affirmations that "Jesus is Messiah" (Mark 8:29; John 11:27); "Jesus is Lord" (Rom. 10:9; Phil. 2:11; Col. 2:6); and "Jesus is the Son of God (Matt. 14:33; Acts 8:37).[171]

Many of these elements will be further explored in chapter 6.

The other major early criticism, as earlier noted, came from Jerry R. Flora. Appearing as a PhD dissertation in 1972 (only a year after Bauer's work was translated into English), Flora concluded that, "What became the dogma of the church ca. AD 200 was 'a religious life which [was] determined throughout by Jesus Christ' and reflected upon its faith-commitment in a variety of ways."[172] In other words, contrary to Bauer (and others like Harnack), the "church's movement toward what became the old catholicism appears to have been not the victory of a disciplined minority [Rome] over the diverse masses by means of aggressive Roman

---

170. Hartog, "From Völker to this Volume," 237.
171. Köstenberger and Kruger, *Heresy of Orthodoxy*, 34.
172. Flora, "Critical Analysis of Walter Bauer's Theory," 219.

leadership as Bauer maintained."¹⁷³ He, therefore, rejected the "Bauer thesis."

Finally, mention should be made of both I. Howard Marshall and Thomas Robinson. Marshall, professor of New Testament exegesis at Aberdeen, "critiqued Bauer from a New Testament vantage point by establishing the presence of early orthodoxy."¹⁷⁴ After surveying some key NT texts, Marshall writes, perhaps taking a cue from Turner:

> Now if this survey is sound, it shows that certain people in the first century, namely the writers of the New Testament, were conscious of the existence of opinions different from their own in the church, that they wrote and used other means to state or show that they were incompatible with the gospel which they believed themselves to have inherited, and that certain groups of people were regarded by them as deviationists and were excluded from the church or took themselves off to form their own groups. And this in my opinion is evidence that Bauer's thesis does not work when it is applied to the first century.¹⁷⁵

Thus, according to him, the "New Testament writers one and all regard themselves as upholders of the truth of the gospel, and they often see quite clearly where the lines of what is compatible with the gospel and what is not compatible are to be drawn."¹⁷⁶ And, although he concedes that Bauer is correct that "it is possible that in some places the beginnings of Christianity came from people later regarded as heretical,"¹⁷⁷ he nevertheless argues that Bauer was wrong to suggest that orthodoxy was a later development.

Robinson's work, a revision of his McMaster PhD dissertation, is entitled *The Bauer Thesis Examined: The Geography of Heresy in the Early Christian Church*. Robinson did what Bauer did—tracing heresy and orthodox in the first century by "reviewing the evidence region by region."¹⁷⁸ In so doing, he was able to even rebut other works that had built on the foundation of Bauer. He concluded that Bauer's work was only helpful in pointing out that early Christianity was diverse. Indeed, as Köstenberger and Kruger comment, "In direct opposition to Bauer,

---

173. Flora, "Critical Analysis of Walter Bauer's Theory," 247.
174. Köstenberger and Kruger, *Heresy of Orthodoxy*, 35.
175. Marshall, "Orthodoxy and Heresy."
176. Marshall, "Orthodoxy and Heresy," 13.
177. Marshall, "Orthodoxy and Heresy," 13.
178. Köstenberger and Kruger, *Heresy of Orthodoxy*, 36.

Robinson argued that heresy in Ephesus and western Asia Minor, where evidence is more readily available, was neither early nor strong; rather, orthodoxy preceded heresy and was numerically larger."[179] One is justified to say that Robinson here turns Bauer's thesis on its head. He further deduces that the "failure of [Bauer's] thesis in the only area where it can be adequately tested casts suspicion on the other areas of Bauer's investigation."[180] While one would have expected this conclusion to move scholarship past Bauer, this has not been the case. Indeed, as it will be shown in the next chapter, the thesis has gone "mainstream."

Before concluding this chapter, two more criticisms deserve to be further highlighted: that of Frederick Norris and Paul Trebilco. As noted earlier, Bauer made a number of conjectures in his argument. Both Norris and Trebilco's criticism focus on methodological issues pertaining to his presentation of the church fathers' orthodoxy. As noted above, Bauer's two main pieces of evidence include his conjecture based on his reading of Ignatian corpus (that orthodoxy most probably was the minority view in the churches to whom Ignatian addressed some of his letters or from whom he received emissaries) and his reconstruction of the most probable scenarios in key early Christian centers such as Edessa and Alexandria. Again, as it has been argued, many reviewers have contested Bauer's reading of the evidence. Additionally, here, the reader's attention will be briefly drawn to the recent and thorough response by P. Trebilco, focusing specifically on his interpretation of Ignatius's situation. Trebilco argues that, instead of providing evidence for the Bauer thesis, "Ignatius is actually a witness against Bauer."[181] He then adduces a four-point response. A few of these are pertinent here.

Trebilco's first counterpoint pertains to Bauer's presumed opponents of Ignatius. It is helpful to remember that, as far as the actual opponents of Ignatius in Asia Minor are concerned, Bauer identified them as Gnosticism and Marcionism. According to Bauer, "a real connection between John [the writer of Revelation] and Ignatius does appear in the fact that John's letters find him in opposition to a false teaching of an unmistakably gnostic brand—a heresy which pursues its path within the

---

179. Köstenberger and Kruger, *Heresy of Orthodoxy*, 36.

180. Robinson, *Bauer Thesis Examined*, 104. Of course, the selected critiques here are not the only ones. The list, in other words, is far from being exhaustive. See also McCue, "Bauer's Rechtgläubigkeit Und Ketzerei"; Martin, "Some Reflections"; Köstenberger, "Diversity and Unity."

181. Trebilco, "Christian Communities," 21.

churches themselves."[182] But is this historically accurate? Were the opponents of Ignatian Gnostics? Trebilco rightly observes that since Bauer published his work, there have been a lot more studies done especially on Gnosticism and its relationship to the key centers of early Christianity. As a result, it "now seems most likely that Ignatius faced two sets of opponents—Judaizers in Magnesia and Philadelphia and docetists in Tralles and Smyrna and of whom he warned in Ephesus."[183] Thus, because of these studies, "It is important to note that most scholars would not now want to argue that Ignatius faced fully-developed 'Gnosticism.'" This realization and scholarly conclusion is extremely significant because the identity of Ignatius's opponents is very central to the Bauer thesis. Rather, it is more historically correct to identify these opponents with Docetism and Judaizers than Gnosticism and Marcionism.

Not only does it seem that Bauer misidentified Ignatius's opponents especially in western Asia Minor, but also, possibly, in his insistence that what is known as "heresy" preceded what later came to be known as "orthodoxy," as noted above, may be an unsustainable claim. As we may recall, Bauer argued that Ignatius's letters show a frantic concern for communities that, in his estimation, were being threatened by the tyranny of the numbers of their opponents. Frederick Norris summarizes Bauer's point here, noting that, according to him, "The peril was depicted so clearly that bishop Polycarp wanted to leave troubled Smyrna and himself travel as a delegate to Antioch."[184] However, as Norris further observes, even Bauer himself changed his view on this crucial anchor of his thesis. That is, "First, he viewed the possibility of their being a majority as unlikely because of Ignatius's frantic arguments and efforts. Then he suggested that they probably comprised smaller or larger majorities in Ephesus, Magnesia, Tralles, and Philadelphia."[185] Consequently, Norris adduces two key points in response to this handling of the evidence by Bauer. First, he notes that it is impossible to substantiate Bauer's claim that Ignatius's views originated from a minority position "on his [Bauer's] reading of the evidence, unless he can prove that these three cities had 'orthodox' minorities prior to Ignatius, or demonstrate that there were

---

182. Bauer, *Orthodoxy and Heresy*, 78.

183. Trebilco, "Christian Communities," 22.

184. Norris, "Ignatius, Polycarp," 24. See also Norris, "Asia Minor before Ignatius," vii

185. Norris, "Ignatius, Polycarp," 24.

Walter Bauer and the "Priority of Heresy" Historiography 115

no truly monarchical bishops in those communities."[186] However, "Bauer made no attempt to argue that prior to the time of Ignatius, Magnesia, Tralles, and Philadelphia had 'orthodox' minorities. He tried to indicate that Ephesus could have been no 'center of orthodoxy' before Ignatius."[187] In other words, Bauer provides no evidence for such a key tenet of his thesis. Second, as Norris argues, Bauer "posited a 'gnostic anti-bishop' or someone acting in that way although he did not wish to quarrel about semantics."[188] Bauer conjectures, from the words of Polycarp in the letter to the *Philippians* 1.1, that there is a reference to a presbyter by the name of Valens, "who apparently was unassailable doctrinally,"[189] that this was a gnostic bishop. Here, again, Bauer fails to marshal enough evidence to reach such a conclusion. Additionally, Bauer's argument here faces a self-created conundrum. Norris captures this clearly. "Furthermore," he writes, "since Bauer insisted that in Smyrna during Polycarp's lifetime there was no 'separation between ecclesiastical Christianity and heresy,' on his reading of the evidence, there was no 'heretical' group outside the community to which Ignatius wrote."[190] This makes it impossible for Bauer to talk about "majority" and "minority" groups. "Therefore," Norris rightly concludes, "Bauer has been unable to prove that ecclesiastical Christianity was a minority among the Christians in Smyrna." This is a major methodological problem for Bauer.

While Trebilco's other salient points, such as the fact that Ignatius's concerns were not just theological as Bauer posits, as well as the fact that there was still continued Pauline influence in Asia Minor despite Bauer's argument, are important,[191] his discussion on the actual state of affairs in Asia Minor provides the most helpful summation. According to him, indeed, if we look at the New Testament literature from western Asia Minor, "we find a strong element of drawing of what we might call 'exclusionary lines' of belief and practice, and of drawing these lines in such a way that they are in continuity with later orthodoxy."[192] What he has

---

186. Norris, "Ignatius, Polycarp," 24–25.
187. Norris, "Ignatius, Polycarp," 25.
188. Norris, "Ignatius, Polycarp," 25.
189. Bauer, *Orthodoxy and Heresy*, 73–74.
190. Norris, "Ignatius, Polycarp," 26. See also Turner, *Pattern of Christian Truth*, 64.
191. Trebilco, "Christian Communities," 22.
192. Trebilco, "Christian Communities," 22. This point will be further pursued in chapter 6 of this work.

in mind here are the NT documents known as the Pastoral Epistles as well as the Johannine Letters, all of which were "written in or to western Asia Minor."[193] This observation clearly cuts into the heart of the Bauer thesis, that is, that orthodoxy was a later development. Trebilco further elucidates:

> In both cases we see *lines of exclusion emerging*. The opponents in view in the Pastorals had an overrealized eschatology and so thought the resurrection had already arrived, practised asceticism, maintained the validity of part of the Jewish Law and their behavior led to adverse comment from outsiders. In response, in the Pastorals we see "boundary lines" being drawn with regard to eschatology, asceticism, the Law, and behavior. For 1 John, the crucial matter was the Christology of the secessionists; it seems likely that they so emphasised the divinity of Christ that they marginalised his humanity. In response, 1 John emphasises the importance of the "flesh" of Jesus.[194]

Therefore, because of these and other methodological issues, the evidence that is solely based on Bauer's reconstruction of the possible scenarios in Asia Minor fails to adequately support his overarching thesis.

These methodological issues mar Bauer's second piece of evidence, a problem already noted in the earlier presentation of the Bauer thesis. This analysis will not be belabored here.[195] However, what about Rome, which,

---

193. Trebilco, "Christian Communities," 22.

194. Trebilco, "Christian Communities," 41–42. Trebilco, further cutting into the heart of the Bauer thesis, rightly comments: "Thus the roots of later 'orthodoxy' are to be found here. 'Orthodoxy' is not to be seen as a later victory by those in power, or something determined by politics. It goes back to and is an organic development from the much earlier period. And although in that earlier period it would be anachronistic to speak of 'orthodoxy,' the polemic against 'opponents' in literature from western Asia Minor reveals a strong sense of doctrinal self-consciousness on the part of the canonical authors. For the authors show that they are aware of holding a doctrinal or behavioral position that they wish to defend. This sense of a limit, self-consciously adopted, is a very significant feature of western Asia Minor, then. And what is self-consciously adopted and defended is in continuity with later orthodoxy" (Trebilco, "Christian Communities," 43).

195. As noted, this brings into mind Turner's questioning of the very first geographical location that Bauer brings up as evidence: Edessa. Turner writes: "Bauer's thesis is not wholly well served even by his opening witness. The evidence is too scanty and in many respects too flimsy to support any theory so trenchant and clear-cut as Bauer proposes. Yet his skepticism on many points of detail appears excessive, and his tendency to postpone the development of recognizably orthodox life far from conclusive. There is no satisfactory evidence Edessene Christianity had a Marcionite origin,

according to Bauer, alone was the important center of "orthodoxy" in the second century?[196]

Bauer's presentation of Rome as the center of orthodoxy in early Christianity almost catches his readers by surprise since, as Turner observes, "surprisingly, for a Lutheran, Bauer finds the hero (or villain) of the piece to be the Church of Rome."[197] But Bauer was able to trace the unfolding movement of "orthodox" Christianity from Rome reaching out to places like North Africa, Corinth, and elsewhere, concluding, Rome "was from the very beginning the center and chief source of power for the 'orthodox' movement within Christianity.'"[198] Indeed, his meticulous tracing of the historical developments of doctrine in one geographical area through a given period to see changes in opinion and action, as well as continuity of position and procedure, has been hailed as "one of the strongest points of Bauer's presentation."[199] However, as great as this reconstruction seems, it fails to take into account several other factors that are clearly pertinent to other key early Christian centers as well.

According to Norris, one of these factors pertains to what Bauer leaves out in his presentation of the evidence for the sole centrality of Rome in terms of early "orthodoxy." He points out that the Pastorals and the Apocalypse, which are chronologically earlier than the literature that Bauer is interested in, "give evidence of cross influences of various centers in Asia Minor."[200] More significantly, even in the writings of both Polycarp and Ignatius, there is discernible evidence of large theological influence/spread over the entirety of Asia Minor. "Polycarp," he writes, "wrote to Philippi in Macedonia in response to a letter from that community."[201] And Ignatius, on his part,

> shows a wide geographical range of influence and concern. He not only wrote to instruct communities in western Asia Minor about faith and practices, but also sent an epistle to Rome with instructions not to interfere in his martyrdom. The occasion of

---

and a substratum of truth may be found in the traditions of the Church even before the time of Palut [bishop of Edessa in the second century]" (Turner, *Pattern of Christian Truth*, 45).

196. Turner, *Pattern of Christian Truth*, 40.
197. Turner, *Pattern of Christian Truth*, 40.
198. Bauer, *Orthodoxy and Heresy*, 229.
199. Norris, "Ignatius, Polycarp," 37.
200. Norris, "Ignatius, Polycarp," 37.
201. Norris, "Ignatius, Polycarp," 38.

his writings was his journey to suffer death, but he used that opportunity to influence the various communities he wrote. The tone of the Roman letter is more favorable than any of the others. Ignatius does not hesitate, however, to warn that community of the consequences if they interfere in his going to God through the martyr's act. Nor does he fail to assert his own position as bishop of Syria paralleled to Rome's position in its region. [Thus] The literature of this period shows a pattern of territorial intervention or interpenetration from many Christian centers.[202]

In other words, what one sees here is a consistent pattern in terms of dealing with the evidence, that is, falling into the fallacy of appeal to selective evidence. That is "an instance where there has been so selective a use of evidence that other evidence has been illegitimately excluded."[203] The result, in the case of Bauer, is this uncontrolled historical reconstruction based on piecemeal evidence. Thus, this second piece of Bauer's thesis is "called into question because he did not recognize the strength of centers elsewhere in the Mediterranean and their contributions to the development of 'orthodoxy.'"[204] This is a noted tendency throughout Bauer's work.

Finally, in order to succeed in the advancement of his thesis, Bauer frequently falls into the fallacy of historical anachronism. "He [Bauer] also has a questionable tendency," argues Norris, "however, to read lines of development backwards, seeing later events in earlier texts. He based the third-century interventions of Rome in the first-century epistle of I Clement."[205] The problem with this kind of approach is that, in the case of Rome's centrality, "the evidence from the second century does not demand that Rome imposed its will on other areas far removed from its local concerns until the dramatic action of Victor."[206] Even in cases where Rome attempted to exert influence (e.g., the Paschal controversy of 154, a controversy concerned with the correct date for Paschal observance), this did not go uncontested by other Christian centers.[207] Therefore, a care-

---

202. Norris, "Ignatius, Polycarp," 38.
203. Carson, *Exegetical Fallacies*, 93.
204. Norris, "Ignatius, Polycarp," 39.
205. Norris, "Ignatius, Polycarp," 39.
206. Norris, "Ignatius, Polycarp," 39.
207. Norris, "Ignatius, Polycarp," 39. After discussing the back and forth between Anicetus and Polycarp on the matter, Norris adds: "Bauer is incorrect to suppose that

ful reading of the historical evidence of the relationship between Rome and other centers of early Christianity, leads to the inevitable conclusion that Bauer's thesis fails because of underestimating the influence of these other centers. "Bauer's second thesis," Norris concludes, "fails to stand up to scrutiny because he underrated the strength and influence of centers in Asia Minor and Syria and because by imputing later developments into his interpretations of earlier ones, he pushed Roman centrality back to a point in history where it did not exist."[208] Unfortunately, these methodological issues continue to plague those who continue to advocate for an unfettered acceptance of Bauer's early church historiography.

CONCLUSION

This chapter has addressed one of the most significant building stones of the quest for early church historiography: the "Bauer thesis." As it has been argued, so epoch-making was this thesis that, as opposed to the time before Bauer, today, "many scholars no longer use the terms *orthodoxy* and *heresy* without accompanying quotation marks."[209] However, as this chapter has argued, it is a mistake to look at the "Bauer thesis" in isolation from the historiographical shift that started with F. C. Baur. As it has been demonstrated, although this reality is recognized by a few scholars here and there, it needs to be stressed more. Again, as Varner argues, the Bauer hypothesis is the natural implication of the Baur hypothesis extended a step further beyond Paul to the early church.[210]

After the initial presentation of the key tenets of the "Bauer thesis," the chapter proceeded to provide initial appropriation of the thesis in the thought of such scholars as R. Bultmann and many of his students and colleagues including A. Ehrhardt, H. Conzelmann, E. Käsemann, J. Robinson, and H. Koester. All of these scholars, in one way or another, helped advance either in whole or an aspect of the "Bauer thesis," with the latter making it their goal to make sure that they indigenize the thesis (under the auspices of Bultmannianism) on American soil.

---

in these events the Roman powers were strategically biding their time until Asia Minor weakened" (Norris, "Ignatius, Polycarp," 39).

208. Norris, "Ignatius, Polycarp," 41.
209. Köstenberger and Kruger, *Heresy of Orthodoxy*, 38.
210. Varner, "Baur to Bauer," 95.

Next, the chapter also interacted with some of the leading critics of the thesis. This presentation started with the earliest critics such as the German church historian W. Völker, H. W. Turner, J. R. Flora, I. H. Marshall, and T. Robinson, among others. The criticisms of P. Trebilco and F. Norris were especially noted for their in-depth rebuttal of Bauer's methodologies. As it was shown, most of these scholars have offered legitimate criticisms of the "Bauer thesis" either in part or in whole. Most, if not all, have accused Bauer of exaggerating the argument from silence and/or simplifying complex issues in both the New Testament and the early church. Particularly, his understanding of doctrinal "diversity" seems to ignore some key unifying themes in the New Testament and the early church. However, instead of the theory phasing out, it has, over time, gained a significant amount of attention and support through the works of such scholars as B. Ehrman, E. Pagels, Karen King, and members of the "Jesus Seminar," among others. While the work now turns to these scholars, it helps to remind ourselves of these two methodological contributions of the work of Bauer: first, he drew attention to the need for examining the available evidence from the relevant geographical regions for early Christianity[211] as well as drawing attention to the argument that "the Church Fathers overstated their case that Christianity emerged from a single, doctrinally unified movement."[212] Both of these factors are explored in the succeeding chapters.

---

211. Köstenberger and Kruger, *Heresy of Orthodoxy*, 39–40.
212. Köstenberger and Kruger, *Heresy of Orthodoxy*, 40.

CHAPTER 5

The Historiography of Bart Ehrman and His Contemporaries

Extreme Historicism

The argument of this work is that the early church historiographical "tree" whose "roots" are found in the thought and work of C. F. Baur, eventually, had its greatest "fruit" in the thought and work of B. Ehrman. Our attention in this chapter now shifts to Ehrman and others who are responsible for the dissemination of the "Bauer thesis" in America presently.

BART EHRMAN'S EARLY CHURCH HISTORIOGRAPHY: BAUER RECONSTRUCTED

The last chapter explored in detail the emergence and dissemination of the "Bauer thesis." However, the chapter focused on scholars who interacted with the thesis primarily within their peers in the academy. While the same trend continues to some extent in this chapter, emphasis is laid upon those scholars who "chose to extend the discussion [of the 'Bauer thesis'] to a popular audience."[1] Among others, focus here will be on Ehrman and Pagels. They are treated in this order here.

It is impossible to estimate the impact of the prolific speaker and author of multiple books, and the James A. Gray Professor and Chair of the Department of Religious Studies at the University of North Carolina,

---

1. Köstenberger and Kruger, *Heresy of Orthodoxy*, 31.

Chapel Hill, Bart D. Ehrman (1955–).[2] While scholarship is still grappling with the place of Ehrman, to say that he is influential is almost an understatement. Through his many books and journal articles (as well as his popular debates with other scholars, both conservative and mainline evangelical), Ehrman has widely managed to carve a place for himself by popularizing his views. His influence came to light once again, when, in the Evangelical Theological Society's 69th Annual Conference held in Providence, Rhode Island, in November 2017, a session was entitled "Growing Up in the Ehrman Era: Retrospect & Prospect on Our Text-Critical Apologetic." Therefore, he is by far the most eloquent and effective popularizer of the Bauer thesis.

Ehrman's own religious pilgrimage from Christian conservative to losing his faith (agnostic atheist?) is an interesting story in itself. He personally documents this voyage in at least these two books: *Misquoting Jesus* and *Jesus, Interrupted*. Ehrman summarizes concerning his early years:

> For most of my life I was a devout and committed Christian. I was baptized in a Congregational church and reared as an Episcopalian, becoming an altar boy when I was twelve and continuing all the way through high school. Early in my high school days I started attending a Youth for Christ club and had a "born again" experience—which, looking back, seems a bit strange: I had been involved in church, believing in Christ, praying to God, confessing my sins, and so on for years. What exactly did I convert from? I think I was converting from hell—I didn't want to experience eternal torment with the poor souls who had not been "saved"; I much preferred the option of heaven. In any event, when I became born again it was like ratcheting my religion up a notch. I became very serious about my faith and chose to go off to a fundamentalist Bible college—Moody Bible Institute in Chicago—where I began training for ministry.[3]

Further, Ehrman explains:

> I continued to be a Christian—a completely committed Christian—for many years after I left the evangelical fold. Eventually, though, I felt compelled to leave Christianity altogether. I did not go easily. On the contrary, I left kicking and screaming,

---

2. His many works include: *Lost Christianities*; *The Orthodox Corruption of Scripture*; *Misquoting Jesus*, *God's Problem*; *How Jesus Became God*; and *Jesus, Interrupted*.

3. Ehrman, *God's Problem*, 1.

wanting desperately to hold on to the faith I had known since childhood... I could no longer explain how there can be a good and all-powerful God actively involved with this world, given the state of things. For many people who inhabit this planet, life is a cesspool of misery and suffering. I came to a point where I simply could not believe that there is a good and kindly disposed Ruler who is in charge of it.[4]

But what was Ehrman's "turning point," such that, as Andreas Köstenberger, Darrell Bock, and Josh Chatraw note, "By the time Bart Ehrman emerged from Princeton Seminary with his master of divinity and PhD degrees, he was no longer the fundamentalist Christian he believed himself to be when he entered Moody Bible Institute as an undergrad[?]"[5] Fortunately, Ehrman answers this question for us. He explains what happened between his years as a student at Moody Bible Institute through Wheaton College to Princeton Theological Seminary where he studied under the renowned textual critic Bruce M. Metzger.[6] He documents his turning point when a certain Professor Story made a comment on his paper on a textual issue in the Gospel of Mark that "Maybe Mark just made a mistake."[7] He comments that, out of this comment (poor Professor Story!), "the floodgates opened. For if there could be one little picayune mistake in Mark 2, maybe there could be mistakes in other places as well."[8] Eventually, Ehrman left Christianity altogether. He, however, admits that this was not at all an easy decision.[9] But as

---

4. Ehrman, *God's Problem*, 3.
5. Köstenberger, Bock, and Chatraw, *Truth Matters*, 1.
6. Decker, "Rehabilitation of Heresy." He explains that "Ehrman was one of Metzger's last two PhD students in textual criticism at Princeton (the other being Michael Holmes) and he was selected to prepare the most recent revision of Metzger's standard textbook, *Text of the New Testament: Its Transmission, Corruption, and Restoration* (New York: Oxford, 2005)" (Decker, "Rehabilitation of Heresy"). Further, he describes Ehrman this way: "One of the current writers in the media spotlight is Bart Ehrman. He is not the first nor only voice advocating a radical overhaul of our conception of early Christianity. He has been, however, one of the more visible and influential voices. This is due to several factors. First, he is a credentialed scholar in a related discipline, NT textual criticism. In this regard he seems to have benefited from his association with the 'dean' of that field, Bruce Metzger. He is also a good writer and effective communicator. In addition, he has achieved broad media exposure for his popularization of more scholarly work" (Decker, "Rehabilitation of Heresy," 3).
7. Ehrman, *God's Problem*, 9.
8. Ehrman, *God's Problem*, 9.
9. He writes, for example, in *Jesus, Interrupted*: "Some things don't go as planned.

soon as the turn was made, for Ehrman, there was no turning back. His thought and scholarship in the area of New Testament and early Christianity has been guided by his religious (or lack thereof) inclination.[10]

Ehrman's early church historiography, though decipherable from various places, comes out clearly in his *Lost Christianities*. As the title suggests, in this work, Ehrman purports to present to the reader versions of early Christianities that were lost in history. Comparing them with the current scenario where all kinds of groups claim to be Christians, Ehrman presents several of these "Christianities" that were present in the second and third centuries. "The wide diversity of early Christianity," he writes, "may be seen above all in the theological beliefs embraced by people who understood themselves to be followers of Jesus."[11] He continues by noting that in the second and third centuries, "there were, of course, Christians who believed in one God. But there were others who insisted that there were two. Some said there were thirty. Others claimed there were 365."[12] In addition to the concept of God, according to Ehrman, most other variegated views were in the areas of cosmology and Christology.

Concerning cosmology, Ehrman explains that in the second and third centuries, "there were Christians who believed that God had created the world."[13] However, according to him, "others believed that this world

---

What I actually did learn at Princeton led me to change my mind about the Bible. I did not change my mind willingly—I went down kicking and screaming. I prayed (lots) about it, I wrestled (strenuously) with it. I resisted it with all my might. But at the same time I thought that if I was truly committed to God, I also had to be fully committed to the truth. And it became clear to me over a long period of time that my former views of the Bible as the inerrant revelation from God were flat out wrong. My choice was either to hold on to views that I had come to realize were in error or to follow where I believed the truth was leading me. In the end, it was no choice. If anything was true, it was true; if not, no" (Ehrman, *Jesus, Interrupted*, xi).

10. Concerning Ehrman's demeanor, I certainly agree with Randy Alcorn, who has perceptively observed: "While I will criticize Ehrman, I should clarify that sometimes I find him likable. He can be overconfident, yet occasionally admits his uncertainties. He avoids the bombastic approach that some atheist—and some Christian—authors display" (Alcorn, *If God Is Good*, 95). Alcorn further comments, "Unfortunately, Ehrman's Christian-to-non-theist testimony gives apparent credibility to his claims, so he functions as a winsome evangelist for atheism. While he says he doesn't intend to cause believers to lose their faith, it's easy to wonder why else he would write such a book" (Alcorn, *If God Is Good*, 95).

11. Ehrman, *Lost Christianities*, 2.

12. Ehrman, *Lost Christianities*, 2.

13. Ehrman, *Lost Christianities*, 2.

had been created by a subordinate, ignorant divinity."[14] The evidence for this, according to him, was the presence of suffering and misery. "Yet other Christians," he writes, "thought it was worse than that, that this world was a cosmic mistake created by a malevolent divinity as a place of imprisonment, to trap humans and subject them to pain and suffering."[15] However, it is in Christology where Ehrman sees most of these various views.

After pointing out to the various views concerning the Jewish Scripture (Old Testament) in the second and third centuries (some believed that it was inspired by God, while others believed it was either inspired by an evil deity or not inspired at all),[16] Ehrman now focuses on the doctrine of Christ. He elaborates:

> In the second and third centuries, there were Christians who believed that Jesus was both divine and human, God and man. There were other Christians who argued that he was completely divine and not human at all. (For them divinity and humanity were incommensurate entities: God can no more be a man than a man can be a rock.) There were others who insisted that Jesus was a full flesh-and-blood human, adopted by God to be his son but not himself divine. There were yet other Christians who claimed that Jesus Christ was two things: a full flesh-and-blood human, Jesus, and a fully divine being, Christ, who temporarily inhabited Jesus' body during his ministry and left him prior to his death, inspiring his teachings and miracles but avoiding the suffering in its aftermath.[17]

And, finally, in terms of soteriology, Ehrman also argued that there were differing Christian groups with different views. According to him, there were Christians "who believed that Jesus' death brought about the salvation of the world,"[18] while there were other Christians who "thought that Jesus' death had nothing to do with the salvation of the world."[19] Lastly, there were those who "said that Jesus never died."[20] So, what is the basis for Ehrman's views?

14. Ehrman, *Lost Christianities*, 2.
15. Ehrman, *Lost Christianities*, 2.
16. Ehrman, *Lost Christianities*, 2.
17. Ehrman, *Lost Christianities*, 2.
18. Ehrman, *Lost Christianities*, 2.
19. Ehrman, *Lost Christianities*, 2.
20. Ehrman, *Lost Christianities*, 2.

Ehrman argues that these views could all be considered "Christian" because "there was no New Testament."²¹ While, by this time, all the books that were to be later recognized as the canonical New Testament had been written, "they had not yet been gathered into a widely recognized and authoritative canon of Scripture."²² For him, therefore, such teachings were contained in many other books, "written as well, with equally impressive pedigree—other Gospels, Acts, Epistles, and the Apocalypses claiming to be written by the earthly apostles of Jesus."²³ Consequently, Ehrman uses many of the chapters in the books exploring these writings, something he does in his twin work to *Lost Christianities*, aptly entitled *Lost Scriptures: Books That Did Not Make It into the New Testament*.²⁴

To be sure, Ehrman is not the first one to make such a contention. Historically, there have been occasional attempts to argue that there were other Christianities in the early centuries, all of equal credence to what has been bequeathed to us as the "orthodox" understanding, according to them. Even before the discoveries at Nag Hammadi in 1945 of the key treatises there, which are primarily what Ehrman is referring to, there were occasional arguments for the existence of these "Christianities." Philip Jenkins summarizes, concerning these:

> Nor are the "new" findings touted in recent years all that new: contrary to some recent writings, the scholarly world did not flounder in darkness until illumination came from Nag Hammadi. Basic to the dramatic account of the rediscovered gospels is the idea that they restored to the world knowledge which had been lost for many centuries. At last, we are told, after 1600 years, we finally hear the heretics speak for themselves. The problem with this approach is that many of the insights about early Christianity found in the lost texts had been known for many years before the Nag Hammadi discoveries, and had in fact already penetrated a mass audience.²⁵

While he sees these developments as having continued over time, increased activity took place between 1880 and 1920, when "a cascade of new discoveries transformed attitudes to early Christianity, both the

---

21. Ehrman, *Lost Christianities*, 3.
22. Ehrman, *Lost Christianities*, 3.
23. Ehrman, *Lost Christianities*, 3.
24. See Ehrman, *Lost Scriptures*.
25. Jenkins, *Hidden Gospels*, 13.

mainstream and the heretical fridges."[26] He argues that this development was catapulted by the exciting find of the *Gospel of Thomas* in Egypt as well as the *Gospel of Peter*.

But, by far, it was the discovery of the Nag Hammadi codices that has led such scholars as Ehrman to reconfigure and take the "Bauer thesis" mainstream (the domestication of the "Bauer thesis"). These writings, popularly known as "the Nag Hammadi library," were discovered by an Egyptian peasant, Muhammad ʿAli, near the city of Nag Hammadi in Upper Egypt. Concerning the occasion and importance of this discovery, Charles W. Hedrick writes:

> In 1945 in Upper Egypt near the large modern village of Nag Hammadi a peasant accidentally discovered a collection of twelve leather-bound papyrus books of one individual tractate. The texts contains some fifty-one individual writings, the bulk of which were unknown to scholarship prior to their discovery. In general, they may be described as heretical Christian-gnostic writings, although they are really more diverse than that general designation implies.[27]

Indeed, on his part, Ehrman believes that "no form of lost Christianity has so intrigued modern readers and befuddled modern scholars as early Christian Gnosticism," adding that "the intrigue is easy to understand especially in view of the discovery of Nag Hammadi library."[28] Although the question of Gnosticism will be picked up later, suffice here to say that these discoveries provided Ehrman and others with the impetus to reconfigure the "Bauer thesis."

Ehrman, after exploring these writings in a lengthy manner, helpfully traces the thread that has led to his conclusions. He traces this in the thoughts of Hermann Reimarus (1694–1768), F. C. Baur (1792–1860), and Walter Bauer (1877–1960). However, he focusses on the latter,

---

26. Jenkins, *Hidden Gospels*, 13. "Even the special role of women," Jenkins continues, "which has attracted so much comment in recent years, was already being discussed in that epoch. The image of Jesus choosing Mary Magdalen as his especially beloved disciple runs through a large Gnostic work called the *Pistis Sophia*, which was available in a popular English translation as far back as 1896. The notion was quoted in feminist and New Age writings of the early twentieth century—and though this tends to be forgotten in modern writings, both feminists and New Age adherents wrote extensively on early Christianity in this period. Radical perspectives on religion were not an innovation of the 1960s" (Jenkins, *Hidden Gospels*, 14).

27. Hedrick, "Introduction: Nag Hammadi," 4.

28. Ehrman, *Lost Christianities*, 113.

whose *Orthodoxy and Heresy*, according to him, "was arguably the most important book on the history of early Christianity to appear in the twentieth century."[29] Calling Bauer a "scholar of great range and massive erudition,"[30] Ehrman, after rehearsing the "Bauer thesis," argues that Bauer's book was so monumental that the "repercussions are still felt today, as Bauer's analysis has changed forever how we look at the theological controversies prior to the fourth century."[31] Ehrman sees especially helpful Bauer's objection to the use of the terms "orthodoxy" and "heresy" as helpful debate terms in the study of early church history. "For him," he writes concerning Bauer, "historians cannot use the words *orthodoxy* to mean right belief and *heresy* to mean wrong belief."[32] This is because these "[words] are value judgements about theological 'truths.' But the historian is no more able to pronounce on ultimate 'truth' than anyone else,"[33] he contends. Thus, Ehrman sees Bauer's model as the best theory to account for the history of the early church because, for him, "Speaking about orthodoxy in the earlier period . . . is a kind of intentional anachronism that highlights the problem by using its own terms."[34] So, how does Ehrman configure his own early church historiography in relation to the "Bauer thesis," which he so much praises, then?

Bingham contends that Ehrman's work "presents us with a revised version of Bauer's argument."[35] In other words, Ehrman "moves the reader away from the classical theory of developments in early Christianity to one which echoes and extends that of Bauer."[36] Ehrman does this by casting suspicion, first on the Gospel accounts themselves. Regurgitating the skepticism of Reimarus on the perceived discrepancies in the Gospels, Ehrman concludes, concerning the Gospel writers, for example:

> Some of the differences are much larger, involving the purpose of Jesus' mission and the understanding of his character. What all the differences show, great and small, is that each Gospel writer has an agenda—a point of view he wants to get across, an

---

29. Ehrman, *Lost Christianities*, 173.
30. Ehrman, *Lost Christianities*, 173.
31. Ehrman, *Lost Christianities*, 173.
32. Ehrman, *Lost Christianities*, 173.
33. Ehrman, *Lost Christianities*, 173–74.
34. Ehrman, *Lost Christianities*, 174.
35. Bingham, "Development and Diversity," 59.
36. Bingham, "Development and Diversity," 59.

understanding of Jesus he wants his readers to share. And he has told his stories in such a way as to convey that agenda.[37]

Thus, for him, instead of telling the story of the life of Jesus from different viewpoints based on their respective occasions for writing, the Gospel writers were each advancing a specific agenda. Indeed, concerning these discrepancies, taking a cue from Reimarus, Ehrman contends:

> The basis evidence for this point of view [the view by Reimarus, that the disciples began a religion contrary to what Jesus intended] involves some of the major points that Reimarus himself made: There are differences among the Gospel accounts that cannot be reconciled: Did Jesus die the afternoon before the Passover meal was eaten, as in John (see 19:14), or the morning afterwards, as in Mark (see 14:12, 22; 15:25)? Did Joseph and Mary flee to Egypt after Jesus' birth as in Matthew (12:13–23), or did they return to Nazareth (2:39)? Was Jairus's daughter sick and dying when he came to ask Jesus for help as in Mark (6:23, 35), or had she already died, as in Matthew (9:18)? After Jesus' resurrection, did the disciples stay in Jerusalem until he had ascended into heaven, as in Luke (24:1–52), or did they straightaway go to Galilee, as in Matthew (28:1–20)?[38]

In fact, Ehrman does not limit his skepticism to the Gospel writers. He moves the reader through the same process in "the Acts of the Apostles, and Eusebius, and the literature and polemics of proto-orthodoxy."[39] He extends the same extreme historicism to the early church, writing:

> But once we begin to suspect the historical accuracy of our Gospel sources, and find influence that corroborates our suspicions, where does that lead us? With regard to our questions about the nature of orthodoxy and heresy in early Christianity, it leads us away from the classical notion that orthodoxy is rooted in the apostles' teaching as accurately preserved in the New Testament Gospels and to the realization that the doctrines of orthodox Christianity must have developed at a time later than the historical Jesus and his apostles, later even than our earliest Christian writings.[40]

37. Ehrman, *Lost Christianities*, 170.
38. Ehrman, *Lost Christianities*, 169–70.
39. Bingham, "Development and Diversity," 59.
40. Ehrman, *Lost Christianities*, 170. Bingham aptly summarizes Ehrman's historiography, explaining that, for Ehrman, "(1) 'the doctrines of orthodox Christianity must have developed at a time later than the historical Jesus and his apostles, later even

In Ehrman, therefore, the "Bauer thesis" has reached its fullest outworking.[41]

---

than our earliest Christian writings'; (2) the extent of proto-orthodoxy in the second and third centuries was even less than Bauer had estimated; (3) 'early Christianity was even less tidy and more diversified' than Bauer had realized; and (4) the victory of the proto-orthodoxy group had less to do with the influence of Rome than with polemical strategies in the art of literary combat. Ehrman presents us with a revised version of Bauer's argument. Development in early Christianity is a movement away from an originally broad variety of Christianities, ideologically in conflict with proto-orthodoxy, to a later, but strategically superior, 'orthodoxy'" (Bingham, "Development and Diversity," 59).

41. After a lengthy section entitled "In Support of Bauer's Basic Thesis: A Modern Assessment of Early Christian Diversity" (chapters 9–11), Ehrman, then, in the last chapter, discusses seven themes which he sees in the attacks by the proto-orthodox heresiologists. Decker summarizes: "1) Unity and diversity: if there is not agreement, something is wrong (and there was great diversity within Gnosticism). 2) Sense and nonsense: beliefs that are not logical are wrong (though Ehrman suggests that Gnostic myth was mistaken for propositional truth. 3) Truth and error: heresy is a perversion of pre-existing truth. 4) Apostolic succession: everything must be traceable back to the apostles. 5) Rule of faith and creeds: the *regula fidei* and later the creeds define truth. 6) Interpretation of Scripture: literal interpretation of the text is primary; figurative interpretations only used to support truth established on literal grounds (Marcion and the Gnostics emphasized figurative, allegorical interpretations). 7) Charges of reprobate activity: traditional rhetoric accused the heretics of immorality: false teaching is matched by promiscuity" (Decker, "Rehabilitation of Heresy," 24). However, the question of whether or not there is truth in these "accusations" is not convincingly resolved in Ehrman's work. Indeed, concerning the final accusation, Decker perceptively observes: "At this point Ehrman uses what he considers an extreme, shocking case: the charges by Epiphanius of orgiastic and cannibalistic practices of a Gnostic group. Ehrman asks rhetorically, 'Can this tale of unbridled lust and ritual cannibalism be true?' (200). He is clear that Epiphanius certainly can't be trusted on this point; the accusations are fabricated for rhetorical, heresiological purposes and have no basis in reality. The picture is quite grotesque and offensive to our sensibilities—and Ehrman spares no details in his (deliberately) shocking portrait. It is quite interesting, however, that Stephen Gero has documented just such a practice in a Gnostic group . . . If this is valid for the Borbotites [gnostic group], perhaps Epiphanius may be right about the Phibionites! We may be repulsed by the description, but that does not make it unhistorical or inaccurate. Ehrman's only evidence against Epiphanius's charge (rather than making his rhetorical 'it couldn't be true') is that the Nag Hammadi library of Gnostic documents consistently lean toward an ascetic emphasis (201). But despite his claim that Nag Hammad represents a 'bewildering variety' of Gnostic schools, there are only four dozen texts involved . . . *If* these documents originate from a monastery several miles away (which is not certain though often suggested), then one would expect them to focus on texts which supported ascetic lifestyle rather than more libertine forms of Gnosticism. In other words, Nag Hammadi may not be widely representative of Gnosticism" (Decker, "Rehabilitation of Heresy," 24–25n59). Thus, the criterion that Ehrman uses to test the truthfulness of Epiphanius's accusation (i.e., an affront to our

In conclusion, not only does Ehrman appropriate the "Bauer thesis," but he goes event beyond Bauer, insisting, "the extent of proto-orthodoxy in the second and third centuries was even less than Bauer had estimated."[42] Indeed, according to him, "if anything, early Christianity was even less tidy and more diversified than he [Bauer] realized."[43] Fully stated, therefore, Ehrman's historiography goes something like this: "Development in early Christianity is a movement away from an originally broad variety of Christianities, ideologically in conflict with proto-orthodoxy, to a later, but strategically superior, 'orthodoxy.'"[44] However, instead of seeing this process as taking place naturally through the "thesis-synthesis-antithesis" cycle, as F. C. Baur conceived it, for Ehrman, "this victory came about through conflicts that are attested in polemical treatises, personal slurs, forgeries, and falsifications."[45] For him, the "final victors were proto-orthodox who got the 'last laugh' by sealing the victory, finalizing the New Testament, and choosing the documents that best suited their purpose and theology."[46] Finally, for him, "posterity is aware of these 'losers' (i.e., 'heretics') only by their sparsely available written remains that the 'winners' excluded from the Bible."[47] Thus, in Ehrman, we have the fullest flowering and complete fruition of the Bauer thesis.

While, as noted above, scholarship is still grappling with Ehrman's popularization of the "Bauer thesis,"[48] several criticisms have so far been raised against Ehrman's early church historiography. Several scholars

---

sensibilities), is itself flawed. See also Gerö, "With Walter Bauer on the Tigris."

42. Bingham, "Development and Diversity," 59.
43. Ehrman, *Lost Christianities*, 176.
44. Ehrman, *Lost Christianities*, 176.
45. Köstenberger and Kruger, *Heresy of Orthodoxy*, 32.
46. Köstenberger and Kruger, *Heresy of Orthodoxy*, 32.
47. Köstenberger and Kruger, *Heresy of Orthodoxy*, 32.
48. As Köstenberger and Kruger further note, Ehrman has managed to popularize his views through a variety of ways. "Besides being a prolific scholar," they write, "having published more than twenty books (some making it onto bestseller lists) and contributing frequently to scholarly journals, Ehrman promotes the Bauer thesis in the mainstream media in an unprecedented way. Ehrman's work has been featured in publications such as *Time*, *The New Yorker*, and the *Washington Post*, and has appeared on *Dateline NBC*, *The Daily Show with Jon Stewart*, CNN, The History Channel, National Geographic, the Discovery Channel, the BBC, NPR, and other major media outlets" (Köstenberger and Kruger, *Heresy of Orthodoxy*, 31–32). A similar approach is evident in the questioning of the standard portrayal of early Christian persecution by Candinda Moss (see Moss, *The Myth of Persecution*).

have criticized several aspects of Ehrman's thought. In one of the most scathing critiques of Ehrman's historiography, Craig Blaising begins by stating that "there are many things that could be said about Bart Ehrman's account of ancient 'Christianities.'"[49] He summarizes:

> The foundation for it all, of course, is a critical theory of NT compositional history which has been contested by evangelical biblical scholars. But you would not know that from Ehrman's book, which presents his critical views as simply the widely accepted results of biblical scholarship. Ehrman, it turns out, is not as interested in diversity as he pretends and has engaged in a little fabrication himself to cover it up. Take away his NT critical views, and later Christian writings acquire a different look. If the NT writings were *not forgeries*, then the early Christian writers were not deceitful in their use of them. If the Gospels give a trustworthy account of Jesus and his teaching, then the early church cannot be faulted for appealing to them to adjudicate conflicting claims about what he said, especially if these claims are found in writings that *are* most likely forgeries. If, in fact, there are authoritative writings from the days of Jesus and his apostles, it is sound to consult them.[50]

Thus, according to Blaising, Ehrman seems to put a lot more trust in documents that are more likely to be forgeries, and, consequently, using them to judge those documents that are less likely to be forged! And while, as Blaising points out, this is not to say that early non-canonical writers "were without any fault in their discourse, in some of their characterizations or arguments,"[51] it is unfair to impugn "their claim of faithfulness to Jesus Christ in accordance with his Word."[52] Indeed, he blames this obsession with diversity on the post-modern culture, a tendency that has affected all fields including theology and Christian historiography.

Finally, Blaising sees the historiography of Ehrman as steeped in postmodern fascination with diversity, as documented by Kathryn Tanner in her work entitled *Theories of Culture: A New Agenda for Theology*.[53] Critiquing the post-liberal theologies of George Lindbeck and Hans Frei,

---

49. Blaising, "Faithfulness: A Prescription," 8.
50. Blaising, "Faithfulness: A Prescription," 8–9.
51. Blaising, "Faithfulness: A Prescription," 9.
52. Blaising, "Faithfulness: A Prescription," 9.
53. Tanner, *Theories of Culture*. For a classic post-liberal approach to doing theology, see Lindbeck, *Nature of Doctrine*.

The Historiography of Bart Ehrman and His Contemporaries

Tanner argues for the concept of the "free Word of God" (Barthianism).[54] According to her, "the free Word can never be identified with human words or human practices which are at best time-bound and culture-bound testimonies to the Free, Unbounded, Unrestrained Word."[55] And therefore, whether stated or not, this postmodern theology is the full outworking of the "Bauer thesis," emphasizing cultural diversity of theology as well. As Blaising concludes, "a postmodern theology of culture sees the Free Word working across and through both inter-cultural and extra-cultural diversity."[56] Thus, "there may exist at any particular time a 'common way of believing and thinking theologically,' but it is always contestable and may actually be or become oppressive to the 'sincere' beliefs of any of the constituency as these beliefs come into existence and develop."[57] Therefore, not only has the "Bauer thesis" been now domesticated, but its implications have taken root in several disciplines of study.

EHRMAN'S CONTEMPORARIES

Elaine Pagels, Harrington Spear Paine Professor at Princeton University, engaged the "Bauer thesis" in her 2003 work entitled *Beyond Belief: The Secret Gospel of Thomas*. In an approach reminiscent of Ehrman, Pagels introduces the work by treating the reader to her own religious journey, which begins with a fatal disease, pulmonary hypertension,[58] and losing him when he was only six years old. This led her to seek help in religion.[59] She explains how she was fascinated by the sight of worship that she saw in progress at the Church of the Heavenly Rest in New York—"the soaring harmonies of the choir singing with the congregation; and the priest, a woman in bright gold and white vestments, proclaiming prayers in a clear, resonant voice."[60] She explains that this attracted her as she saw the

---

54. Blaising, "Faithfulness: A Prescription," 10.

55. Blaising, "Faithfulness: A Prescription," 10.

56. Blaising, "Faithfulness: A Prescription," 10.

57. Blaising, "Faithfulness: A Prescription," 10. See also Geertz, *Interpretation of Cultures*.

58. Pagels, *Beyond Belief*, 4.

59. She follows the same theme in her memoir (Pagels, *Why Religion?*). She experienced another loss, just fifteen months after her son's death—the death of her husband in a climbing accident.

60. Pagels, *Beyond Belief*, 3.

church as a "family that knows how to face death."[61] She explains that she returned to the church "not looking for faith but because, in the presence of that worship and the people gathered there—and in a smaller group that met on weekdays in the church basement for mutual encouragement—my defenses fell away, exposing storms of grief and fear."[62] Then she raises this crucial question—what is faith?

It is in her attempt to respond to this question that Pagels reengages the "Bauer thesis." She argues that it is a mistake to define faith as simply an assent to set beliefs, commenting:

> When people would say to me, "Your faith must be of great help to you," I would wonder, What do they mean? What is faith? Certainly not a simple assent to the set beliefs that worshippers in that church recited every week ("We believe in one God, the Father, the Almighty maker of heaven and earth . . .")—traditional statements that sounded strange to me, like barely intelligible signals from the surface, heard at the bottom of the sea. Such statements seemed to me then to have little to do with whatever transactions we were making with one another ourselves, and—so it was said—with invisible beings. I was acutely aware that we met driven by need and desire; yet sometimes I dared hope that such communion has the potential to transform us.[63]

Again, rejecting the idea that Christianity is synonymous to assent to a certain set of beliefs, she argues that from her historical reading, she knew that "Christianity had survived brutal persecution and flourished for generations—even centuries—*before* Christians formulated what they believed into creeds."[64] Certainly, one detects language reminiscent of that of Adolf Harnack here. Consequently, after describing how this Christianity looked before the creeds, she argues that, contrary to this period, "since the fourth century, most churches have required those who would join such communion to profess a complex set of beliefs about God and Jesus—beliefs formulated by fourth-century bishops into ancient creeds."[65] Thus, according to her, the problem arose with these creedal formulations in the fourth century.

---

61. Pagels, *Beyond Belief*, 3.
62. Pagels, *Beyond Belief*, 3.
63. Pagels, *Beyond Belief*, 5.
64. Pagels, *Beyond Belief*, 5.
65. Pagels, *Beyond Belief*, 27.

Pagels credits the discovery of the gnostic Gospels at Nag Hammadi in 1945 with her understanding of Christian life before the codification by the fourth century bishops. "Furthermore," she writes, "the astonishing discovery of the gnostic gospels—a cache of ancient secret gospels and other revelations attributed to Jesus and his disciples—has revealed a much wider range of Christian groups than we have ever known before."[66] This discovery led her to argue from her study of the *Gospel of Thomas* that "modern Christians should move beyond belief in rigid dogmas to a healthy plurality of religious views since the early Christians were likewise not dogmatic but extremely diverse."[67] Speaking of this diversity, and comparing the canonical Gospels with the Nag Hammadi ones, she writes:

> after the gospels of Mark, Matthew, and Luke were joined with John's gospel and Paul's letters to become the "New Testament"— a process that took place over some two hundred years (c. 160 to 360 CE)—most Christians came to read these earlier gospels through John's lens, and thus to find in all of them evidence of John's conviction that Jesus is "Lord and God." The gospels discovered in 1945 in Upper Egypt, however, offer different perspectives. For if Matthew, Mark and Luke had been joined with the Gospel of Thomas instead of with John, for example, or had *both* John and Thomas been included in the New Testament

---

66. Pagels, *Beyond Belief*, 28. Her own journey towards discovering these documents is interesting as it brings into focus some scholars already discussed in this work. She writes: "After college I studied dance at the Martha Graham School in New York. I loved dance, but I still wondered what it was about Christianity that I found so compelling and at the same time so frustrating. I decided to look for the 'real Christianity'—believing, as Christians traditionally have, that I might find it by immersing myself in the earliest Christian sources, composed soon after Jesus and his disciples wandered in Galilee. When I entered the Harvard doctoral program, I was astonished to hear from the other students that Professors Helmut Koester and George MacRae, who taught the early history of Christianity, had file cabinets filled with 'gospels' and 'apocrypha' written during the first centuries, many of them secret writings of which I'd never heard. These writings, containing sayings, rituals, and dialogues attributed to Jesus and his disciples, were found in 1945 among a cache of texts from the beginning of the Christian era, unearthed near Nag Hammadi in Upper Egypt. When my fellow students and I investigated these sources, we found that they revealed diversity within the Christian movement that later 'official' versions of Christian history had suppressed so effectively that only now, in the Harvard graduate school, did we hear about them. So we asked who wrote these alternative gospels, and when. And how do these relate to—and differ from—the gospels and other writings familiar from the New Testament?" (Pagels, *Beyond Belief*, 32).

67. Köstenberger and Kruger, *Heresy of Orthodoxy*, 31.

canon, Christians probably would have read the first three gospels quite differently. The gospels of Thomas and John speak for different groups of Jesus' followers engaged in discussion, even argument, toward the end of the first century.[68]

This is the gist of the entire book. She identifies the contested issues between what can be termed as the "Johannine tradition" and the "Thomas tradition" as this: "Who is Jesus, and what is the 'good news' (in Greek *euangellion*, 'gospel') about him?"[69] Her emphasis, therefore, is the diversity on these subjects that existed before the canonization of the New Testament as well as the creedal formulations of the fourth century.

Therefore, Pagels, like Ehrman, reengages the "Bauer thesis." According to her, as the second century emerged, "Christians became increasingly narrow in their doctrinal views."[70] She attributes the theological controversies of the second century to this "narrowing." For her, "the group espousing 'orthodoxy' arose in the context of this theological narrowing and subsequently came to outnumber and conquer the Gnostics and other 'heretics.'"[71] Her call for the church is to go back to the

---

68. Pagels, *Beyond Belief*, 38. It is important to note that, for Pagels, the author of John is not necessarily the apostle of Jesus. She argues that, possibly, whoever wrote John did so in order to refute the *Gospel of Thomas*. "I was amazed when I went back to the Gospel of John after reading Thomas," she writes, "for Thomas and John clearly draw upon similar language and images, and both, apparently, begin with similar 'secret teaching.' But John takes this teaching to mean something so different from Thomas that I wondered whether John could have written his gospel to refute what Thomas teaches. For months I investigated this possibility, and explored the work of other scholars who also have compared these sources, and I was finally convinced that this is what happened. As the scholar Gregory Riley points out, John—and only John—presents a challenging and critical portrait of the disciple he calls 'Thomas, the one called Didymus,' and, as Riley suggests, it is John who invented the character we call *Doubting* Thomas, perhaps as a way of caricaturing those who revered a teacher—and a version of Jesus' teaching—that he regarded as faithfulness and false. The writer called John may have met Thomas Christians among people he knew in his own city [she posits this to be Ephesus]—and may have worried that their teachings would spread to Christian groups elsewhere. John probably knew that certain Jewish groups—as well as many pagans who read and admired Genesis 1—also taught that the 'image of God' was within humankind; in any case, John decided to write his own gospel insisting that it is Jesus—and only Jesus—who embodies God's word, and therefore, speaks with divine authority" (Pagels, *Beyond Belief*, 57–58).

69. Pagels, *Beyond Belief*, 38.

70. Köstenberger and Kruger, *Heresy of Orthodoxy*, 31.

71. Köstenberger and Kruger, *Heresy of Orthodoxy*, 31. Pagels, however, is careful not to ascribe entirely political motives to this dogmatization of the faith. She makes this caveat: "The sketch of what happened during the fourth century does not support

diverse faith expressed by diverse Christians before this narrowing. For her, therefore, like Harnack and others already surveyed in this work, doctrinal development amounted to dogmatization of the faith.

The other noted historian who has appropriated the "Bauer thesis" in his own way is the Valentinian scholar Einar Thomassen, Professor Emeritus, Study of Religion, University of Bergen, Norway. Born in Bergen in 1951, Thomassen was educated in Sweden, France, and Scotland. He holds a PhD from the University of St. Andrews in Scotland. Among his many works especially in the area of Gnosticism include his PhD dissertation entitled "The Tripartite Tractate from Nag Hammadi: A New Translation with Introduction and Commentary," *The Spiritual Seed: The Church of the "Valentinians," Canon and Canonicity: The Formation and Use of Scripture, The Coherence of "Gnosticism,"* and *How Valentinian Is the Gospel of Philip?* However, it is in his article on orthodoxy and heresy in second-century Rome where he reconfigures the "Bauer thesis."

Thomassen focusses on the part of the "Bauer thesis" pertaining to the centrality of Rome in the development of "orthodoxy" in the early church. As the reader recalls, according to Bauer, Rome was the earliest center of orthodoxy and uniformity of the early church.[72] Thomassen, however, takes the "Bauer thesis" to task particularly in this aspect. Arguing that we must "try to avoid thinking in static categories" when it comes to the situation in Rome, be those categories "conglomeration of disconnected congregations or a unified and centrally led 'church,'" Thomassen holds that it is more helpful "a dynamic model, in which relations among the several groups of Christians in Rome are characterized by tension between decentralizing and centralizing forces."[73] Rejecting Bauer's contention that orthodoxy was already centralized in Rome by 100 CE, Thomassen argues that the church of Rome was more diverse than Bauer conceived. "Walter Bauer," he writes, "in his seminal work *Rechtgläubigkeit und Ketzerei im ältesten Christentum* . . . regarded Rome

---

the simplistic view often expressed by historians in the past—namely, that catholic Christianity prevailed only because it received imperial patronage, or that people participated because their leaders somehow succeeded in coercing them" (Pagels, *Beyond Belief*, 179).

72. Bauer, *Orthodoxy and Heresy*, 95–129. He concludes, concerning Rome: "Essentially *unanimous* in the faith and in the standards of Christian living, tightly organized and methodically governed by the monarchical bishop, the Roman church toward the close of the second century feels inclined and able to extend further the boundaries of her influence" (Bauer, *Orthodoxy and Heresy*, 129, emphasis added).

73. Thomassen, "Orthodoxy and Heresy," 248.

as the exception to his general thesis that 'heretical' forms of Christianity predominated in the early history of the Church."[74] As he further explains, Bauer argued that in Rome, "what was later to become orthodoxy was firmly established already around 100, and the Roman church subsequently managed to export its form of Christianity to communities elsewhere." But, as indicated, he bluntly points out that "we cannot accept this view of early Roman orthodoxy and uniformity."[75] Thomassen provided a "range of factors" that may have contributed to this decentralization and diversity in Rome. He writes:

> First, the material infrastructure of the church in Rome was composed mostly of modest private dwellings. Second, as the Christian population grew, new congregations proliferated. Third, Christianity in Rome was a religion of immigrants: it recruited people from all over the empire, persons with backgrounds in a variety of local Christian traditions. Fourth, the social and educational levels—in addition to personalities and temperaments—varied. Fifth, the Roman church may have followed existing models of decentralized religious organization, such as the private clubs of the *collegium* type, the cells of mystery religions, and the relatively autonomous Jewish synagogues.[76]

Not only does Thomassen see this early diversity in Rome, but he specifically sees other groups in addition to Valentinianism and Marcionism as operating in Rome. "All these factors," he writes, "favored diversity. And diversity there was. Other gnostics besides Valentinus and Marcion operated in Rome in the mid-second century."[77] Therefore, for Thomassen, as Bingham explains, there "was no Roman exception and until the middle of the second century no group had excluded others from the general definition of 'Christian.'"[78] This is how Thomassen adopts but also significantly reconfigures the "Bauer thesis."

74. Thomassen, "Orthodoxy and Heresy," 250n38.
75. Thomassen, "Orthodoxy and Heresy," 250n38.
76. Thomassen, "Orthodoxy and Heresy," 248.
77. Thomassen, "Orthodoxy and Heresy," 248.
78. Bingham, "Development and Diversity," 60. Thomassen observes especially concerning the conflicts seen in *The Shepherd of Hermas* concerning questions of rank and authority among presbyters and local leaders: "Such conflicts may be interpreted as expressions of a struggle between the decentralizing and the centralizing forces. In Hermas's time, the decentralizing forces were apparently so strong that efforts to realize the ideal of the unity of the church tended to increase division rather than to reduce

Even when orthodoxy and centralization finally took place in the Roman church, according to Thomassen, the agents of this centralization were Hermas, Marcion, and Valentinus. According to him, in spite of the existing differences between these three "reformers," "they all shared a desire for reform. Each of the three reacted against the current lack of unity among Christians as being contrary to the ideal of 'the church.'"[79] This is an interesting argument by Thomassen because, as Bingham observes, he argues that, in addition to Hermas, "the first Roman 'orthodox' Christians were the 'heretics' Marcion and Valentinus." Thomassen concludes:

> The picture that emerges, then, of the development of Christianity in Rome in the second century, is this: Until about the middle of the century, we cannot speak of either orthodoxy or heresy in a sociological sense. Roman Christianity was divided into a number of communities that alternated between cooperation and conflict in their attitudes to one another, but no group had taken the decisive step of declaring any of the others to be outside the general category of Christianity; if such attempts were made, they were of little consequence. The concepts of orthodoxy and heresy become valid only when one group asserts itself as the only bearer of true Christianity, to the exclusion of the others. The driving forces behind such a self-conception are the inherited ideal of "the church" as a unity and the associated sectarian mentality. In our sources, Hermas, Marcion, and Valentinus would actualize this ideal. Only Marcion and Valentinus, however, went so far as to define the unity of the church in terms of doctrine and to follow up their ideas by action: Marcion declared a break with the rest of the Christians; Valentinus effected a more subtle withdrawal. Here we have, for the first time in Rome, examples of an impulse to establish a form of restrictive orthodoxy.[80]

---

it. Thus an unstable situation obtained, wherein relationships fluctuated between collaboration, conflict, and resigned passivity. It was unclear who belonged within and who stood outside 'the church,' understood as the people with whom one co-operated or whom one regarded as fellow Christians; such notions would have varied from one group to the other, and from one point in time to the next. In this context it is quite conceivable that accusations of doctrinal deviation may have shaped conflicts, but stable definitions of orthodoxy and heresy had not yet been developed" (Thomassen, "Orthodoxy and Heresy," 250).

79. Thomassen, "Orthodoxy and Heresy," 251.
80. Thomassen, "Orthodoxy and Heresy," 255.

And, therefore, as Bingham contends, in this reconfiguration of the "Bauer thesis," "we have the orthodoxy of heresy."[81] Thus, Thomassen accepts large parts of the "Bauer thesis" (especially Bauer's concept of the dominance of what came to be known as "heresy" as opposed to the "classical view." But when it comes to the situation in Rome in earliest Christianity, Thomassen rejects Bauer's idea of an early centralization of orthodoxy, arguing for dynamic development towards later centralization (from the middle of the second century).

BEYOND EHRMAN?

While there are others who have attempted to appropriate the "Bauer thesis" in their own ways, at this point, it would help to briefly explore how, in the recent years, the quest for early church historiography has attempted to move beyond Hellenization and syncretism to hybridity (still, in my opinion, based on this thesis).[82] For example, as Bingham explains, in her presidential address to the North American Patristic Society in 2002, Rebecca Lyman, emeritus professor of religious studies at San Diego State University, "moved forcefully beyond Bauer and Ehrman and the classical historicism of Robinson and Koester."[83] Rather, she argued for an early church historiography based on the "hybridity" postcolonial approach based on the work of Homi Bhabha entitled *The Location of Culture*.[84]

In her address, Lyman, borrowing from postcolonial theories, argues that "the ancient history of Christian theological controversies should no longer rest on oppositions between 'orthodoxy' and 'heresy' or Christianity."[85] According to her, "further attention must be given to recent studies which challenge the polarities usually assumed by European imperialism to define cultural contexts and cultural production."[86] As she

---

81. Bingham, "Development and Diversity," 60.

82. Bingham, "Development and Diversity," 60–63.

83. Bingham, "Development and Diversity," 60. See Lyman, "Hellenism and Heresy." See also Lyman, "Natural Resources"; Lyman, "Politics of Passing"; and, Lyman, "Justin and Hellenism."

84. Bhabha, *The Location of Culture*.

85. Lyman, "Hellenism and Heresy," 209.

86. Bingham, "Development and Diversity," 60. As Bingham further notes, "The polarity of East and West, she argues, is as false in its clarity as the polarity between Christianity and Hellenism. To attempt to comprehend the development and diversity

sees it, therefore, "Christianity before Nicea needs to be understood, not as a translation of an essential orthodoxy into categories of Roman Hellenism, but as an 'intellectual creation by particular individuals within Roman Hellenism.'"[87] For her, "heresy" in the second century was an invention by specific individuals in response to cultural changes within the Roman Hellenistic culture. She writes:

> If recent studies in literary theory, historiography, and culture continue to chip away at our traditional narratives of theology, they also allow us new ways to examine and represent the complexity of social, political and religious life in late antiquity. Drawing on these new insights, I want to look at the "invention of heresiology" in the second century as an intellectual creation by particular individuals in response to issues of social identity and philosophical meaning within Roman Hellenism itself, rather than as a cultural translation of an essential Christian exclusivity. This is an attempt to recover the intentions of ancient authors as agents of complex personal commitments in particular religious and social contexts rather than as narrative representatives of a particular historical causality or an *a priori* orthodoxy.[88]

She, therefore, argues that rather than seeing second Christianity as "defecting" from the Roman Hellenistic culture, we should "conceive of Christians as participating in a cultural movement within Hellenism."[89] In other words, second-century apologists and polemicists such as Justin, Irenaeus, and Clement "should be understood as participants within a 'larger cultural discussion on ancestral origins and the transcendent truth within a plurality of religions.'"[90] And, as noted, her arguments are based on Bhabha's postcolonial theories of "hybridity" and "mimicry." Bingham summarizes, concerning these terms as Bhabha uses them:

> "Hybridity," for Bhabha, created the possibility of negotiation, instead of negation, a position in between. It offers a construct which is not identified with the essentialism of the received

---

of early Christianity within the limits of the latter polarity is to miss the 'cultural and historical realities of second-century provincial life'" (Bingham, "Development and Diversity," 60).

87. Bingham, "Development and Diversity," 61.
88. Lyman, "Hellenism and Heresy," 211–12.
89. Bingham, "Development and Diversity," 61.
90. Bingham, "Development and Diversity," 61.

tradition, but which unsettles it, which deconstructs the polarities, and conveys the reality that political, or philosophical, referents are not primordial or natural, but historical. History is not teleological or transcendent. "Mimicry," a "difference that is almost the same, but not quite," results from the desire for an other which can be recognized, but which is altered. Such mimesis, as "hybridity," subverts established authorities viewed as being essentialist.[91]

Therefore, rather than an insistence on an orthodox essentialism, these early Christian writers were, like the other Roman Hellenistic intellectuals, participating in the search for some form of unity as the current pluralism was seen as in the process of decline.

Lyman sees the thought of Justin Martyr as a key piece of evidence for her early church historiography of "hybridity." She writes, concerning especially his concept or *Logos Spermatikos*:

> My brief example here for a new interpretation of a problematic "hybrid" will be Justin Martyr, the acknowledged early inventor of heresiology who maintained overt commitments to both philosophy and Christianity as an "Apologist" in the second century. Justin is a self-identified philosopher and Christian, appealed in his extant writings to a transcendent universality based on hierarchies of contemporary traditions. His highly original exposition of the ultimate authority of divine revelation in prophetic texts and of Jesus as the incarnate Logos, the ancient and now complete truth sought by human philosophers, was confrontational, but it was religiously powerful precisely because the themes address problems within Roman Hellenism.[92]

And, making the connection between Justin's approach and the postcolonial theory of "hybridity," she continues:

> Returning to the concept of "hybridity," we see that Justin's defense of Christian philosophy alone as "safe and profitable" reflected both resistance to and negotiation of existing authorities. In bringing together revealed texts of the Jewish tradition and the history of Greek philosophy, he shifted cultural categories rather than destroyed their validity. He displaced the sole cultural authority of Hellenistic philosophy, yet the truth of his own "philosophy" rested on acknowledged and shared cultural

---

91. Bingham, "Development and Diversity," 61–62.
92. Lyman, "Hellenism and Heresy," 217.

concepts of transcendence and mediation as well as biblical authority or revelation. The transcendent unity of Pythagorean Platonism allowed Justin, like Numenius or Plutarch, to disassemble contemporary traditions and retrieve fresh readings, claiming, for example, monotheism in philosophy and Hebrew scripture, while criticizing the religious practices of polytheism and Hebrew law. Such a "hybrid" authorizes his Christian exegesis of culture as the only true reading, yet I argue that the move is coherent only for a Hellenist who accepts the underlying unity of truth and the hierarchy of cultures and literatures rather than their opposition.[93]

Thus, according to her, for Justin, "Christianity may be superior to philosophy, but it is congruent with it, and therefore, truth and error 'remain intertwined within the multiplicity of locative religions, texts, stories, and competing philosophies.'"[94] And, although, within this "hybridity" and "mimicry," Justin can still talk about "heresy," he is not using the term in the standard definition seen especially in the "classical view" of early church historiography. Rather, as Lyman contends, "The mimetic construction of 'almost the same, but not quite' or 'almost totally different, but not quite' creates an indeterminacy in human reception of truth and error, which is not strictly equivalent to a border between Christianity and culture or philosophy and revelation."[95] However, if this is what Justin is doing in his *Apologies* (i.e., creating this "hybridity" and "mimicry" amongst "Christianity, Hellenism and Judaism"), what about his use of such terms as "heresy?" Lyman responds by arguing that, for Justin, "'Heretics' are the improper imitation of a common truth shared by philosophers, Jews, and Christians, just as idolatry mocks transcendent monotheism."[96] Essentially, therefore, "Transcendent truth as well as

---

93. Lyman, "Hellenism and Heresy," 217.
94. Bingham, "Development and Diversity," 62.
95. Lyman, "Hellenism and Heresy," 219.
96. Lyman, "Hellenism and Heresy," 219. As Lyman further clarifies, "although Justin notes a separate and false succession for 'heresy,' with demonic origin, he acknowledges the contemporary confusion among those called 'Christians.' Heresy may be alien to truth, but in Justin's heresiology truth itself is diffuse; error and truth may appear internally or externally to all traditions as a means of discord or evidence of the Logos . . . If we read Justin's theology only as 'apologetic strategy,' then we assume a pre-existing definition of tradition or a separation between Christian identity and Hellenism [and Judaism] that does not do justice to his original philosophy of Logos *spermatikos*" (Lyman, "Hellenism and Heresy," 219). For a similar argument, see also Pagels, *Origin of Satan*.

error is found in sources other than those identified as Christian."[97] This is her "hybridity" in a nutshell.

In sum, as it has been demonstrated, Lyman has attempted to move beyond the previous historiographies by arguing for an early church historiography based on the postcolonial theories of "hybridity" and "mimicry" based on the work of Bhabha. Using the example of Justin's *Apologies*, she argues that "development of early Christianity, then, is a participation in Hellenism, resulting in something truly 'Christian' and 'Hellenistic,' not something 'Hellenistic' or 'Christian.'"[98] However, as already observed, despite her protestations, this is not a significant move beyond Bauer. As Bingham observes, for proponents of "hybridity," "Bauer's diversity, then, at least in part, it seems, needs to be seen as multiple instances in which locality and individuality produced different versions of negotiations between universalism and traditions within Roman Hellenism."[99] Thus, even with her attempt to move past Bauer, Ehrman, Robinson, and Koester, Lyman's early church historiography of "hybridity" and "mimicry" is still steeped in the "Bauer thesis" in some significant ways.

It is helpful, as we conclude, to note that other scholars, such as Daniel Boyarin (Hermann P. and Sophia Taubman Professor of Talmudic Culture in the Departments of Near Eastern Studies and Rhetoric at the University of California Berkeley) and Virginia Burrus (Bishop W. Earl Ledden Distinguished Professor of Religion, Syracuse University), have extended the application of hybridity beyond the fourth century to Athanasius of Alexandria.[100] However, as they argue, with shifting political situations in the empire, the process of "hybridizing" in the fourth century takes a slightly different turn. They write:

---

97. Bingham, "Development and Diversity," 62.
98. Bingham, "Development and Diversity," 62.
99. Bingham, "Development and Diversity," 62.
100. Boyarin and Burrus, "Hybridity as Subversion."

> When, in the 4th century AD, Christianity shifts from a "colonized" position toward one of political and cultural hegemony, the discourse of heresiology initially forged by earlier Christians as well as Jews in a period of shared persecution comes to be voiced by Christian bishops who collude, however ambivalently, with imperial power. For Judaism, the context also shifts: no longer positioned by Christians as a competing "heretical" sect, the Rabbis adapt to the recolonized position as subjects of a Christian empire.[101]

In other words, according to them, what was happening in the fourth century is not only the "triumph" of Christianity. It was also "the birth of 'religion' constituted as a 'totalizing'—indeed, an imperializing discourse."[102] Indeed, they bluntly argue that "even when conceived as an 'orthodoxy,' religious identity is never pure: all subjects are hybrid, differential, marked by the trace of their others."[103] This is an interesting analysis especially given Athanasius's attempt to deal with Arianism.

According to them, even when Athanasius is dealing with the heresy of the Arians, he adapts an approach that can be characterized using the postcolonial theory of "mimicry." They write:

> Yet heresiological discourse constructs the relationship of heresy to orthodoxy not simply as one of negation but also, and rather more ambivalently, as one of mimicry . . . Thus, Athanasius suggests that heretics skillfully mimic true Christianity, above all by decking their teachings in scriptural dress: the Arian heresy, "in her craft and cunning, affects to array herself in Scripture language . . . that with the pretense of Christianity, her smooth sophistry (for reason she has none) may deceive men into wrong thoughts of Christ" (Ar. 1.1). The problem with heresy, then, is that it looks much like true Christianity. In Bhabha's terms, the heretic is a mimic, "not quite" Christian (thus also very nearly Christian), and the consequence of this, it would seem, is that the Christian is "not quite" (thus also very nearly) heretical.[104]

While several other examples can be adduced as to make the same point, Athanasius's interaction with the Arians, the authors believe, presents a perfect case of "mimicry." "Intriguingly," they write, "the

---

101. Boyarin and Burrus, "Hybridity as Subversion," 432–33.
102. Boyarin and Burrus, "Hybridity as Subversion," 433.
103. Boyarin and Burrus, "Hybridity as Subversion," 433.
104. Boyarin and Burrus, "Hybridity as Subversion," 434.

issue of mimesis is at the heart of Athanasius's theological debate with his Arian opponents."[105] In this case, "Athanasius aligns himself with the divine Word who is the perfect image of the Father, placing the Arians on the side of stage actors mouthing frivolous and made-up lines—their words, in effect, created out of nothing, mimicking their own claims that amounts to a pseudo-Son."[106] According to them, Athanasius's opponents use his language mockingly. They write:

> While he [Athanasius] understands that the Son is ever begotten by the one who is ever Father, he complains that the Arians take up his language of Fatherhood and Sonship *mockingly*: "They turn to silly women, and address them in turn in this womanish language: "hadst thou a son before bearing? now, as thou hadst not, so neither was the Son of God before His generation"" (Ar. 1.22). Athanasius refuses to take part in such wildly inappropriate "sport and revel", sternly insisting on the distinction between the Original and its mere copies.[107]

Additionally, according to Boyarin and Burrus, Athanasius extends the same approach in dealing with the "Talmudic heresiology." This refers to some Jewish scholars (especially Rabbi Akiva), who, according to Athanasius, were Jews who "mimic" the Christian ideal of martyrdom for their adherence to the Torah. Boyarin and Burrus explain:

> In the tale of the proto-martyr Rabbi Akiva, we find an explicit appropriation of Christian martyrology ... The mimicking of martyrology is, moreover, directed to the service of an anti-Christian heresiology that opens up all of the hybridity of the rabbinic orthodox project. In one story, a highly problematic Jewish figure, Papos ben Yehuda, invites Rabbi Akiva to abandon his study and practice of Torah during a period of imperial persecution. Rabbi Akiva refuses the invitation, producing a

---

105. Boyarin and Burrus, "Hybridity as Subversion," 435.

106. Boyarin and Burrus, "Hybridity as Subversion," 435.

107. Boyarin and Burrus, "Hybridity as Subversion," 435. As Boyarin and Burrus add, "Behind this assertion [that is, the contrast between the fatherhood of God the Father and that of earthly fathers] lies the distinction between the exact reproduction of the Father (the divine Son) and the inexact mimesis (mimicry?) at work in creation (human 'sons,' begotten of fathers *and* mothers). The Arians, in their mockery of the favored Athanasian theological terminology of Fatherhood and Sonship, get it all backwards: they imply that the divine begetting imitates mere human generation. For this they themselves will surely 'incur much derision and mockery' (Ar. 1.23)" (Boyarin and Burrus, "Hybridity as Subversion," 435).

parable to support his refusal. In the parable, the Jews are the fish whom certain men (obviously symbols of the empire) wish to catch, and Papos is the fox who tempts them to join him on land, where they will be safe. The fish answer that if they are endangered in their natural habitat, the water, they will be in even greater danger if they abandon that habitat.[108]

Thus, while not going into details of how Athanasius uses this parable to illustrate his point, if, for him the problem "is that Jews and Judaizing heretics imitate orthodox Christianity,"[109] in a similar manner, "for the Rabbis who told the story of Rabbi Akiva and Papos, the Christianizing heretic, the double and deeply paradoxical moment of 'orthodox' hybridity is likewise situated in the Jews' mimicry of Christians—but it is the Jewish mimicry that is now positioned as authentic."[110] In so doing, "the originary status of Christianity is reframed as poor imitation."[111] In so doing, therefore, Athanasius, according to Boyarin and Burrus, is able to extend this mimicry from his Arian heretical opponents to the OT Jews. As he argues, failure to recognize Jesus as the one who was prophesied in the Scriptures, Arians were aligning themselves with the Jews. And, thus, if "Arians are virtual Jews, the Jews are also, like all heretics, Christian apostates."[112] This is how these authors see Athanasius employing mimicry in his apologetics.

In sum, therefore, in the thought of Boyarin and Burrus, the postcolonial theories of hybridity and mimicry, first applied to such early church fathers as Justin Martyr, are now applied to the fourth century theologian, Athanasius. However, in their application of these theories in the thought of Athanasius, both Boyarin and Burrus add the caveat that "we must acknowledge the potential menace of hybridity itself, which can all too easily be turned toward imperialist ends."[113] What they mean by this is that hybridity itself "not only can continue to 'colonize' the other but can serve the purposes of inscribing a virtual oneness (not quite one, but close enough) in opposition to a purely externalized other with whom there can be no effective negotiation."[114] It is significant to

108. Boyarin and Burrus, "Hybridity as Subversion," 436–37.
109. Boyarin and Burrus, "Hybridity as Subversion," 439.
110. Boyarin and Burrus, "Hybridity as Subversion," 439.
111. Boyarin and Burrus, "Hybridity as Subversion," 439.
112. Boyarin and Burrus, "Hybridity as Subversion," 434.
113. Boyarin and Burrus, "Hybridity as Subversion," 439.
114. Boyarin and Burrus, "Hybridity as Subversion," 439–40.

notice that Boyarin and Burrus choose, as an example of a place to apply this caveat, the "Judeo-Christianity"[115] hybridity. Thus, instead of seeing this hybridity as a positive development (as Lyman sees it especially in the early church), they caution that it easily leads to imperialism of some sort. "In our current political moment," they write, "any productive mobilization of consciously hybridized identities must refuse the limit to negotiation."[116] In other words, they urge this negotiation to be able to "give rise to the ambivalent and agnostic negotiation of identities not only of Jews and Christians but of Jews, Christians, and Muslims."[117] Although they do not use this language, what Boyarin and Burrus seem to be proposing here is the application of an almost Hegelian-type theory of history akin to that of F. C. Baur (thesis-antithesis-synthesis, with the synthesis eventually becoming the new thesis in the form of an imperialized hybrid—especially in the form of "Judeo-Christianity"). In other words, with their application of the postcolonial theories of hybridity and mimicry, we have come full circle! The careful observer, however, wonders about whether there are any guarantees that their proposed final hybridity of Jews, Christians, and Muslims is itself not subject to becoming imperialistic as well. This concern does not arise in their work.

CONCLUSION

This chapter has explored the early church historiographies of such current early church historians as Bart Ehrman, Elaine Pagels, Einar Thomassen, as well as those who have attempted to move beyond the "Bauer-Ehrman" thesis, such as Rebecca Lyman, Daniel Boyarin, and Virginia Burrus. As it has been argued, the historiography of Ehrman attempts to reconstruct the "Bauer thesis." However, his conviction is that Bauer did not go far enough because he granted too much "proto-orthodoxy," which he saw as evident in the second and third centuries. Rather, according to Ehrman, what we have in these earliest times of Christianity are versions of Christianities whose works were suppressed by the "official" church (or lost), only to be discovered in Nag Hammadi in Egypt in 1945. Thus, according to him, rather than a situation where there was some kind of a competition of some "orthodoxy" and "heresy,"

---

115. Boyarin and Burrus, "Hybridity as Subversion," 139.
116. Boyarin and Burrus, "Hybridity as Subversion," 440.
117. Boyarin and Burrus, "Hybridity as Subversion," 440.

The Historiography of Bart Ehrman and His Contemporaries 149

there were "Christianities." While this is beyond this work, Ehrman takes the same approach in his exploration of the process of the canonization of the books of the New Testament.

As it was argued, this approach to the understanding of the history of the early church is continued in the thought of Elaine Pagels. In her re-engagement with the "Bauer thesis," Pagels insists that Christians should move beyond the prescribed "belief" (especially the fourth-century doctrinal formulations) to the pre-creedal Christianity which, in her understanding, was characterized by a beautiful diversity and freedom. She sees this as detectable in the Nag Hammadi Codices. Like Harnack before her, Pagels rejects the dogmatization of the faith that she sees as having taken place with the creedal formulations of the early church.

In his case, Valentinian scholar Einar Thomassen focuses his attention in the second part of the "Bauer thesis." This is the issue of the centrality of Rome in Bauer's argument. In an attempt to adopt and also significantly reconfigure the "Bauer thesis," Thomassen argues that we should not think in static categories in early Christianity. Rejecting Bauer's understanding of the state of the church in Rome in early Christianity, Thomassen, in language reminiscent of that of Ehrman, argues that the church in Rome was more diverse than Bauer conceived. For him, in the city of Rome, in addition to the Roman church, religion included Valentinianism and Marcionism. This was a result of such factors as the presence of migrants and other social factors. In other words, he accepts yet further significantly reframes the "Bauer thesis."

Finally, the chapter explored what looks like an attempt to move beyond both Hellenization and syncretism (Ehrman) in the conception of the history of early Christianity. This attempt, seen in the works of such historians as Lyman, Boyarin, and Burrus, utilizes such postcolonial theories as hybridity and mimicry to interpret early Christianity. Following the theories of Homi Bhabha, these historians have attempted to understand early Christianity not in terms of "orthodoxy" and/or "heresy" but, rather, as part of an intellectual movement within Roman Hellenism itself. Thus, "orthodoxy" in this case is, as Lyman puts it (and as already noted), "an intellectual creation of particular individuals in response to issues of social identity and philosophical meaning within Roman Hellenism itself."[118] And, again, as demonstrated, Boyarin and Burrus have extended these postcolonial theories to the fourth-century theologian

---

118. Lyman, "Hellenism and Heresy," 211.

Athanasius of Alexandria in his engagements with Arianism and other Jewish groups. However, for them, there should be a caveat in the application of these theories, as it can lead to "imperialized hybridity," as in the case of "Judeo-Christianity." And, as argued, while they would like to see the same kind of "negotiations" extended to interreligious discussions among Christians, Jews, and Muslims, there is no guarantee that the resulting "hybridity" would not be immune from their conceived imperialism (a possible reverting to the Hegelian conception of history in terms of thesis-antithesis-synthesis—with the resulting synthesis still prone to becoming itself the new thesis).

This concludes our investigation into historiographical theories that have been proposed as challenges to the "classical view" to account for the development of doctrine and other issues in early Christianity. With especially these latest proposals as highlighted in this chapter, key questions need to be raised: Was Christianity in its earliest forms that amorphous—to the extent that there were no defined (albeit rudimentary) parameters for determining orthodoxy and heresy? Were there "versions" of Christianities, in other words? Indeed, were there Christianities that were eventually "lost," as Ehrman's book title insinuates? These and other related issues are picked up in the following chapter.

CHAPTER 6

Determination of Orthodoxy and Heresy in Early Christianity

The Quest For Criteria

INTRODUCTION

THE PRECEDING CHAPTERS HAVE especially focused on the historiographical challenges to the "classical view" pertaining to the conception of the history of early Christianity. In the presentation of these theories, it has become consistently clear that, for their proponents, categories that were already accepted in the "classical view" as having been clearly defined in the early church, such as "orthodoxy" and "heresy," are to be rejected (or, in some cases, severely modified). Thus, in various ways, each of these alternative views has sought to re-interpret language embedded in the "classical view" in its own way. What has remained consistent, however, is the fact that there is a detectable ideological genealogy that stretches from the clearly Hegelian historiography of F. C. Baur through the pivotal "Bauer thesis" to that of current early church historians such as B. Ehrman and E. Pagels.

However, especially with Ehrman's assertion that, instead of seeing the situation in the early church in terms of such categories as "orthodoxy" (or, to use Bauer's language, "proto-orthodoxy") and "heresy," it is better to conceive it in terms of versions of "Christianities," it has become particularly significant to even investigate the situation further.[1]

---

1. As Kruger and Köstenberger explain, "the Bauer-Ehrman thesis contends that 'orthodoxy' is not a first-century phenomenon but only a later concept that allowed

As Bingham emphasizes, "an [early church] evangelical historiographical model ought to reflect continuity with other theological commitments concerning diversity and development."[2] The question, however, remains: How does one even begin to conceive of such a historiography? What are the parameters that need to be kept in one's mind while doing so? In other words, is it possible to establish the exact doctrinal situation both in the documents that were later to be recognized as the inspired books of the New Testament as well as in the life and thought of the early church fathers? Is there, in other words, criteria (albeit rudimentary) for determining "orthodoxy" and "heresy" in earliest Christianity?

This chapter will try to address these questions. In so doing, the chapter will proceed from dealing with the thorny issue of whether or not one can speak of "orthodoxy" and "heresy" in the New Testament since, as Kruger and Köstenberger contend, it is only through "an investigation of the New Testament data regarding orthodoxy and heresy"[3] that we can be able to "move beyond Bauer's biased account to a proper understanding of the actual first-century condition of *earliest* Christianity."[4] This will be achieved through an examination of language that is evident in the documents that were later recognized as the canonical New Testament which seems to suggest some clear early criteria on the determination of orthodoxy and heresy in some key doctrinal areas. In other words, it will be contended that from her inception at Pentecost, evidence suggests that the early church held to a rudimentary body of propositional truths, a body so tenaciously held such that to deny it either completely or in part amounted to one being accorded a heretic. That is, from the cursory mentions in the New Testament to fully developed statements in the early church, there is a traceable body of propositional truth against which everything else was measured. And, therefore, as it will be demonstrated, the concept of truth and falsity (orthodoxy and heresy), was not a mere construction of church fathers (heresiologists). It is rather the working out of that which was explicit in the New Testament itself. Indeed, in addition to this pre-creedal language, early Christian rites and ceremonies also played a significant role in early doctrinal definition. For example, as Turner observes, the development of the doctrine of the Holy Trinity

---

the Roman church to squelch alternate versions of Christianity" (Kruger and Köstenberger, *Heresy of Orthodoxy*, 70).

2. Bingham, "Development and Diversity," 63.
3. Köstenberger and Kruger, *Heresy of Orthodoxy*, 69.
4. Köstenberger and Kruger, *Heresy of Orthodoxy*, 69–70.

Determination of Orthodoxy and Heresy in Early Christianity 153

"might almost be described as a theological commentary upon the Baptismal Formula."[5] Similar observations can be made concerning almost any other major doctrine of concern in earliest Christianity, as will be demonstrated.

In the second part, the chapter will trace the development of the conception of orthodoxy and heresy in the thought of the early church fathers. While, as many have observed, it is impossible to continue to insist that the categories of "orthodoxy" and "heresy" were static in the early church, the accounting for the doctrinal diversity and continuity in the thought of the fathers needs to be done carefully. In other words, the focus of this section will be on how, as John Behr argues, the "theology that emanated from the New Testament continued through the church fathers, was guarded by the apologists and solidified in the ecumenical councils."[6] The idea here is to attempt to reconstruct the criteria, albeit rudimentary, that these fathers employed in determining heresy from orthodoxy in these formative years of Christianity.

Finally, the chapter will propose an early church historiography based on the arguments of the preceding sections. As Bingham contends, any meaningful early church historiography must take into account the shared elements between early Christianity and the Roman-Hellenistic enterprise as well as the *differences*. "But although early Christianity's journey shared elements with Roman-Hellenism's enterprise," he writes, "this conceptualization fails to satisfy the restrictions of the early Christian theological commitments."[7] Rather, "Christianity was not the only religion seeking to formulate a concept of its exclusivity, but it sought to do so differently than Roman-Hellenism." Thus, a "theologically conditioned historiography"[8] is demanded.

EARLY CONCEPTIONS OF ORTHODOXY AND HERESY: COMPETING DEFINITIONS

As can easily be deciphered from the discussion up to this point, much of the contest pertaining to the history of the early church concerns the origin, age, and usage of these terms: *orthodoxy* and *heresy*, terms that

5. Turner, *Pattern of Christian Truth*, 318.
6. Köstenberger and Kruger, *Heresy of Orthodoxy*, 53. See Behr, *The Way to Nicea*.
7. Bingham, "Development and Diversity," 65.
8. Bingham, "Development and Diversity," 66.

Bauer considered so significant that they basically became the title of his work. Thus, it becomes imperative that the beginning point would be to attempt to define these terms.

So, what does the term *orthodoxy* mean? According to J. I. Packer, in its standard usage, the term is the "English equivalent of Greek orthodoxia (from *orthos*, 'right,' and *doxa*, 'opinion') meaning right belief, as opposed to heresy or heterodoxy."[9] Packer further explains that although the term is not originally biblical and that "no secular or Christian writer uses it before the second century, though the verb *orthodoxein* is in Aristotle ... [it] expresses the idea that certain statements accurately embody the revealed truth content of Christianity and are therefore in their own nature normative for the universal church."[10] Thus, according to him, the term *orthodoxy* refers to statements that reflect correctly the body of truth believed by Christianity. Stanley Grenz and others also capture this idea, explaining that literally, the term *orthodoxy* refers to "'right praise' or 'right belief' (as opposed to *heresy)."[11] According to them, being orthodox refers to "being characterized by consistency in belief and worship with the Christian faith."[12] They add that this important fact, that the concept of orthodoxy is believed to be "witnessed to in Scripture, the early Christian writers and the official teachings, *creeds and *liturgy of the church."[13] While these concepts are further elucidated below, one final definition of the term "orthodoxy" needs to be highlighted. According to Köstenberger and Kruger, the term *orthodoxy* means the "correct teaching regarding the person and work of Jesus Christ, including the way of salvation, in contrast to teaching regarding Jesus that deviates from standard norms of Christian doctrine."[14] As it can be observed, this definition limits the meaning of the term *orthodoxy* to matters of Christology and soteriology. For this reason, for our present purposes, the earlier definitions are more accurate as they relate to the entirety of Christian doctrine. Thus, the definition of the term *orthodoxy* adopted in this work emphasizes the "right" belief (and practice, sometimes referred to as *orthopraxy*—a tenet already imbedded in the definition of

---

9. Packer, "Orthodoxy," 875.
10. Packer, "Orthodoxy," 875. See also Aristotle, *Nicomachean Ethics* 1151a19.
11. Grenz, Guretzki, and Nordling, *Pocket Dictionary*.
12. Grenz, Guretzki, and Nordling, *Pocket Dictionary*, 87–88.
13. Grenz, Guretzki, and Nordling, *Pocket Dictionary*, 88.
14. Köstenberger and Kruger, *Heresy of Orthodoxy*, 70–71.

orthodoxy) as opposed to what would be considered "wrong" belief. Scholarly debate has, however, centered on how far back one goes as the time of the conception of the term in these parameters is concerned. This, as well, applies to the counter term, *heresy*.

The English term *heresy* is the transliteration of the Greek term *hairesis* (αἵρεσις) "which originally meant an action or belief chosen from among several options but in time came to mean an unorthodox opinion held by a group—sometimes even a majority—within the church."[15] As such, in its early usages in the New Testament, the term seemed to have mixed meanings with context being the determining factor. Nijay Gupta and Jonah Sandford elucidate concerning the use of the term in the NT:

> Αἱρέσεις (FPN LF: αἵρεσις) can refer to "parties" or "sects" within a religious body (sometimes in a neutral sense, e.g., Sadducees and Pharisees; cf. Acts 5:17; 15:5), or it can refer to (threatening) sectarian teachings or "heresies" (cf. 2 Pt 2:1, αἱρέσεις ἀπωλείας). Here, as in 1 Cor 11:19 (the only other Pauline occurrence), it refers negatively to divisive factions.[16]

However, as time progressed, the term gained a technical meaning, emphasizing deviation from the truth.

Rick further helpfully insists that the term can only have meaning where there is a defined body of truth. "The concept of 'heresy,'" he writes, "is grounded in the conviction that there exists one revealed truth, and that other opinions are intentional distortions or denials of that truth."[17] As expected, of course, with this understanding, critics would easily argue that the definition of heresy is still based on the "classical view" of the history of early Christianity.[18]

---

15. Rick, "Heresy," 550.

16. Gupta and Sandford, *Intermediate Biblical Greek Reader*, 115.

17. Grenz, Guretzki, and Nordling, *Pocket Dictionary*, 88. Grenz and others further explain that the term "heresy" came to refer to "Any teaching rejected by the Christian community as contrary to Scripture and hence to *orthodox doctrine" (Grenz, Guretzki and Nordling, *Pocket Dictionary*, 58). They further helpfully explain: "Most of the teachings that have been declared heretical have to do with either the nature of God or the person of Jesus Christ. The term *heresy* is not generally used to characterize non-Christian belief. That is to say, systems of belief such as *atheism or *agnosticism, or non-Christian religions such as Buddhism or Islam are not technically heresy. [Rather] The term heresy is generally reserved for any belief that claims to be Christian and scriptural but has been rejected by the church as sub-Christian or antiscriptural" (Rick, "Heresy," 550).

18. Indeed, according to Rick, this question has been raised especially in the

This particular issue, as already suggested, was brought to the forefront by Bauer in his *Orthodoxy and Heresy*. Instead of defining the terms *orthodoxy* and *heresy* in terms of their content, Bauer's definition focused on influence, power, and numbers. In a very telling paragraph, he writes:

> Perhaps—I repeat, *perhaps*—certain manifestations of Christian life that the authors of the church renounce as "heretics" originally had not been such at all, but at least here and there, were the only form of the new religion—that is, for those regions they were simply "Christianity." The possibility also exists that their adherents constituted the majority, and that they looked down with hatred and scorn on the orthodox, who for them were the false believers.[19]

For him, therefore, not only does Bauer see the usage of these terms in the early church as fluid, but, significantly, their meaning seems to be based on the numbers. In this case, the majority in each given geographical region would be seen as the "orthodoxy" and vice versa. Again, he commends:

> I do not say this in order to introduce some special use of language for the investigations which follow, so that "orthodoxy" designates the preference of the given majority, while "heresy" is characterized by the fact that only the minority adhere to it. Majority and minority can change places and then such a use of language, which would be able to represent this change only with difficulty, would easily lead to obscurities and misunderstanding. No, even in this book, "orthodoxy" and "heresy" will refer to what one would customarily and usually understands them to mean. There is only this proviso, that we will not hear the two of them discussed by the church—that is, by the one party—but by history.[20]

Thus, it is clear that, as Georg Strecker comments, Bauer "does not intend to use 'orthodoxy/heresy' as value judgements—despite the fact that in their 'traditional and usual use' they normally do involve value

---

twentieth century. "In the twentieth century," he writes, "many churchmen (until recently, more often clergy than laity) have questioned whether truth can be discerned with sufficient clarity to justify the contemporary use of the concept of 'heresy'" (Rick, "Heresy," 551).

19. Bauer, *Orthodoxy and Heresy*, xxii.
20. Bauer, *Orthodoxy and Heresy*, xxii.

judgments."[21] As Hultgren and Haggmark contend, for Bauer, orthodoxy "'represented the form of Christianity supported by the majority in Rome' that became ascendant in the second century and victorious in other areas to the east around AD 200."[22] The reason for this ascendancy, according to Bauer, was because of the church of Rome's "superior organizational powers."[23] But, again, it is as though Bauer painted himself into a corner. That is, while, on the one hand, he saw no clear definitions of *orthodoxy* and *heresy* in earliest Christianity, on the other hand, his central thesis that heresy preceded orthodoxy in the key early centers of Christianity demands that there were clear demarcations between these concepts in the earliest times of Christianity. Indeed, this is a key issue that followers of Bauer must contend with. "If it is the case that heresy preceded orthodoxy in many areas," so correctly argue Hultgren and Haggmark, "it follows that the so-called heretical views may well go back to the very beginning, the earliest interpretations of Jesus and his message."[24] Not only do I agree with Bauer at this point, but I believe that the concepts of orthodoxy and heresy, however rudimentary, go back to the New Testament itself. However, as I will attempt to demonstrate in the following pages, the conclusion reached by Bauer and others, that, since these concepts are so early, "the so-called heretical views (as in Gnosticism) may be regarded as alternative, rather than incorrect (and 'heretical'), interpretations,"[25] does not take the entirety of the evidence into consideration. As already noted, critics of Bauer have demonstrated that he skillfully ignored New Testament evidence to this effect. Kruger and Köstenberger correctly observe:

> Bauer virtually ignores the New Testament evidence while believing to find evidence for early heresy and late orthodoxy in various urban centers of the second century. Ehrman, likewise, makes much of second-century diversity and assigns the notion of orthodoxy to later church councils. The precursors of orthodox, Ehrman calls "proto-orthodox," even though it must, of course, be remembered that at the time this group was not

---

21. Strecker, "Appendix 2: The Reception of the Book," 312n28.
22. Hultgren and Haggmark, *Earliest Christian Heretics*, 6.
23. Hultgren and Haggmark, *Earliest Christian Heretics*, 6.
24. Hultgren and Haggmark, *Earliest Christian Heretics*, 6.
25. Hultgren and Haggmark, *Earliest Christian Heretics*, 6.

the only legitimate representative of Christianity according to Ehrman, which renders the expression anachronistic.[26]

However, contrary to these assertions by Bauer and Ehrman, the New Testament documents that were later recognized as canonical show "a fixed set of early core beliefs that were shared by apostolic mainstream while allowing for flexibility in nonessential areas."[27] And, while one can legitimately say that these documents were still in circulation and had not yet been put together as one document, it is clear that these works were available in many key centers of Christianity, most of which were recipients of these letter. So, how do these documents present this early set of core beliefs?

CONCEPTIONS OF ORTHODOXY IN THE DOCUMENTS OF THE NEW TESTAMENT

While, as already noted, some scholars continue to insist that the categories of *orthodoxy* and *heresy* developed later (with heresy being assigned to the second century and orthodoxy to the fourth century), it is demonstrable that there is clear evidence of conceptions of these categories (albeit, in their rudimentary form) in the documents that were later recognized as the canonical books of the New Testament. This evidence comes to us in the form of both pre-creedal doctrinal formulations as well as Christian rituals. These are selectively treated in this order here.

Pre-Creedal Formulations in the New Testament

Although some continue to insist that creeds were later developments in the church signifying the concretization of early Catholicism, evidence exists to suggest that, even before the books of the New Testament were collected, the early church formulated the earliest versions of Christian doctrinal creeds. The term "creed" is from the Latin *credo*, which literally means "I believe." In his attempt to define the term *credo*, Pelikan equates it with the term *creed*, arguing that, for hundreds of years, "Christians have been accustomed to understand by the word *creed* a fixed formula summarizing the essential articles of their religion and enjoying the

---

26. Köstenberger and Kruger, *Heresy of Orthodoxy*, 70.
27. Köstenberger and Kruger, *Heresy of Orthodoxy*, 70.

sanction of ecclesiastical authority."²⁸ As well, as he further explains, from the earliest times, "two of the earliest technical terms employed by the Christian writers to identify such creeds and confessions of faith were 'symbol [Greek *symbolon*, Latin *symbolum*]' and 'rule of faith [Greek *kanôn tēs pisteos*, Latin *regula fidei*],' both of which are still part of the Eastern Orthodox and the Roman Catholic theological vocabularies."²⁹ The contention here is that language that forms the basis for these early creedal formulations emerges from the New Testament documents themselves.

Most of these formulations appear in several texts of the New Testament, being introduced by such phrases as "I passed to you what I received/as I received." A clear example is found in 1 Corinthians 11:23, where Paul writes: ἐγὼ γὰρ παρέλαβον ἀπὸ τοῦ κυρίου, ὃ καὶ παρέδωκα ὑμῖν ("For I received from the Lord that which I also delivered to you,") as well as in 15:3–8. As Behr argues, what is recognized by the end of the second century "as normative Christianity is committed to understanding Christ by engaging with Scripture on the basis of the canon of truth and in the context of tradition (παράδοσις)."³⁰ The other formula used to introduce these creedal statements in the New Testament (especially in the Pastoral Epistles), is this: "this is a trustworthy saying" (πιστὸς ὁ λόγος), which appears in these texts: 1 Tim 1:15a; 3:1a; 4:9; 2 Tim 2:11a; and Titus 3:8.³¹

---

28. Pelikan, *Credo: Historical and Theological Guide*, 3–4.

29. Pelikan, *Credo: Historical and Theological Guide*, 4.

30. Behr, *Way to Nicea*, 15. Behr helpfully further elucidates: "The Gospel which Paul delivered ('traditioned') is from the first 'according to the Scriptures.' Clearly the Scriptures to which Paul is referring here are not the four Gospels, but the Law, the Psalms and the Prophets. The importance of this written reference, repeated twice, is such that the phrase is preserved in later Creeds; Christians who use the Nicene-Constantinopolitan creed still confess that Christ died and rose according to the (same) Scriptures. The point of concern in this basic Christian confession is not the historicity of the events behind their reports, but that the reports are continuous with, in accordance with, Scripture; it is textual, or more accurately an 'intertextual' or interpretative confession. And this scriptural texture of the Gospel is . . . the basis of both canon and tradition as articulated by what emerges as normative Christianity. If 'orthodoxy' is indeed later than 'heresy,' as Bauer claimed and is commonly assumed, it is nevertheless based on nothing other than Gospel as it was delivered at the beginning" (Behr, *Way to Nicea*, 16).

31. I am not oblivious to the fact that each of these appearances is within a particular context. I agree with Timothy Swinson, who argues that "πιστὸς ὁ λόγος plausibly may serve as a concise summation and commendation of the apostolic proclamation of the gospel and that it relates to the basic content of that proclamation while

While the goal here is not to offer a comprehensive treatment of these passages, a select analysis helps demonstrate the fact that enough early creedal language was available to express orthodoxy in such a way that to deviate from it would be to accord oneself a heretic in the eyes of the church. Indeed, it can be demonstrated that these texts form the building blocks of what came to be known as the *regula fidei* (the Rule of Faith) in the early church. As Paul Blowers helpfully explains, "the Rule of Faith (which was always story or associated with Scripture itself) served the primitive Christian hope of metanarrative articulating and authenticating a world-encompassing story or metanarrative of creation, incarnation, redemption, and consummation."[32] Rather, as already noted, instead of a murky picture that is usually painted to indicate that the early church was indeterminate doctrinally, these rudimentary creeds, coalescing into the *regula fidei*, set forth the basic, "'dramatic' structure of a Christian vision of the world, posing as an hermeneutical frame of reference for the interpretation of Christian Scripture and Christian experience, and educing the first principles of Christian theological discourse and of a doctrinal substantiation of Christian faith."[33] A few of these key New Testament texts that served as the foundational building blocks for the earliest version of the *regula fidei* are evaluated here.

First, as noted above, Paul, in 1 Corinthians 11, informs the Corinthian believers that he passed to them the tradition that he himself had received, tradition that finds its origin in the Lord himself. The key terms in his presentation are these: παραλαμβάνειν (*paralambanó*—to receive)

---

permitting the content to assume various forms" (Swinson, "Πιστὸς Ὁ Λόγος," 60). His conclusion, however, is consistent with the argument being made here. "Two things," he writes, "warrant mention at this point. First, while the analysis proposed in this essay has not proceeded from the premise that each occurrence of πιστὸς ὁ λόγος must pertain to salvation or salvific material, it has been argued that, in all five occurrences, the formula probably does pertain to such concerns. Second, while internal coherency does not necessarily translate into the most compelling interpretation, the question of coherency nevertheless must be satisfied in order for any proposed interpretation to receive adoption. On this point also, it must be acknowledged that the approach and interpretation proposed in this study does result in a coherent reading of each text in which πιστὸς ὁ λόγος occurs. Consequently, the construal advocated here, that πιστὸς ὁ λόγος serves as an affirmation and confirmation of the firm reliability of the apostolic gospel message, at the very least may stand as a plausible solution to the riddle of the formula and its referent in each instance and in each letter" (Swinson, "Πιστὸς Ὁ Λόγος," 75).

32. Blowers, "*Regula Fidei*," 202.
33. Blowers, "*Regula Fidei*," 202.

and παραδιδόναι (*paradidonai*—to pass on). In their usage in both Greek and Jewish tradition, these are technical terms, and "are used for the cultivation of the school tradition."[34] Arguably, Paul received the contents of the tradition from the other apostles, as reported in Galatians 1:12. Indeed, Paul argues that what he is passing down is the content of the gospel message, which is what he preaches and what the Corinthians believed (1 Cor 15:2). It is clear that this is not Pauline construction. Rather, together with a few other Pauline texts using similar language, this passage reflects an earlier hymn of a confessional nature. "Many believe that Philippians 2:6–11 and Colossians 1:15–20," write Köstenberger and Kruger, "represent early Christian hymns that Paul incorporated into his letters for various purposes."[35] This idea of a pre-Pauline hymn, as noted above, is also evident in 1 Corinthians 15. John Kloppenborg helpfully explains:

Vocabularic analysis has shown that the bulk of vv. 3–5 is non-Pauline in character and certainly belongs to the tradition. Verses 6b and 8, as well as the connectives *eita . . . epeita . . . epeita . . . eita . . . eschaton* (vv 5b–8) are to be attributed to Paul's hand, while verse 6a (*ōphthē epanō pentakosiois adelphois ephapax*) and v 7 (*ōphthē Iakōbō* [kai?] *tois apostolois pasin*) might be assigned to tradition on the basis of the non-Pauline terms *ōphthe* (five times in Paul), *epanō* (hapaxlegomenon) and *ephapax* (only in Rom 6:10).[36]

However, while it is clear that the formula is originally not Pauline because of the above-mentioned factors, scholarly debate still continues pertaining to its provenance. Two cultural settings are brought up as possible areas of origin for the formula: the earliest Aramaic-speaking community and the Jewish-Hellenistic church.[37] The truth of the mat-

34. Conzelmann, *1 Corinthians*, 195.

35. Köstenberger and Kruger, *Heresy of Orthodoxy*, 77. Concerning especially the antiquity of Philippians 2:6–11, the authors contend: "Regarding the 'Christ hymn' of [Philippians] 2:6–11, arguments for its pre-Pauline origin include (1) its unusual vocabulary; (2) its rhythmic style; (3) the absence of key Pauline themes such as redemption or resurrection" (Köstenberger and Kruger, *Heresy of Orthodoxy*, 77).

36. Kloppenborg, "Analysis of the Pre-Pauline Formula," 351–52.

37. Kloppenborg, "Analysis of the Pre-Pauline Formula," 352. For a detailed discussion of these debates, see Kloppenborg, "Analysis of the Pre-Pauline Formula," 352–57. See also Jeremias, *The Eucharistic Words*, and Conzelmann, "On the Analysis of the Confessional Formula." And, concerning how and from whom Paul received this information, Hunter helpfully explains: "Where did Paul receive this piece of formulated tradition, and when? Did he receive it when he was first admitted into the Christian church? Or when he became a missionary? Or during his fortnight's stay in Jerusalem? We do not certainly know. The usual theory is that this passage is part of

ter, however, is that, in its final form, the formula reflects a multi-faceted origin as it progressed to its final form, the form that Paul now quotes in his letter to the Corinthian church.[38]

The formula is introduced by the means of the ὅτι ("that") clause, an introduction formula that is repeated throughout the creed. With Christ being the subject, the foundation of the formula, argues Conzelmann, is constituted by two double arguments: ἀπέθανεν, ετάφη, "he died, he was buried" and ἐγήγερται, ὤφθη "he was raised up, he appeared."[39] Of these, two verbs are seen as fundamental: ἀπέθανεν (*apethanen*—"He died") and ἐγήγερται (*egēgertai*—"He was raised"), because they "constitute the foundation of the Christological 'work' formula."[40] Contextually, Paul brings up the formula as he argues in defense of the resurrection of Christ in this chapter. While some think that the "resurrection" clause was not present in the earliest form of the formula, this seems untenable. As Kloppenborg comments, since "the argumentation in chap. 15 revolves around the reality of the resurrection; the tradition adduced by Paul in support of his argument must have contained some element of proof of the resurrection (i.e., witnesses)—otherwise there would have been no reason for Paul to adduce it in the first place."[41] Indeed, this understanding is in accordance with the parallel tradition as recorded in

---

what Paul learned when he went up to Jerusalem to 'learn Peter's story'. The form of the passage—it sounds so obviously a bit of catechism—does not suggest something learned in conversation. Much more likely is the view that Paul is here reproducing the baptismal creed of the Damascus church—a creed perhaps taught to him by Ananias before his baptism. This formula, or something like it, must have formed part of the 'catechesis' which Theophilus and other Christians received upon conversion" (Hunter, *Paul and His Predecessors*, 16–17).

38. After assessing the arguments for both sides, Kloppenborg rightly concludes: "Nevertheless, the other indicators (*kata tas graphas, ōphthē*, septuagintal allusions) seem to indicate that the formula at least took final shape in a Jewish-Hellenistic milieu. However, both the fact that Paul came into contact with officials of the Palestinian church (but also the church of Antioch!) and the fact that in 15:11 he specifically aligns himself with Cephas and the Twelve in his *preaching* suggests that the formula, in at least one of its earlier recensions, came from the Palestinian church, although it may have been formulated in Greek. The same may be said of the list of witnesses to the appearance of the risen Lord: the tradition of the appearance to Cephas and the Twelve must have originated in the Palestinian church although it is possible that it was *kerygmatically formulated* elsewhere" (Kloppenborg, "Analysis of the Pre-Pauline Formula," 357).

39. Conzelmann, *1 Corinthians*, 252.

40. Conzelmann, *1 Corinthians*, 252.

41. Conzelmann, *1 Corinthians*, 358.

Determination of Orthodoxy and Heresy in Early Christianity 163

Luke 23:34, where the risen Christ appeared to Simon. Even broader, as Vernon Neufield notes (quoting C. H. Dodd), 1 Cor 15:1–11. is the "*locus classicus* of the kerygma [and as such] represents a summary of the gospel which Paul preached, but one which he also received from the Christian community before him."[42] Thus, this "*kerygma* . . . remains basically consistent throughout the New Testament and represents that body of truth proclaimed by the primitive church."[43] And this body, although, again, still very rudimentary, contained enough creedal truth such that, to deny it would result in one being legitimately accorded a heretic.

Finally, although it would be fascinating to track how the four parts of the formula evidently came together, for the purpose of this work's consideration here, it is better to take it as a unit. As already noted, in terms of its *Sitz im Leben*, "1 Cor 15:3b–5 appears to be a confessional statement, containing the essential elements of the kerygma in an extremely compressed form."[44] Indeed, as it will be demonstrated, this is similar to other creedal formulae evident especially in the Pastoral Epistles of the New Testament. In these, the corresponding formula is introduced by this phrase: πιστος ὁ λογος (*pistos logos*—"the word is faithful"). But these creedal formulae are not limited to 1 Corinthians and the Pastoral Epistles. Again, as Kloppenborg comments, "One might compare similar credal formulae such as 1 Thess 4:14 or Rom 10:9b in which 'believe' with *hoti* ['that'] appears."[45] And, while there are debates pertaining to whether the formula of 1 Corinthians 15:3b–5 comprises a formal catechetical (didactic) or a kerygmatic formula, this is beside the point here. Kloppenborg correctly argues that it comprised both of these genres. "Nevertheless," he writes, "kerygmatic or confessional statements (which represent opposite sides of the same coin) must have formed the basis for catechesis, so to that extent, 'catechetical formula' may have some currency."[46] More will be said especially as we deal with liturgical evidence for early conceptions of orthodoxy.

---

42. Neufield, *Earliest Christian Confessions*, 9. See also Dodd, *The Apostolic Preaching*.

43. Neufield, *Earliest Christian Confessions*, 3.

44. Kloppenborg, "Analysis of the Pre-Pauline Formula," 365.

45. Kloppenborg, "Analysis of the Pre-Pauline Formula," 365.

46. Kloppenborg, "Analysis of the Pre-Pauline Formula," 365–66. Neufield offers this elucidation of the relationship between didactic and kerygmatic contents of 1 Corinthians 15: "The relationship between *didache* and *homologia* is not as clearly discernible as that noted between *kerygma* and *homologia*. *Didache* and *paradosis* . . . are

In summary, the creedal formula quoted by Paul here in his defense of the resurrection of Christ constitutes one of the earliest expressions of the body of the Christian faith. Its presence and contents argue against those who see no criteria for the differentiation of truth and error (orthodoxy and heresy) in earliest Christianity. As Neufield concludes concerning the function of this (and related formulae in the NT), it was "used to combat schismatics (Rom. 16:7), to convince or convict opponents (Tit. 1:9), and to distinguish *true believers* and *heretics* (II Jn. 9, 10)."[47] This understanding of the function of this earliest creedal formula, goes against the continued argument that, during its primitive times, Christianity was so fluid such that it could not necessarily determine orthodoxy from heresy. The investigation now briefly turns to the Pastoral Epistles.

The Pastoral Epistles exhibit a significant amount of formulae that are known as *pre-performed creedal texts*. According to Ryan Wettlaufer, briefly abbreviated as PCT, these are "various sayings, poems, hymns and prose that constituted a confession, or encapsulation, of the Christian faith, which were created, possibly but not necessarily written down, and circulated prior to the composition of the New Testament."[48] Indeed, be-

---

concerned with the basic elements of the Christian faith (such as the gospel, the word of the Lord) which were taught in the church; but more specifically, the instruction included the things about Jesus, the gospel story itself" (Neufield, *Earliest Christian Confessions*, 28).

47. Neufield, *Earliest Christian Confessions*, 29. Emphasis added.

48. Wettflaufer, "Interpretative Discussion," 1. Concerning the criteria for determining these, Wettlaufer adduces these: 1) *Dense theological content*. The idea here is that "the phrase or pericope contains or refers to a multiplicity of central theological concepts" (Wettflaufer, "Interpretative Discussion," 12). 2) *Repetition of theme of motif*. Concerning this criterion, Wettlaufer expounds: "We would expect that a preformed tradition that was popular enough to be quoted by a NT author would perhaps show itself more than once. This is akin to the common trend of any popular saying or text showing up multiple times in a variety of secondary sources, such as the constant quoting of Shakespeare, or the vast army of amateur critics who trot out 'all of western philosophy is a series of footnotes on Plato'" (Wettflaufer, "Interpretative Discussion," 13). 3) *Parallels in other texts*. While this seems to be an extension of the previous criterion, Wettlaufer points out that "the occurrence of parallels in other authors is weighty evidence that a text is PCT" (Wettflaufer, "Interpretative Discussion," 14). 4) *Poetic devices*. The reasoning behind this criterion, Wettlaufer explains, is that poetic language has been proved to be the most effective genre for memorization. "Poetic language," he writes, "as an elevated departure from common speech, has always been more pleasant to the ears and more acceptable to the memory than didactic discourse. This is why people are more likely to commit to memory Psalms or Proverbs, rather than Romans or Galatians; Shakespeare or Tennyson rather than Tolstoy or Dickens" (Wettflaufer, "Interpretative Discussion," 14). 5) *Rare or uncharacteristic word usage.*

cause of the abundance of these creedal texts (either introduced by the phrase πιστὸς ὁ λόγος ("this is a trustworthy saying") or just referenced as deposit (παραθήκην—"what has been deposited to you"), some have argued that the Pastoral Letters are not authentically Pauline. It is argued that, judging from these creedal formulae (among other factors), the letters exhibit an advanced ecclesiological organization that seems to be beyond the circumstances of the first-century church. Representing such a view, for example, Martin Dibelius and Conzelmann write, "In case they are spurious, it is not only the writer's immediate purpose that is characteristic; the couching of the letters as epistles is itself symptomatic for the development of the concept of tradition, and reflects the basic of the second and third generation."[49] The problem, according to them, is this: "How did the kerygma become a 'deposit' (παραθήκην)?"[50] For some other scholars, such as Bart Ehrman, the Pastoral Epistles are just forgeries.

While it is not the purpose here to offer a full defense of Pauline authorship of the Pastoral Epistles, it would suffice to offer a brief response to the opponents. Owing to the now disregarded Baur thesis, scholars tended to date the Pastoral Epistles sometime in the second century.

Concerning this criteria, Wettlaufer further elucidates: "Rare or uncharacteristic word usage is not a sign of PCT because the early church had a penchant for using rare words in their supposedly popular creeds, but rather because it simply stands to reason that unique authorial tendencies make it likely that a creed created by one person and a NT document written by another will have noticeable differences in style and diction. As such, when we find a text that contains words not typically used by the author, we may have grounds to identify the text as PCT" (Wettflaufer, "Interpretative Discussion," 15). 6) *Syntactical variation*. This criterion refers to "any significant differences in syntax vis a vis the surrounding context which could show that the text in question has been interpolated from a different source, namely, a PCT" (Wettflaufer, "Interpretative Discussion," 15.). In many cases, there are changes in person and number. As Wettlaufer explains, according to Cranfield, "we often find sudden changes in the use of the first, second and third persons both singular and plural" (Wettflaufer, "Interpretative Discussion," 15. See Cranfield, "Changes of Person and Number"). 7) *Preceding or proceeding introduction*. According to Wettlaufer, this criterion is the strongest and the easiest to spot (Wettflaufer, "Interpretative Discussion," 17). These introductory formulae include but are not limited to such terminology as ὁμολογία, εὐαγγέλιον, μαρτυρία, πίστις, κήρυγμα, διδαχη and παράδοσις" (Wettflaufer, "Interpretative Discussion," 17). However, he makes this helpful caveat: "We would remind the reader that PCT identification does not rest on the occurrence of a single term, but on the weight of probability compiled by the simultaneous occurrence of a multiplicity of the characteristics we have discussed" (Wettflaufer, "Interpretative Discussion," 17–18).

49. Dibelius and Conzelmann, *Pastoral Epistles*, 1.
50. Dibelius and Conzelmann, *Pastoral Epistles*, 1.

That is, in the earliest Tübingen reconstruction of the history of early Christianity, together with 2 Peter and other writings, the Pastorals were seen as later attempts to rehabilitate Paul, whose earlier writings such groups as Marcionites and the gnostics had domesticated for their use.[51] However, it was left for Walter Bauer to fully situate the Pastoral Letters in the second century. Again, the main reason for this, according to Bauer, was to attempt to rescue Paul from aspects of Gnosticism that had fully domesticated him. Rensberger further summarizes:

> Where do the letters of Paul fit into Bauer's reconstruction? Hegesippus is at first said only never to have heard of them. But Papias is assigned a "negative attitude" toward the epistles (along with the gospels of Luke and John, on which he is also silent), because they had been compromised by Marcion and other heretics. Justin's failure to mention Paul or make any significant use of his letters can only be deliberate, given his time and place of writing, and again Marcion is probably the cause. Polycarp's use of Paul is only possible before Marcion's appearance.[52]

In other words, in the reconstruction of Bauer, Paul's letters are not well known or used by these main second-century writers because of their use by Marcion and other heretics. "Of course," writes Rensberger concerning this theory, "beside Marcion many others of 'the heretics' appealed to Paul—Valentinus and his followers, Basilides, the Montanists, and more."[53] Thus, according to this view, one can understand the "reluctance" with which the church in the second century approached Paul's letters. But, somehow, the church had to find a way to recover Paul, since his letters had been used by the church in Rome and elsewhere too often. The solution was, according to Bauer's reconstruction, to compose the Pastoral Epistles. Again, Rensberger explains:

> To drop Paul in favor of the Twelve [apostles] was now impossible, since Rome and the church had already appealed to him too often (to 1 Corinthians if not to Romans). Therefore, to make Paul unambiguously orthodox and antiheretical, to "eliminate the lack of confidence in him in ecclesiastical circles," the Pastoral Epistles were composed. A Paul stripped of his individuality, subservient to the Twelve, became influential in the church through its scriptures; the Pastorals "made the collection

---

51. Rensberger, "As the Apostle Teaches," 9–10.
52. Rensberger, "As the Apostle Teaches," 33.
53. Rensberger, "As the Apostle Teaches," 33.

of Paul's letters ecclesiastically viable for the very first time" [essentially].[54]

Although it is not our purpose here to offer a thorough response to arguments against Pauline authorship of the Pastoral Epistles (hereafter, just PE), it is important to emphasize that, of all reasons provided for their pseudepigraphic nature, a few deserve further exploration.[55]

First, opponents of Paul's authorship of the PE insist that they fit nowhere in the known chronology of Paul's life. As it is stated in the second half of the book of Acts, "we find the story of Paul's multiple missionary journeys, during which he meets Timothy and evangelises the Ephesian church."[56] As noted, the story ends with Paul being arrested and on his way to Rome. Thus, "The problem is that 1 Tim paints a picture of Paul as a free-travelling evangelist, making trips not mentioned in the Acts narrative."[57] However, it is highly probable that Paul wrote 1 Tim "*after* the events recorded in Acts."[58] This is the view held by Eusebius in his *EH* 2.22.1–2.[59] In this case, "we expect that it was in the time *after* the first imprisonment recorded in the end of Acts, but *before* the second unrecorded imprisonment which led to his death, while he travelled around on one last missionary endeavour, under the reign of Nero, that Paul wrote his first letter to Timothy."[60] This is even more significant for those who support a later pseudepigrapher as having perfectly captured what would have been the mind of Paul in such matters several decades later.

54. Rensberger, "As the Apostle Teaches," 33.

55. For a good defense of Pauline authorship of the PE, see Fee, *1 & 2 Timothy and Titus*; Guthrie, *Pastoral Epistles*; Johnson, *First and Second Letters*; Mounce, *Pastoral Epistles*; and Oden, *First and Second Timothy and Titus*.

56. Wettflaufer, "Interpretative Discussion," 26.

57. Wettflaufer, "Interpretative Discussion," 26.

58. Wettflaufer, "Interpretative Discussion," 26.

59. Eusebius writes in *EH* 2.22.1–2: "Festus was sent by Nero to be Felix's successor. Under him Paul, having made his defense, was sent bound to Rome. Aristarchus was with him, whom he also somewhere in his epistles quite naturally calls his fellow-prisoner, Colossians 4:10. And Luke, who wrote the Acts of the Apostles, brought his history to a close at this point, after stating that Paul spent two whole years at Rome as a prisoner at large, and preached the word of God without restraint. Thus after he had made his defense it is said that the apostle was sent again upon the ministry of preaching, and that upon coming to the same city a second time he suffered martyrdom. In this imprisonment he wrote his second epistle to Timothy, in which he mentions his first defense and his impending death."

60. Wettflaufer, "Interpretative Discussion," 26.

As Gordon Fee argues, "the proponents of the above difficulties simply do not take the historical data seriously enough."[61] Further, he argues that "it seems highly unlikely that a pseudepigrapher, writing thirty to forty years later, would have tried to palm off such traditions as Paul's evangelizing Crete, the near capitulation to heresy of the Ephesian church, or a release and second imprisonment of Paul if in fact they had never happened."[62] Thus, an unbiased interaction with the historical data leads to the conclusion that the PE are authentically Pauline.

The second major objection to the authenticity of the PE concerns the message of the letters. As already noted, scholars of this orientation argue that, as far as the heretics addressed by the PE are concerned, they "have in their cross-hairs a form of gnosticism."[63] In this case, since Gnosticism is, historically speaking, a post-Pauline development, "so too must be the PE."[64] Indeed, Walter Bauer and Hans von Campenhausen have argued for the thesis that "the Pastorals were written against Marcion (or even that they were compiled by Polycarp)."[65] Polycarp's suggested authorship is based on especially the similarity between the PE and Polycarp's *Epistle to the Philippians*.

However, in response to this argument, it is helpful to note that even the proponents of this argument—from Bauer to the more recent ones like Ehrman—are not at all clear that the PE were addressing Gnosticism. "The reference *to certain people* in I Tim 1: 3," writes Wettlaufer, "is a most probable sign that the disorder in Ephesus was at least partially the result of particular people working to disrupt the church. However, the opinion of the academy is hardly unanimous as to who these people were

61. Fee, *1 & 2 Timothy and Titus*, 4. Later, Fee convincingly concludes concerning the external evidence in support of the authenticity of the PE: "The external evidence for the Pauline authorship of the PE is as good as for any other of his letters except Romans and I Corinthians. They are quoted as Pauline by Irenaeus, ca. AD 180 (*Against Heresies* 2.14.7; 3.3.3). But they are clearly known much earlier. They are used as early as Polycarp (d. ca. AD 135), who 'cites' their content (*Philippians* 4:1) in the same eclectic but authoritative way he does other Pauline letters. They are missing from Marcion's canon (ca. AD 150), but Tertullian says Marcion rejected them [*Against Marcion* 5.21], which is no wonder, since the content of 1 Timothy 4:1–5 is completely antithetical to Marcionism. By the end of the second century they are firmly fixed in every Christian canon in every part of the empire and are never doubted by anyone until the nineteenth century" (Fee, *1 & 2 Timothy and Titus*, 23).

62. Fee, *1 & 2 Timothy and Titus*, 4.

63. Wettlaufer, "Interpretative Discussion," 27.

64. Wettlaufer, "Interpretative Discussion," 27.

65. Dibelius and Conzelmann, *Pastoral Epistles*, 2.

Determination of Orthodoxy and Heresy in Early Christianity 169

or what they were teaching."[66] Indeed, Fee clearly sees such a reconstruction as untenable for several reasons. He writes:

> The problems with such reconstruction, however, are several: It almost totally fails to locate the Epistles into a *specific* identifiable historical context, for example, Ephesus or Crete at the end of the first century. It therefore tends to see the Epistles as not having genuine logic to their arguments, thus demanding theories of "compositional technique," in which the author is viewed as purposeful in the overall scheme but negligent or without clear reason in the placement of some materials. Furthermore, it must candidly admit that much in these letters does not fit the proposed occasion at all. Most importantly, it never adequately answers the question, Why *three* letters? For example, why write Titus or 1 Timothy, given one or the other, and why from such a considerably different perspective and historical context? And why 2 Timothy at all, since it fails so badly to fit the proposed reconstruction.[67]

In other words, "much in the letters [the PE] have nothing to do with Gnostic claims."[68] Essentially, this pseudepigraphical reconstruction ignores the occasions for the composition of the letters. As Wettlaufer contends (while responding to a different objection), "we can confidently say that in contrast to the rest of the Pauline corpus, the PE are paraenetic letters, and as such, differences in the quantity or type of theology are only to be expected, and are anything but a cause for authorial consternation."[69] Thus, the occasions for the PE are different from those of other works in the entire Pauline corpus. Frankly, an acceptance of this reality alleviates most of the issues identified by those who are opposed to the works' authenticity. As Wettlaufer concludes, because the key objections against the authenticity of the PE cannot be demonstrably sustained, "we are left with the historical presumption that the letters were in fact written by Paul, and that they accurately describe their own occasion and purpose."[70] And, therefore, the PE provide us with a glimpse into the earliest creedal formulations that act as the precursor to the *regula fidei*, and, as such, provide us with some of the earliest criteria

66. Wettlaufer, "Interpretative Discussion," 27.
67. Fee, *1 & 2 Timothy and Titus*, 6.
68. Wettlaufer, "Interpretative Discussion," 27.
69. Wettlaufer, "Interpretative Discussion," 29.
70. Wettlaufer, "Interpretative Discussion," 33.

for determination of orthodoxy and heresy. This, of course, is in contrast to the current insistence that such criteria never existed. To some of these PCTs we now turn.

To recap, the acronym "PCT" has been adopted to refer to a genre found in the New Testament that comes to us in the form of poems, hymns, and prose that form a succinct summary of the key tenets of the Christian faith. According to Earl Ellis, a significant amount of the NT consists of these kinds of writings. Wettlaufer quotes Ellis as stating that "it is fair to say, I think, that most New Testament letters contain a substantial amount of preformed traditions, a number of them not composed by the letter's author."[71] Indeed, according to Ellis, many NT books exhibit a high percentage of these PCTs. According to him, the distribution looks like this: "Ephesians 54%; Colossians; 42%; I Timothy 43%; Titus 46%; I Peter 39%; II Peter 33% or 55% . . . II Thessalonians 24% and II Timothy 16%."[72] For the sake of space and for our purposes, only the key PCTs found in the PE will be highlighted here.

Concerning the actual determination of the PCTs, perhaps the most influential attempt was the already-noted Neufeld's *The Earliest Christian Confession*. He focused on introductory formulae terminology as the way to determining the PCTs. "His survey of introductory terms covers," writes Wettlaufer, "(including cognates): ὁμολογία, εὐαγγέλιον, μαρτυρία, πίστις, κήρυγμα, διδαχή, and παράδοσις."[73] Highlighting specifically the term ὁμολογία, Neufeld argues that it was clearly a marker of orthodoxy in that it "was the confession of Jesus with specific reference

---

71. Ellis, *History & Interpretation*, 141, quoted in Wettlaufler, "Interpretative Discussion," 1.

72. Ellis, *History & Interpretation*, 140, quoted Wettlaufler, "Interpretative Discussion," 1n4. See also Kelly, *Early Christian Creeds*. However, in language reminiscent of Kelly's attempt to play down any seemingly clear theological formulation that early, he writes: "The reader of the NT is continually coming across creedlike slogans and tags, catchwords which at the time of writing were being consecrated by popular usage. In addition, he lights upon longer passages which, while still fluid in their phrasing, betray by their context, rhythm and general pattern, as well as by their content, that they derive from a community tradition rather than from the writer's untrammelled invention. To explain them as excerpts from or echoes of an official ecclesiastical formula, as used to be fashionable, is unnecessary and misleading. Since the very existence of a creed in the precise sense implied is pure hypothesis, and unlikely hypothesis at that, it is more natural to treat them as independent units and examine them on their merits" (Kelly, *Early Christian Creeds*, 13).

73. Wettlaufer, "Interpretative Discussion," 10.

to his person or work, and was therefore Christological in character."[74] In short, the "*homologia* was an open declaration of this faith, whether expressed in public worship (Phil. 2.11), in some special service (I Tim. 6.12), in preaching (Rom. 10.8–10), or in controversy with Jews (Jn. 9.22; 12.42), with pagans (I Tim. 6.13), or with heretics (I Jn. 4.2, 3)." He further elaborates:

> References in early Christian literature utilizing ὁμολογία (or its verbal form) are concerned with the *content* of the confession and not the act of confession. The syntactical structure sometimes suggests specific formulas or statements; e.g. ὁμολογεῖν ὅτι introducing either direct or indirect quotations, and ὁμολογεῖν with the double accusative or with the infinitive. All introduce references to or fragments of the *homologia* itself.[75]

Essentially, therefore, these introductory formulae establish the content of the faith. The same is true of the PE, where we now turn to highlight a few examples whose introductory formulae consist of the corresponding phrase, πιστὸς ὁ λόγος (or its plural form). As noted, these are 1 Tim 1:15a, 3:1a, 4:9, 2 Tim 2:11a, and Titus 3:8.[76]

Instead of focusing on the specific texts themselves, it is better to analyze the phrase, as it seems like Paul uses it almost uniformly. Sometimes, the phrase occurs as the introductory phrase to the entire pre-creedal pericope (for example, in 1 Tim 1:15a) or even come in the middle or the end of the formulation (e.g., 1 Tim 3:1 and 4:9). According to George Knight, the occurrence of this phrase in the PE is striking "because of the absence of this exact phrase, or even anything closely approximating it, elsewhere in Paul or for that matter in the NT."[77] He adds that equally striking "is the addition 'and worthy of all acceptation' (πάσης ἀποδοχῆς ἄξιος) in two of the five occurrences but not at the

---

74. Neufield, *Earliest Christian Confessions*, 20.

75. Neufield, *Earliest Christian Confessions*, 20.

76. For more information about these PCTs, see Swete, "Faithful Sayings"; Knight, *Faithful Sayings*; and Campbell, "Identifying the Faithful Sayings." Additionally, in his studies in 1971, A. M. Hunter went on to declare that "The phrase πιστὸς ὁ λόγος evidently marks a quotation, and introduces something which the early Christians believed was of the essence of Christian faith and practice. Indeed, when we examine the sayings, most have a clear rhythm, suggesting that they embody early Christian hymns, which have their roots in what Christ had said or done" (Hunter, "Sure Sayings," 127, quoted in Wettflaufer, "Interpretative Discussion," 37).

77. Knight, *Faithful Sayings*, 1.

other three."[78] So, what is the origin of this phrase? How did this PCT act as demarcation between orthodoxy and heresy this early?

Concerning the phrase's origins, Knight locates this in the Classical Greek, beginning with Dionysius of Helicarnassus (1 BCE). He summarizes:

> Dionysius of Helicarnassus (1 BC) and Chrysostom (I–II AD) would appear to be the only other [in addition to Paul in the PE] known authors using the phrase πιστὸς ὁ λόγος. The former says γενήσεται δὲ μου πιστός ὁ λόγος . . . which . . . translates "and my claim will be credible . . ." (*Dionys. Hal.* 3, 23, 17). The latter says ἴσος δὲ οὐδέ φανεῖται πιστός ὁ λόγος . . . which . . . translates "and possibly the statement will not even seem credible . . ." (*Dio Chrys.* 28 [45] 3). Dionysius also uses πιστός εἶναι ὁ λόγος in the statement διά μέν δή ταύτας τὰς αἰτίας οὐκ ἔδοξε μοι πιστός εἶναι ὁ λόγος ("for these reasons, then, this account has not seemed to me to be credible," *Dionys. Hal.* 9, 19, 3).[79]

However, after exploring the possible origins of this phrase, Knight is right in insisting that since the exact parallel of this phrase is quite rare in extrabiblical literature, the LXX, and the Jewish writings, "the meaning of the phrase must be determined by ascertaining the meaning of its individual words as well as by studying the phrase in its [PE] context."[80] Significantly, Knight points out that, in the PE, there are at least two occurrences of the term λόγος that are quite important. First, he mentions the appearance of the term in Titus 1:9. The preceding verses describe the office of the bishop. Interestingly, in his description of the requirements of this office in this verse, Paul, in addition to others, requires the bishop to be the one who is ἀντεχόμενον τοῦ κατὰ τὴν διδαχὴν πιστοῦ λόγου ("holding to the faithful word which is according to the teaching"). He is supposed to hold onto this "faithful word" so that he "may be able to exhort in the sound doctrine (ἐν τῇ διδασκαλίᾳ τῇ ὑγιαινούσῃ), and to convict the gainsayers."[81] Thus, Knight helpfully explains, as it is used here, "Ὁ λόγος is considered πιστός just because it is κατὰ τὴν διδαχὴν."[82] In other words, the message is trustworthy because it "faithfully reflects 'the pattern of teaching' (Rom. vi.17) which the Apostle

78. Knight, *Faithful Sayings*, 1.
79. Knight, *Faithful Sayings*, 5.
80. Knight, *Faithful Sayings*, 7.
81. Knight, *Faithful Sayings*, 10.
82. Knight, *Faithful Sayings*, 10.

himself had delivered."[83] That is, at this point, it "is noticeable that the primitive kerygma is already beginning to take shape as a fixed body of orthodox doctrine."[84] And, essentially, this is the conclusion that those who are vehemently opposed to the existence of early criteria for determination of orthodoxy and heresy must have to come to terms with. For Paul, therefore, the "faithfulness of the word is related to the fact that it is according to teaching which has been taught by a faithful servant of God, and hence comes from God who is faithful." Indeed, it is clear here that "the πιστὸς λόγος is part of the solid core of διδαχὴ which has been faithfully transmitted and received."[85] No wonder, therefore, it is able to "exhort" (παρακαλεῖν) and to "convict" (ἐλέγχειν). But there is another key passage.

In 1 Timothy 1:12, Paul thanks Jesus Christ, because he has considered him "faithful" (πιστόν), appointing him to service. The temptation is to see πιστὸς here in the active sense (that is, "one who believes"). However, as Knight points out, "the entire context [of 1 Tim] and the use of the verb (ἡγήσατο ['he considered'])."[86] Further;

> Hebrews 11:11 is a noteworthy parallel in the New Testament because there also πιστὸς and ἡγέομαι are used together. The passage reads that Sarah "counted him faithful who had promised" (πιστὸν ἡγήσατο τὸν ἐπαγγειλάμενον). The passive meaning of πιστὸς is beyond question. The similarity points to the same sense in the 1 Tim. 1:12 passage. In 1 Cor. 4:1–5 Paul refers to his ministry, as he does in 1 Tim., and also uses the word πιστὸς in reference to it. There πιστὸς clearly means faithful.[87]

Therefore, it seems it is better to take πιστὸς here as passive. In other words, Paul, as "one who is entrusted with the εὐαγγέλιον, he may with this apostolic power from God declare authoritatively πιστὸς ὁ λόγος."[88] Indeed, here, "again, we see πιστὸς intimately related to God and his Son

---

83. Knight, *Faithful Sayings*, 10n27.

84. Knight, *Faithful Sayings*, 10n27. See also Kelly, *Commentary on the Pastoral Epistles*.

85. Knight, *Faithful Sayings*, 11.

86. Knight, *Faithful Sayings*, 11.

87. Knight, *Faithful Sayings*, 11.

88. Knight, *Faithful Sayings*, 12.

Jesus Christ."[89] It is, in other words, for Paul and these early Christians, the content of the gospel message!

Finally, a word needs to be said about whether the phrase πιστὸς ὁ λόγος and the statements to which it refers were oral or written. This is a debated issue in scholarship. Obviously, as Wettlaufer observes, some were written down, as "all the PCT we know of were in fact written down."[90] The issue is exacerbated by the fact that it is "apparent that in those very same books of the N.T. where λόγος is used to refer to that which is oral, it is used to refer to that which is written (*e.g.*, Acts in which cf. 2:41; 20:7 to those previously cited; 2 Thess; 2 Cor side by side in 10:10 and 11)."[91] With this understanding, as Wettlaufer observes, the "true question though is whether or not these creedal sayings were in written form before being utilised by the NT authors. From another point of view, the same question could be: did the creedal sayings circulate in written or oral form?"[92] Even more, since we have the ones that were written down, another question would be: How many were not eventually written down, and how far back do these go?

It has to be admitted that there are no satisfactory answers to these questions. It is perhaps best to conclude that, even in the five-fold occurrences of the in the PE, the formula "πιστὸς ὁ λόγος might refer in some cases to that which was oral and in others to that which was written."[93] And, as Wettlaufer concludes, "given that fact, it is certainly possible, and perhaps even plausible that someone wrote a few of them down. If such did occur, no manuscript evidence has survived, and without such

---

89. Knight, *Faithful Sayings*, 12. Knight explains this interesting take by Theodore of Mopsuestia concerning the origin and meaning of the phrase πιστὸς ὁ λόγος in the NT. "Theodore of Mopsuestia," he writes, "saw a relation between the πιστὸς ὁ λόγος and ἀμὴν λέγω in the Gospels. The latter is found in the form Ἀμὴν λέγω or in the form of ἀμὴν ἀμὴν λέγω on the lips of Jesus. Ἀμὴν is used by Jesus with λέγω and with the saying which he wishes to declare. Thus it serves as an introductory formula of asserveration to a λόγος that Jesus says (λέγω). 'The point of Amen before Jesus' own sayings is rather to show that as such they are reliable and true, and that they are so as because Jesus Himself in His Amen acknowledges them to be His own saying and thus makes them valid.' This usage of Jesus may have provided a background for the origin of the formula πιστὸς ὁ λόγος. The relationship would then be more of similar concepts than that of linguistic relationship" (Knight, *Faithful Sayings*, 12–13).

90. Wettlaufer, "Interpretative Discussion," 5.

91. Knight, *Faithful Sayings*, 16.

92. Wettlaufer, "Interpretative Discussion," 5.

93. Knight, *Faithful Sayings*, 17.

evidence we could never assert the idea dogmatically."[94] However, when all is said, it is evident that "in the Pastoral Letters . . . λόγος in πιστὸς ὁ λόγος refers to a statement, to a series of words."[95] But, as we shall argue, these PCTs and other similar formulations formed the basis for the later orally-transmitted *regula fidei*.

In summary, the PE exhibit five specific πιστὸς ὁ λόγος formulaic constructions, each of which addresses either one or more key tenets of the Christian faith. In 1 Timothy 1:15, the doctrines of Christology and soteriology are addressed. It, in other words, focusses on some very key aspects of Christology. Knight helpfully summarizes:

> 1 Tim 1:15 depicts pointedly Christ Jesus as Savior. He is the one who has come to save sinners. This and no other reason is given as the purpose for Christ's coming. 1 Tim 1:15 specifies explicitly the incarnation ("came into the world") and in doing so embraces all that the Johannine phrase implies concerning the person and work of the one who has come. The second part of the saying in synoptic terminology describes the condition of men and the action Christ Jesus has wrought to make them whole and deliver them from their condition. The saying pinpoints the act of God in history in Christ Jesus for man's salvation. In a few words it defines who the Savior is and what we men are. With one telling verb ("to save") it describes the whole work of Christ Jesus and its effect upon us lost men.[96]

Even more significantly, the appearance of the phrase in Titus 3 takes the Trinitarian form. Here, the "movement within the saying proceeds from the action on God's part in history (his kindness and love toward man appearing) to the action within us by His Spirit."[97] As well, it also "connects the Holy Spirit's work with the work of Jesus Christ as Savior and shows that the Holy Spirit is poured forth by him because he is the Savior."[98] Indeed, the same theological concepts continue with the other occurrences of this phrase, although, as in the case of 1 Timothy 4:8 and 2 Timothy 2:11–13, the focus is on man's needed activity. However, even

---

94. Wettflaufer, "Interpretative Discussion," 5.
95. Knight, *Faithful Sayings*, 18.
96. Knight, *Faithful Sayings*, 139.
97. Knight, *Faithful Sayings*, 139.
98. Knight, *Faithful Sayings*, 140.

with these variations, the theological delineations especially concerning the person and the work of Christ in these sayings cannot be missed.[99]

Questions have been raised concerning the exact relationship between the PCT and the so-called *kerygma* in the early church. The *kerygma* refers to the "primitive preaching" of the early church. C. H. Dodd famously summarized the kerygma as comprising of these elements: "(1) the Davidic descent of Jesus Christ (thus, he is qualified as the Messiah);[100] (2) His death according to the Scriptures based on the determinate council and foreknowledge of God;[101] (3) His resurrection from the dead according to the Scriptures, as well as his consequent exaltation at the right hand of God where he is now the "messianic head of the new Israel," and Lord and Christ (deity);[102] (4) the consummation of the messianic age at Christ's return; and, (5) the fact that "the *kerygma* always closes with an appeal for repentance, the offer of forgiveness and of the Holy Spirit, and the promise of 'salvation,' that is of 'the life of the age to come,' and those who enter the elect community."[103] So, how do the "faithful sayings" as explored here relate to the *kerygma*?

A careful observation indicates that, while both refer to the work of Christ (especially the one in 1 Tim 1:15), the saying "refers to the work of Christ in a much briefer way than does the *kerygma*."[104] It is possible, as Knight argues, that the *kerygma*, like the other noted formulae, forms the background for the sayings.[105] However, this was not an unqualified transference. In other words, "the sayings are not completely built upon

---

99. Knight provides this helpful summary of the theological demarcations of these sayings: "The delineation of the work of Christ in the three sayings is diverse and noteworthy (1 Tim. 1:15; Titus 3:4–7; 2 Tim. 2:11–13). All relate that work to the salvation of sinful mankind. 1 Tim 1:15 speaks in a compressed way of the great deed of Christ coming to save sinners. The emphasis would appear to be on the historical act of Christ Jesus coming into the world. Through this great act in history, with all that it involves, Christ saves sinners. Titus 3:4–7 encompasses this element of 1 Tim. 1:15 but builds on it. It refers not only to the appearing in history of God's kindness and love toward man but also of that which has taken place within those who are saved. And the saying views the entire sweep of the history of salvation, from Christ's coming until our inheritance of eternal life as heirs" (Knight, *Faithful Sayings*, 142).

100. Dodd, *Apostolic Preaching*, 26.
101. Dodd, *Apostolic Preaching*, 26.
102. Dodd, *Apostolic Preaching*, 27.
103. Dodd, *Apostolic Preaching*, 28–29.
104. Knight, *Faithful Sayings*, 147.
105. Knight, *Faithful Sayings*, 147.

Determination of Orthodoxy and Heresy in Early Christianity 177

the previous *kerygma* without any transition."¹⁰⁶ That is, while the sayings are not "purely ethical and hortatory," they "apply Christ's work to the believer and encourage and exhort him on that basis."¹⁰⁷ Essentially, according to Knight, the most important difference between the *kerygma* and the faithful sayings "lies in the fact that the former is a rather well-defined summary for evangelism whereas the latter cover various aspects of the life and work of the church and are concerned with the Christian life as well."¹⁰⁸ It seems like here one begins to see the transition into later creedal formulations, transitions that go through the second century pre-creedal *regula fidei*. Before looking at the *regula fidei*, however, something needs to be said about liturgical material that seems to describe orthodoxy even before the recognition of the NT canon.

Liturgical Material Predating the New Testament

In addition to the discussed pre-creedal formulations, scholars have also identified another indication of the core doctrinal beliefs of the early church through "the likely inclusion of hymns and other preexisting materials in the writings of the New Testament."¹⁰⁹ For example, "many believe that Philippians 2:6–11 and Colossians 1:15–20 represent early Christians hymns that Paul incorporated into his letters for various purposes."¹¹⁰ We will briefly treat these here in the same order.

There have been some scholarly debates concerning whether Philippians 2:6–11 was originally a hymn. Those who argue that it was a Christological hymn point to some distinguishing marks. Fee summarizes these, commenting that "What seems to favor this view are (1) the obvious poetic nature of vv. 6–8, (2) that it begins with ὅς, which is how two other apparent hymns begin (Col 1:15; 1 Tim 3:16); (3) that it seems to be a self-contained piece, not all of which . . . seems to fit the context (esp. vv 9–11), and (4) some unusual wording, especially for Paul."¹¹¹

---

106. Knight, *Faithful Sayings*, 147.
107. Knight, *Faithful Sayings*, 147.
108. Knight, *Faithful Sayings*, 148.
109. Köstenberger and Kruger, *Heresy of Orthodoxy*, 77.
110. Köstenberger and Kruger, *Heresy of Orthodoxy*, 77.
111. Fee, *Paul's Letter to the Philippians*, 193. Fee adds that those who are opposed to the "hymn thesis" bring up these arguments: "(1) the word ὕμνος in Greek, including the LXX, is used exclusively to describe songs or poems written in praise of a deity (or honored person), which include an ascription of praise and the reasons for

Köstenberger and Kruger argue that, indeed, there are indicators that the hymn is actually pre-Pauline. These include "(1) its unusual vocabulary; (2) its rhythmic style; (3) the absence of key Pauline themes such as redemption or resurrection."[112] Again, the main debate has been whether this is a pre-Pauline hymn, and, if so, then the questions of its actual origins arises.

While it is impossible to resolve these issues here, among all the possible views, it seems that Larry Hurtado's conclusions on the issues need to be highlighted. While arguing that the larger Greco-Roman culture within which the hymn probably originated, Hurtado contends that "the primary consideration in determining the meaning of Jesus' actions in [Phil] 2:6–8 must be the use of the *terminology of early Christianity*."[113] Hurtado writes:

> The language used to describe Jesus' actions qualitatively in 2:6–8 is drawn from the language of early Christian paraenesis and possibly from the Jesus tradition of the Pauline period. This suggests that the tradition of the earthly Jesus was influential in shaping both this description of his actions, and possibly early Christian paraenesis. Further, this evidence suggests strongly that Jesus' actions are so described as to present them as a pattern to which the readers are to conform their behavior.[114]

---

it . . . (2) that no one has yet produced an analogy (either stylistically or linguistically) that even remotely resembles the structures of our passage; and (3) that vv. 9–11 have almost nothing hymnic about them; the combination of διό ('therefore'), followed by a ἵνα clause ('so that') concluding with a ὅτι clause (serving as the object of 'confess') is not the stuff of hymns but of argumentation" (Fee, *Paul's Letter to the Philippians*, 193). For a good summary of the possible origins of this likely hymn, see Reumann, *Philippians*, 333–39. After surveying all the possible sources of the hymn, Reumann correctly concludes that "No one background unlocks the problem in 2:6–11 . . . There are OT aspects, via the LXX and Hellenistic Judaism, and reflections of the Greco-Roman world . . . Nagata . . . adds 'the creative theological ability of the Christian community'" (Fee, *Paul's Letter to the Philippians*, 338). Although the last source (organic doctrinal growth arising from the Christian community) is sometimes overlooked, it is a major impetus to early doctrinal development.

112. Köstenberger and Kruger, *Heresy of Orthodoxy*, 77. Like Fee, Köstenberger and Kruger note that opponents of the "hymn theory" raise these counter points: "(1) other Pauline passages contain as many unusual words within a comparable space; (2) other passages convey a rhythmic style; and (3) Paul need not mention all of his theology in every page" (Köstenberger and Kruger, *Heresy of Orthodoxy*, 77).

113. O'Brien, *Epistle to the Philippians*, 197.

114. Hurtado, "Jesus as Lordly Example," 126.

Determination of Orthodoxy and Heresy in Early Christianity 179

For Hurtado, therefore, most likely the language of this hymn developed organically with the Christian community.[115] Indeed, irrespective of the origin, the reader cannot miss the high Christology presented in this hymn. Hurtado helpfully summarizes the Christological message of this text. He writes:

> As to content, it is patently clear that Philippians 2:6–11 is concerned with "Christology" (that is, with affirmations about the significance of Jesus). The clear thrust of the passage is an affirmation of Jesus' special significance. Indeed, virtually all of the earliest, sizeable, and significant Christological passages in the New Testament appear to be remnants of early Christian hymns, and it seems that such odes to and about Jesus may have been a crucial mode in which Jesus' exalted significance was articulated in the earliest years of Christianity. Under the impact of the religious fervor characteristic of earliest Christian circles, which they understood as the manifestation of God's Spirit, believers were moved to express their devotion to Jesus in composing and chanting odes that celebrated his deeds and high status.[116]

Thus, it is very clear that, from this and other early Christological hymns, the early church was very clear on the parameters that set orthodoxy from heresy in these key beliefs concerning the Person of Jesus Christ. In these hymns, "Jesus is equated with God (Phil. 2:6; Col. 1:15, 19), and presented as the exalted Lord (Phil. 2:9–11; Col. 1:15–18)."[117] Thus, by this time, language indicating the deity of Jesus Christ had already become commonplace in the Christian community. Colossians follows the same pattern as well.

The final Christological passage where Paul emphasizes the supremacy of Christ is Colossians 1:15–20. However, just like the Philippians'

---

115. Interestingly, O'Brien points out that G. F. Hawthorne arrives at a similar conclusion. "Independently," he writes, "G. F. Hawthorne suggested the particular shape given to the hymn—indeed, the very existence of the hymn itself—may have been the result of deep meditation by Paul, or some other Christian if Paul was not the author, on one particular event from the life of Christ, namely, Jesus' washing his disciples' feet (Jn. 13:3–17); on this view 'δοῦλος emphasizes the fact that in the incarnation Christ entered the stream of human life as a slave, that is, as a person without advantage, with no rights or privileges of his own for the express purpose of placing himself completely at the service of all mankind'" (Hawthorne, *Philippians*, 77, 78, quoted in O'Brien, *Epistle to the Philippians*, 197–98).

116. Hurtado, *How on Earth Did Jesus Become a God?*, 86. See also Nagata, "Philippians 2:5–11."

117. Köstenberger and Kruger, *Heresy of Orthodoxy*, 78.

passage, this one has also been marred by the same debates. In this passage, Paul declares that Jesus is the "image of the invisible God, the firstborn over all creation" ("εἰκὼν τοῦ θεοῦ τοῦ ἀοράτου, πρωτότοκος πάσης κτίσεως"). As in the case of the Philippian passage, the debate has been on whether this is a pre-Pauline hymn or by Paul himself.[118] While we cannot exhaust the wealth of the historical scholarly engagement on these issues, suffice it here to say that a majority of opinions points to this as being a Christological hymn. For example, Markus Barth and Helmut Blanke point out some key hymnal identifying marks. They write:

> The text [of] 1:15-20 exhibits the typical distinguishing features of the (oriental) hymnic style... Characteristic is the participial as well as relative sentence style of predicates, and the description of the praised person in the third person. Therefore vv 15-20 must be designated as a hymnic piece and the two cited parallel sections are properly called stanzas.[119]

Lohse expresses similar sentiments, arguing that "Christological statements about the exaltation are introduced twice by a relative clause (ὅς ἐστιν 1:15, 18b), and each in turn is followed by a causal clause beginning with ὅτι (1:16, 19)."[120] Further, he notes that "Vss 17 and 18 respectively are joined by a καὶ αὐτός ('and he...'), and v 20 is attached by καὶ δι' αὐτοῦ ('and through him')."[121] Finally, the hymn itself is "concluded by the pleonastic phrase, 'making peace the blood of his cross, through him, whether on earth or in the heaven' (εἰρηνοποιήσας διὰ τοῦ αἵματος τοῦ σταυροῦ αὐτοῦ, δι' αὐτοῦ εἴτε τὰ ἐπὶ τῆς γῆς εἴτε τὰ ἐν τοῖς οὐρανοῖς)."[122] On his part, Scot McKnight, after clarifying that he will not speculate as to what Paul added to the so-called pre-Pauline hymn, recognizes the "full possibility that Paul composed the entire hymn himself or he was its genius, perhaps on the basis of preexisting confessional lines that he perhaps also had a hand in himself."[123] This conclusion coheres with the earlier conclusion that the Christological language in Philippians 2 also emerged from the Christian community (albeit with the possibility of

---

118. For a brief summary of the history of the scholarship of this hymn, see O'Brien, *Colossians, Philemon*, 32–42.

119. Barth and Blanke, *Colossians*, 228.

120. Lohse, *Colossians and Philemon*, 41.

121. Lohse, *Colossians and Philemon*, 41.

122. Lohse, *Colossians and Philemon*, 41–42.

123. McKnight, *Letter to the Colossians*, 136–37.

some earlier versions). Thus, there is a consensus that, whatever its origin, this passage is a significant Christological hymn of the early church.[124]

Regardless of the view one takes on these matters, it is clear that, in this passage, Paul provides us with an early Christian hymn that celebrates the deity of Jesus Christ. It, in other words, "celebrates in song the Jewish Messiah as creator and reconciler of the universe, who has now acceded to his reign not only over Israel, but over all of creation."[125] There is nothing ambiguous about this. Indeed, as it will be highlighted, Paul's declaration that Jesus is not only the Jewish Messiah, but the Lord of his creation, means that all the other contrary viewpoints are heretical. As Barth and Blanke explain, for Paul, since the Messiah is lord over all things, "the religious viewpoints and prescriptions that are cited in chapter 2 [of Colossians] can be refuted as 'empty deception'; the orientation toward the glorified Messiah who is celebrated in 1:15–20 determines also the ethical appeals in chaps. 3+4 (cf. especially 3:15)."[126] This

---

124. O'Brien adds this helpful caveat: "In describing the passage in this way [as a hymn] it should be noted that the term 'hymn' is not employed in the modern sense of what we understand by congregational hymns with metrical verses. Nor are we to think in terms of Greek poetic form. The category is used broadly, similar to that of 'creed,' and includes dogmatic, confessional, polemical or doxological material" (O'Brien, *Colossians, Philemon*, 32–33). It should be noted that not all agree on the hymnal nature of this passage. For example, through the application of form-criticism, Benjamin Endsall and Jennifer Strawbridge argue that there is simply too much silence surrounding the Philippian and Colossian passages to warrant identifying them as "hymns." "Of course," they write, "one cannot draw strong conclusions from silence. What we are arguing, however, is that it is this silence that needs to be recognized. The default position for analyzing these passages needs to be simply that they are heightened prose as part of a letter. Given that starting point, the burden of proof is on those who wish to argue for the Philippian and Colossian passages being hymns. Significantly, the weakness of classical form-critical criteria and silence throughout early Christian reception makes any positive statement about their hymnic status extremely difficult, to say the least. It may be that some subsequent textual discovery will demonstrate conclusively that these passages were used as hymns in antiquity. Until that time, however, we should be content with the descriptor *Christuslob*, a conclusion supported by early Christian reception, and which emphasizes the need to reset how these two pericopes might be understood, read and interpreted" (Benjamin and Strawbridge, "The Songs We Used to Sing?," 306. However, I think that the authors define the term ὕμνος (hymn) in an extremely restricted manner. As McKnight observes, in these cases, "the term 'hymn' is no more preferable than the term 'poetic' to describe 1:15–20. So, call it hymn or poetry" (McKnight, *Letter to the Colossians*,137).

125. Barth and Blanke, *Colossians*, 194.

126. Barth and Blanke, *Colossians*, 194. As Köstenberger and Kruger further note, there are many other confessional formulae scattered throughout the NT. "Another important indication of early orthodoxy in the New Testament writings," they write,

hymn, therefore, is a major criterion for the determination of not only Christological orthodoxy but also heresy.

While many examples of clear identification of heresy in the documents of the NT can be adduced, the case of the identifiable "Colossian heresy" suffices here. Scholars agree that the major impetus for Paul's letter to the Colossians was the presence of a "strange teaching which was being inculcated at Colossae."[127] For him, there was "the need to rebut the error which lay at the heart of this strange aberration of the apostolic kerygma."[128] But what was this heresy? On this point there is simply no scholarly consensus.

Although Paul does not formally define the heresy itself, there is enough information in his letter to help decipher what kind of a heresy it was. Paul uses some terminology to describe his theological and philosophical opponents at Colossae, beginning at chapter 2. In 2:4, he uses this phrase to describe his opponents: "no one will deceive you through arguments" (NET). He continues in 2:8 by telling them to not to allow anyone to deceive them "through an empty, deceitful philosophy that is according to human traditions and the elemental spirits" (NET). Finally, in 2:16 and 18, he urges them not to let anyone judge them or welcome anyone who delights in false humility. As McKnight explains, Paul here "is using language that refers to someone—and probably one front is in view—who is teaching something about which Epaphras, Paul and Timothy have major concerns."[129] So, who were these opponents, and what were they teaching?

In the scholarship of this question, focus has been on the key identifying characteristics that Paul draws attention to.[130] First, as McKnight observes, "*the opponents were operating with a Jewish set of ideas and*

"is the pervasive presence of confessional formulas. These include 'Jesus is Messiah' (Mark 8:29; John 11:27; cf. Matt. 16:16; Acts 2:36; Eph. 1:1); 'Jesus is Lord' (Rom. 10:9; Phil. 2:11; Col. 2:6; cf. John 20:28; Acts 2:36; 1 Pet. 1:3; Jude 17); and 'Jesus is the Son of God' (Matt. 14:33; Mark 1:1; Luke 1:35; John 20:31; Acts 9:20; 2 Cor. 1:19; Heb. 10:29; 1 John 3:8). These formulas represent a set of core beliefs that center on the person of Jesus Christ" (Köstenberger and Kruger, *Heresy of Orthodoxy*, 78–79).

127. O'Brien, *Colossians, Philemon*, xxx.

128. O'Brien, *Colossians, Philemon*, xxx.

129. McKnight, *Letter to the Colossians*, 25.

130. Some of the key studies of this issue are Hooker, "Were There False Teachers in Colossae?," Sappington, *Revelation and Redemption*, Attridge, "On Becoming an Angel," and Royalty, "Dwelling on Visions."

practices."¹³¹ In a manner reminiscent of what Paul addresses in Galatians, "the Jews of Colossae dismissed the claims made by Gentile Christians that they shared inheritance of Israel."¹³² Paul highlights this by the use of the terms "philosophy" (τῆς φιλοσοφίας) in 2:8 and "wisdom" (σοφίας) in 2:13. According to Lohse, the term "philosophy" in Hellenism "was used to describe all sorts of groups, tendencies and points of view, and thus, had become a rather broad term."¹³³ Included in these groups, according to Josephus, would be Jewish sects as the Pharisees, Sadducees, and the Essenes.¹³⁴ As well, "even those who through spells and magic knew how to unleash hidden powers called themselves sages and Philosophers."¹³⁵ These philosophies were all, in a way, appealing to an epistemology of initiation into the mysteries.

According to Lohse, however, for Paul, what these sects offered as "philosophy" "had nothing in common with the critical thinking and discerning knowledge of Greek philosophy, except the name. In an ironic parody of their claims the author says that their philosophy is empty, without content, in truth, nothing but 'empty deceit' (κενὴ ἀπάτη)."¹³⁶ In other words, for Paul, the result of the claims of these philosophies was that "tradition stands against tradition, claim against claim: here the apostolic tradition which the community had accepted (2:6f), there the 'tradition' of philosophy."¹³⁷ But, for Paul, although these groups insisted that their philosophy rested on solid tradition, "in reality, it was nothing other than the 'the tradition of men' (παράδοσις τῶν ἀνθρώπων)."¹³⁸ Paul

---

131. McKnight, *Letter to the Colossians* 29. See also Trebilco, *Jewish Communities in Asia Minor*.

132. McKnight, *Letter to the Colossians* 30.

133. Lohse, *Colossians and Philemon*, 94.

134. Lohse, *Colossians and Philemon*, 94.

135. Lohse, *Colossians and Philemon*, 95.

136. Lohse, *Colossians and Philemon*, 95. Lohse further elaborates concerning the transmission of knowledge in these philosophies: "Philosophical knowledge was transmitted as teaching. The tradition, which stemmed from the earlier philosophers, must be thought through anew. The 'philosophy,' about which the mysteries spoke, was also protected by a sacred tradition. The initiation rites communicated to the devotee of the mysteries the 'sacred word'... which as 'tradition' (παράδοσις) conveyed tidings of divine revelation. And through the tradition, which Gnostic teaching claimed, great pains were taken that the origin of the teachings be protected and the source of all revelation not be obscured" (Lohse, *Colossians and Philemon*, 95–96).

137. McKnight, *Letter to the Colossians*, 96.

138. McKnight, *Letter to the Colossians*, 96. In spite of Paul's language here, some

applied this response to both the Judaizing groups and other Hellenistic philosophical groups that were enticing the Colossian church.

Although there are several other characteristics that Paul brings up concerning this heresy, two more will suffice here: dualistic tendencies

---

have contested the ascription of the term "heresy" to these groups. Owing perhaps to their fascination with the idea of diversity, scholars like James D. G. Dunn have attempted to dissuade their readers not to use the term "heresy" to refer to the Colossian "error." After exploring the issue, he concludes: "One other corollary should also be mentioned. The standard way of speaking of the Colossian philosophy is to refer to it as 'the Colossian heresy', or by reference to 'the Colossian errorists'. Quite apart from whether 'heresy' is an appropriate term at this stage in Christian development, it should now be observed that the terms 'heretics' or 'errorists' may totally misrepresent those alluded to, and may indeed amount to little more than cheap and unworthy name-calling. For titles like 'heretic' or 'errorist' reduce the system represented by those so labelled to the status of no more than a corrupt growth on Christianity as the main plant, their whole system of religion summed up and sweepingly dismissed solely as 'error'. This may be effective populist demagogery, but it is hardly a responsible historical judgment. And if, as I have argued, the Colossian philosophy is a form of diaspora Judaism, then it was certainly more venerable, more established and more esteemed than the Colossian Christians. We do no justice to Christianity if we demean its early rivals by using such language, and incapacitate our texts from serving as role models for a Christianity keen to respond to its contemporary challenges. In short, given the various factors outlined above, including the likely origin of the Colossian church from within synagogue circles, the possibility of Israelite sectarianism in the diaspora, the lack of other evidence of Jewish syncretism in Asia Minor, and the readiness of some Jews to promote their distinctive religious practices in self-confident apology, we need look no further than one or more of the Jewish synagogues in Colossae for the source of whatever influences were thought to threaten the young church there. The more relaxed style of Colossians' polemic, and the absence of anything quite like the fierceness of the reaction in Galatians, further suggests that what was being confronted was not a sustained attempt to undermine or further convert the Colossians, but a synagogue apologetic promoting itself as a credible philosophy more than capable of dealing with whatever heavenly powers might be thought to control or threaten human existence. To describe this as a 'heresy' is quite inappropriate, and to brand it simply as 'false teaching' (maintained by Colossian 'errosists'!) reduces that teaching to its controverted features and completely fails to appreciate the strength and attractiveness of a confident Jewish apologia" (Dunn, "The Colossian Philosophy," 180–81). However, as McKnight responds, "The issue in world religions, not least in our Western pluralist cultures, might make us more sensitive to this kind of accusatory language, but the exegete lets Paul say what he says, and he sees these people as opponents of the gospel, Jewish or not, Christian or not. I suspect Paul would have called them errorists and *heretics*" (McKnight, *Letter to the Colossians*, 31, emphasis added). I agree. Indeed, highlighting some of the issues that I have tried to address here, McKnight further comments: "Scholarship today maximizes diversity, at times with the hope of offending the orthodox, as is the case often with Bart D. Ehrman, but that drill ought not to diminish the reality of [legitimate] early Christian diversity" (McKnight, *Letter to the Colossians*, 31n110). More will be said in the conclusion.

and their "*propensity to entangle themselves with what Paul calls the 'elementary powers of this world.*'"[139] The first of these characteristics (dualism) is more implicit than explicit in Paul's thought. As some have suggested, this dualism is traceable to Middle Platonism.[140] Paul hints at this dualism in 2:11–12. He uses language that suggests practices that were found in the mystery cults as part of their dualism. The reference, for example, of "putting off the body of flesh" (ἀπεκδύσει τοῦ σώματος τῆς σαρκός) in v. 11, "suggests the practices of mystery cults."[141] That is, in their initiation rites, "the devotee had to lay aside what previously had served him as clothing so that he could be filled with divine power."[142] No wonder Paul tells the Colossian believers that their circumcision is not one of hands, but through Jesus Christ (ἐν τῇ περιτομῇ τοῦ Χριστοῦ). However, it is in the more ascetic language of 2:21 where this dualism becomes clearer.

In this passage, Paul provides the example of three regulations that were being held up by some of these groups as aspects of their ascetic requirements: "Do not handle! Do not taste! Do not touch!" (μὴ ἅψῃ μηδὲ γεύσῃ μηδὲ θίγῃς). Although the imperatives do not have any objects to indicate the exact prohibitions, they nevertheless "appear to be an intense caricature of the legalistic commands."[143] Further, it seems like the first and the third verbs are very similar ("handle, touch"). However, there may be a subtle difference. As Lohse observes, "while θιγγάνειν means 'to touch,' ἅπτεσθαι can be somewhat stronger: 'to take hold of something with a view to possessing it.'"[144] In any case, all these restrictions pointed to aspects of asceticism within some of these groups. Lohse further elucidates:

---

139. McKnight, *Letter to the Colossians*, 31. In a helpful summary, Köstenberger and Kruger write: "Paul's opponents in Colossae . . . were probably propagating an eclectic amalgamation of Judaism and incipient Gnosticism, including elements of astrology, asceticism, and pagan mystery cults. They were most likely not considered Christians (Col. 2:8: 'not according to Christ'). The type of Judaism found at Colossae seems less coherent than that in Galatia. It is unclear whether the proponents of the Colossian heresy were a well-organized group and what affinities, if any, they had to other religious groups in the region" (Köstenberger and Kruger, *Heresy of Orthodoxy*, 92).

140. McKnight, *Letter to the Colossians*, 31.

141. Lohse, *Colossians and Philemon*, 102.

142. Lohse, *Colossians and Philemon*, 102.

143. Lohse, *Colossians and Philemon*, 102.

144. Lohse, *Colossians and Philemon*, 123.

> Of course the proponents of the "philosophy" did not think that a person should absolutely not touch anything. Rather, we must assume that their "regulations" included distinct taboos which referred to contact with objects that had been declared unclean or with forbidden foods. To taste such food and drink is strictly prohibited. Such ascetic taboo regulations describe in minute detail what is to be eaten and what not. The fence that is erected by "Do not" restricts the ascetic's area of action. Therefore, he must scrupulously observe the "Do not trespass" signs set up for him: Do not handle—also do not taste—do not even touch![145]

Thus, in their desire to enter into "the depths of mystical experience and ascent into the heavenly world,"[146] members of these groups advocated for this kind of self-denying dualistic asceticism. This brings us to the final characteristic: entangling themselves with "elemental powers of this world."

Paul, in Colossians 2:8, cautions the Colossian believers that the deceitful and empty philosophy of these groups is "according to human traditions and the elemental spirits of the world" (κατὰ τὴν παράδοσιν τῶν ἀνθρώπων, κατὰ τὰ στοιχεῖα τοῦ κόσμου). Later, in 2:20, he argues that since they have died with Christ to "the elemental spirits of the world" (τῶν στοιχείων τοῦ κόσμου), they should not submit to these elements. One of the more debated points pertains to the meaning of the identity of the *stoicheia*, who "create the practices connected to food laws, calendar, false humility, worship of angels, visionary experiences and claims of revelation."[147] Ian Smith offers this helpful summary concerning the worldview that included these "elements":

> The world of evil elemental spirits was both recognized and feared. This fear of the powers of evil led Jews to participate in legalism. The philosophy stressed distinctively Jewish practices such as circumcision, Sabbath observance and dietary restrictions as means whereby the adherents could release themselves from the powers of evil. Such "good" practices would help the errorists overcome the "evil" forces. These practices, however, inasmuch as they were centred upon human obedience rather than divine grace, actually enslaved the Colossians to the very forces from which they wanted to be liberated. Furthermore, submission to such practices denied the sufficiency of the

---

145. McKnight, *Letter to the Colossians*, 123–24.
146. McKnight, *Letter to the Colossians*, 32.
147. McKnight, *Letter to the Colossians*, 281.

atonement by Christ and his lordship over creation, especially over the elemental spirits.[148]

Paul's antidote to this is, once again, Christological: an appeal to the Colossian believers' relationship with Christ. Paul makes it clear to the Colossians: since they died with Christ to these elements, they do not have to submit to them as though they lived in the world. According to Paul, "Co-crucifixion is implicit in the circumcision of Christ (2:11) and in their [Colossians'] baptismal identification with Christ in his death (e.g., Rom 6:1–14); this Christoformity will become more explicit in the next paragraph (3:1–4)."[149] Thus, as Barth and Blanke note, "the premise of this conditional clause is actually existing reality."[150] O'Brien clarifies that, for Paul, "as death breaks the bond which bounds a subject to his ruler so dying with Christ severs the bond that bound the Colossians to the slavery of the principalities and powers."[151] The Colossian believers, therefore, need not submit to these elements because they are not under the worldly systems because they are in Christ, and his death has already spelled an end to these systems.

Summary and Conclusion

This section has raised the question of whether there were early and clear definitions of *orthodoxy* and *heresy* (as well as criteria for determination of these) in the documents of the NT. Through the examination of especially evidence found in the Pastoral Epistles (e.g., the pre-creedal confessional formulae, especially the more occurring πιστος ὁ λογος (*pistos logos*—"the word is faithful"), it was demonstrated that this, indeed, was the case: orthodoxy creedal language, albeit rudimentary at this time,

---

148. Smith, *Heavenly Perspective*, 143. Smith further elaborates: "Within a world view that was dominated by the presence of evil spirits, a dualism that deprecated the physical world was seen in the philosophy. This world view resulted in ascetic practices that longed to mortify the flesh in order to have release from the bondage of the world and entry to heaven. At the time of Paul there were extra-Biblical texts within Judaism which described heavenly ascents where the participants could either witness or join in heavenly worship. Therefore it is consistent that a belief in the determinative power of the evil spirits would lead some Jews to long for a mystical heavenly ascent whereby they could witness (and possibly participate in) the worship that angels directed towards God" (Smith, *Heavenly Perspective*, 143–44).

149. McKnight, *Letter to the Colossians*, 281.

150. Barth and Blanke, *Colossians*, 353.

151. O'Brien, *Colossians, Philemon*, 149.

was early. Additionally, liturgical confessions, which occur in such places as Philippians 2:6–11 and Colossians 1:15–20, point to early crystallization of the church community's theological convictions (especially those pertaining to the Person and work of Jesus Christ).

Lastly, the section has also provided evidence for early definition and identification of *heresy*. While there are many examples of warnings concerning false teachings/teachers in the documents of the NT, the case of the "Colossian heresy" was chosen. The main reason for the choice is that not only did this heresy cover a "multitude of heresies," but, as well, it is one of the most debated ones. As it was demonstrated, although, there are some today who, because of their fascination with religious and ideological diversity, have argued against calling the teachings of these groups' "heresies." Paul does not leave this option out. He is clear that the teachings of these groups amount to error/heresy no matter how one feels about them.

Therefore, through these definitions and identifications of early orthodoxy and heresy, it became increasingly clear that, contrary to some scholarly views today, the early church, going all the way back to the documents that were later recognized as the canonical NT, had clear definitions and criteria for identifying *orthodoxy* and *heresy*. The final section of this chapter briefly looks at the emergence and development of the *regula fidei* in the second century, the final step towards the earliest ecumenical creeds.

THE EMERGENCE AND FUNCTIONS OF THE *REGULA FIDEI*

Towards the end of his lengthy response to the "Bauer thesis," Turner introduced the ancient concept of the "Rule of Faith." According to him, this concept is based on the Greek idea of the κανών which, in its original usage, "denoted a carpenter's rule or a builder's plumb-line, and by an easy transference of meaning it could be applied to a rule, standard, or norm whether in the arts of music and rhetoric or to the set of opinions of a philosophical school."[152] As a reference to the doctrinal standard of the early church, this term begins to be prevalent in the writings of such fathers as Clement, Irenaeus, and Tertullian. Turner further clarifies:

---

152. Turner, *Pattern of Christian Truth*, 348–49.

The phrase "The Rule of Truth" (κανών τῆς ἀληθείας, *regula veritas*) occurs freely in the writings of St. Irenaeus. A single passage in the Armenian translation of the *Epideixis* [the Armenian version of Irenaeus's *The Demonstration of Apostolic Preaching*] presupposes "the Rule of Faith" as its original, but this form is otherwise paralleled in St. Irenaeus. That the genitive is one of apposition is proved by a passage in which both elements in the phrase are set side by side as objects of a common verb. In close conjunction to the Rule of Truth stand words like faith, its content or subject matter (ὑπόθεσις, *argumentum, argumentation*), and proclamation or preaching (κήρυγμα, *praedicatio*). Perhaps with its original meaning in mind it is once described as fixed or unbending (ἀκλινῆ, *immobilem*).[153]

However, while the usage of this term seems to have been commonplace in the second century (see, for example, 1 *Clem*. 46.6; Irenaeus, *Epid*. 6 and *Adv. Haer*. 1.10.1), questions pertaining its origins and precise content continue to be sources of debate in scholarship. Blowers identifies these critical questions, wondering; "What *kind* of rule was the Rule of Faith? How was it definitive and authoritative among Christian communities when a Christian biblical canon was still in formation and when the episcopate was not yet fully networked as an ecclesiastical and magisterial infrastructure?"[154] The answers to these two questions form a critical link in the progress of the argument here.

Concerning the origin of the *regula fidei*, Tomas Bokedal argues convincingly that the real origins of the term κανών are to be located in pre-Pauline and Pauline literature. For example, he highlights Paul's use of the term in Galatians 6:16. As Paul uses it "in a conflict situation referring to the uncompromisable essence of the truth of the gospel associated with the universality of the gospel and the concept of 'new creation.'"[155] As he further observes, it seems like Tertullian is alluding to this passage when he writes in *Against Marcion*: "'Let us see . . . to what rule *of faith*

---

153. Turner, *Pattern of Christian Truth*, 349: "In the New Testament and the apostolic Fathers (especially in I *Clement*)," Turner writes, "the word κανών is used of a rule of life or a pattern of conduct. Towards the end of the second century it is applied to doctrinal norms, while by the fourth century it is customarily used of the itemized decisions of a Council or in the technical sense of the Canon of Scripture."

154. Blowers, "*Regula Fidei*," 199.

155. Bokedal, "Rule of Faith," 236. See also Farmer, "Galatians and the Second-Century," 143–70.

the Galatians were brought for correction' (*Marc.* 4, 5.1)."[156] So, how did it become commonplace in the second century?

Consistent with his theory of development of early Christianity as degeneration into concrete forms in the name of creeds and the episcopate, Harnack argued that the "*regula fidei* was a kind of hard copy of primitive baptismal confessions, a traditionalizing of the gospel."[157] According to him, what Irenaeus set forth as the "rule of truth" or "tradition" or simply "faith" was "undoubtedly, as far as he himself is concerned, based on the facts that he had already a rigidly formulated creed before him and that he had no doubt as to its interpretation."[158] In other words, Harnack understood Irenaeus as seeing the *regula fidei* as already creedalized (facsimiled) by his time. Further, as Osborn demonstrates, from Tertullian's *Praescr.* 21, 32, and 36, Harnack saw the *regula fidei* as an early coalescing of three early standards, "viz, the apostolic doctrine, the apostolic canon of scripture, and guarantee of apostolic authority, afforded by the organization of the Church, that is, by the episcopate, and traced back to the apostolic institution."[159] In so arguing, one easily senses what was identified earlier as "Hanarckian historiography" which sees doctrinal development in the early church as scientific concretization of the faith at the expense of the gospel message, itself having originated as a "joyous celebration." Is this the case, though?[160]

---

156. Bokedal, "Rule of Faith," 236. As Eric Osborn explains elsewhere, "For Tertullian the rule is a fixed form, unshakeable, irreformable, identical with the totality of revelation from God, and prior to all heresy. It runs straight back to the apostles and Christ. Heresy is secondary; truth is primary, total and the same in its many presentations" (Osborn, "Reason and Rule of Faith," 45).

157. Blowers, "*Regula Fidei*," 200.

158. Harnack, *History of Dogma*, 2.27.

159. Osborn, "Reason and Rule of Faith," 43. According to Blowers, William Farmer argued that it was Marcion's "conter-*regula*" that was "ultimately the most important catalyst to the solidification of the catholic *regula fidei* of the second century, with its affirmation of the oneness of God, Creator *and* Father of Jesus Christ" (Blowers, "Regula Fidei," 202).

160. Osborn helpfully clarifies that "While the interdependence of the ideas [the sources that Harnack identifies] is clear, their relation cannot be defined with precision. The baptismal hypothesis must be rejected; it was once confidently claimed that by the middle of the second century the Roman church had a fixed baptismal creed which was the source of the rule of faith. This theory was based on two false assumptions—that the rule of faith was the same as the creed and that the declaratory creeds were always in baptism; but it is useless to look to the baptismal liturgy as the source for declaratory creed at this time" (Osborn, "Reason and Rule of Faith," 43). Harnack's identification of the *regula fidei* with the Roman church's baptismal formula is akin to

However, as it will be suggested in the next chapter, it seems that the formation of the Rule of Faith was part of "legitimate diversity." As Blowers has successfully demonstrated, *regula fidei* developed as an aspect of the struggle for "Christian" identity; the Christian narrative in continuity with earlier pre-creedal formulations. He explains:

> At bottom, the Rule of Faith (which was always associated with Scripture itself) served the primitive Christian hope of articulating and authenticating a world-encompassing story or metanarrative of creation, incarnation, redemption, and consummation . . . in the crucial "proto-canonical" era in the history of Christianity, the Rule, being a narrative construction, set forth the basic "dramatic" structure of a Christian vision of the world, posing as an hermeneutical frame of reference for the interpretation of Christian Scripture and Christian experience, and educing the first principles of Christian theological discourse and of a doctrinal substantiation of Christian faith.[161]

That is, rather than seeing the *regula fidei* as a concrete formula that had been codified before the writings of the fathers, it is better to see it as a growing consensus on the key doctrines of the Bible as the early church struggled to respond to questions about these doctrines. "Attempts to set out the core of the Christian faith in the form or a *regula*," writes Blowers, "arose from complex centrifugal and centripetal forces at work among churches that claimed apostolic status but remained distinguished by significant differences of tradition-history, hermeneutics, theological conceptualization, and patterns of symbolism."[162] Indeed, this understanding is in conformity with the well-known theory of doctrinal development: the church develops doctrinally as a result of either internal or external questions that force her to refine beliefs based on her hermeneutical considerations.

However, while the *regula fidei* developed as an aspect of Christianity's attempt towards self-identity, in terms of its content, it clearly identified parameters outside of which one would be considered not a Christian (or, at least, an *orthodox* Christian). Blowers helpfully further elucidates:

Bauer's disputed argument of an early centralization of the Roman church.

161. Blowers, "Regula Fidei," 202. See also Bray, *Holiness and the Will of God*, 97–104.

162. Blowers, "Regula Fidei," 203.

> Whether or not one accepts the thesis that the Rule of Faith was "imposed" on Scripture by the church as a summary of right doctrine or as a principle of interpretation, it is doubtless true that the earliest exponents of a Christian *regula* regarded it as representing the kind of authority which "Scripture" (broadly speaking) conveyed: essentially the authority of a story, or a divine gospel (Gal. 1:11) enshrined within a grand story, with God himself as the primary narrator. It was a drama gradually unfolded with a coherent plot, climaxing in the coming of Jesus, who held the secret to the story's ending. And yet the denouement, while "certain" insofar as the earlier plot of the story pointed to it, remained mysterious, enlisting the crucial participation of the "audience" of the drama, that is, the audience's own "performance" in the drama's last act.[163]

Thus, as Köstenberger and Kruger observe, although the church fathers never explicitly spelled out the exact content of the *regula fidei*, "there is relative consensus among scholars that it served as a minimal statement concerning the church's common faith."[164] This is a point that even Ehrman concurs with, writing that "The [*regula fidei*] included the basic and fundamental beliefs that, according to the proto-orthodox, all Christians were to subscribe to, as these had been taught by the apostles themselves."[165] Thus, it was correctly referred to as a "concise statement of early Christian public preaching and communal belief, a normative compendium of the *kerygma*."[166] In this sense, rather than being an exact creed, it was more than a creed. It was the essence of the gospel message. As Hartog correctly observes, in some renditions of the *regula fidei*, it is clear that it is conceived as a "metanarrative" encompassing God's nature, originating work, and interaction with his creation. "The developed Rule is the depiction of the work of the Godhead in creation," he writes, "the gracious election of the patriarchs, the administration of the Law, the proclamation of the prophets, the incarnation of the Word, the bestowal of the Spirit, the building of the church, and the future final eschaton."[167]

---

163. Blowers, "Regula Fidei," 205.
164. Köstenberger and Kruger, *Heresy of Orthodoxy*, 54.
165. Ehrman, *Lost Christianities*, 194.
166. Köstenberger and Kruger, *Heresy of Orthodoxy*, 54.
167. Paul Hartog, "'Rule of Faith' and Patristic Biblical Exegesis," 70. It would help to remember Irenaeus's illustration of how the heretics (Valentinians) misarrange the precious jewels, and, in so doing, produce the figure of a fox instead of the beautiful figure of a king (Irenaeus, *Adv. Haer.* 1.8).

Determination of Orthodoxy and Heresy in Early Christianity

In other words, the Rule attempts to show that the Scriptures are coherent, something that, according to Irenaeus, the heretics have no sense of.

As noted above, there are several mentions of the Rule of Faith in the writings of the ante-Nicene fathers. The references are too many to analyze here, however.[168] Thus, only a few will suffice.[169] Beginning with the initial formulations in Ignatian corpus (*Mag.* 8.2; *Eph.* 15.3; 18.2, *Rom. Praescr.*, 3.3; *Pol.* 8.3) through *1 Clement* (46.6), the formula finds its most references in the writings of Irenaeus and Tertullian. The former continues this tradition in *Adv. Haer.* 1.3.6; 1.10, 3.4.2; 4.33.7 and *Epid.* 6 among others while the latter picks it up in *Praescr.* 36 and *Virg.* 1. A distinctive of Irenaeus's usage of the *regula fidei* is his endeavor "toward comprehensiveness."[170]

Out of the many mentions of the Rule of Faith by the great second-century polemicist and theologian Irenaeus of Lyons, two deserve attention: *Adv. Haer.* 1.10 and *Epideixis* (*Proof of Apostolic Preaching*) 3. As Kelly argues, for Irenaeus, "the Church's faith was everywhere one and the same."[171] The basis for his claim was his understanding that, although the church is scattered from one end of the earth to the other, "it shared one system of belief derived from the Apostles and their disciples, and that while languages of mankind were various, 'the substance of the tradition (ἡ δύναμις τῆς παραδοσεως)' was identical in all places."[172] This "system of belief" by which Irenaeus "did not mean a single universally accepted creed, or indeed any kind of formula as such, but rather the

---

168. For a thorough analyses, see Bokedal, "Rule of Faith."

169. As Bokedal explains, concerning the variation of the Rule of Faith/Truth, it seems like, in its usage in the fathers, sometimes it refers to a summary of the Christian faith, while at other times it refers to whole content of the Christian faith (Bokedal, "Rule of Faith," 255). As well, William Countryman elucidates especially concerning Tertullian's usage of this phrase: "Sometimes this phrase makes sweeping reference to the whole content of Christian faith; at other times, however, it refers to a specific summary of the faith to which Tertullian appealed in the midst of controversy" (Countryman, "Tertullian and the Regula Fidei," 208.) For a recent analysis of the scholarship of the *regula fidei*, see Ferguson, *Rule of Faith*.

170. Bokedal, "Rule of Faith," 246.

171. Kelly, *Early Christian Creeds*, 76.

172. Kelly, *Early Christian Creeds*, 76. As Bingham explains, "What distinguished Irenaeus from the heretics was his theme of unity and his interpreting Scripture within the parameters of the faith passed down from apostle to bishop. What has been entrusted from one faithful Christian to another always plays an important role in interpretation" (Bingham, *Pocket History*, 42).

doctrinal content of the Christian faith as handed down,"[173] was, for him, the Rule of Faith ("the canon of the truth").

While it is clear that Irenaeus's version of the *regula fidei* in *Adv. Haer.* 1.10 pertains to the Trinity, it is also clear that, instead of the shorter version of the *regula fidei*, it employs what Kelly identifies as "one-membered, two-membered and three-membered"[174] confessions of faith. In other words, as Bokedal contends, "In *Haer.* 1, 10.1, he [Irenaeus] seems to enclose a one-limbed (the Christological supplement), two-limbed (the one-God, one-Lord pattern) and three-limbed formula (Father, Son, and Spirit) in one all-inclusive formula."[175] If this is what Irenaeus does here, then it becomes evident that either a restrictive understanding of the *regula fidei* as only the baptismal formula of the Roman church or the overly broadened concept encompassing everything that everyone taught in the early church is to be rejected. In other words, Irenaeus here seemingly "combines such formulas—earlier confessional patterns integrated into one single confession, signifying the sum content of apostolic teaching."[176] Similarly, Tertullian shows the same approach in his usages of the *regula fidei*.

173. Kelly, *Early Christian Creeds*, 76.

174. Kelly, *Early Christian Creeds*, 76.

175. Bokedal, "Rule of Faith," 246. Irenaeus writes in *Adv. Haer.* 1.10.1: "The Church, though dispersed throughout the whole world, even to the ends of the earth, has received from the apostles and their disciples this faith: [She believes] in one God, the Father Almighty, Maker of heaven, and earth, and the sea, and all things that are in them; and in one Christ Jesus, the Son of God, who became incarnate for our salvation; and in the Holy Spirit, who proclaimed through the prophets the dispensations of God, and the advents, and the birth from a virgin, and the passion, and the resurrection from the dead, and the ascension into heaven in the flesh of the beloved Christ Jesus, our Lord, and His [future] manifestation from heaven in the glory of the Father to gather all things in one, and to raise up anew all flesh of the whole human race, in order that to Christ Jesus, our Lord, and God, and Saviour, and King, according to the will of the invisible Father, every knee should bow, of things in heaven, and things in earth, and things under the earth, and that every tongue should confess to Him, and that He should execute just judgment towards all; that He may send 'spiritual wickednesses,' and the angels who transgressed and became apostates, together with the ungodly, and unrighteous, and wicked, and profane among men, into everlasting fire; but may, in the exercise of His grace, confer immortality on the righteous, and holy, and those who have kept His commandments, and have persevered in His love, some from the beginning [of their Christian course], and others from [the date of] their repentance, and may surround them with everlasting glory."

176. Bokedal, "Rule of Faith," 246. As Kelly argues, this representation is comparable to others that were contemporary to it in other early Christian centers. For example, Kelly sees a parallel between Irenaeus's *regula fidei* here and the one produced by

It helps to remember that Irenaeus employed the *regula fidei* formula mainly in his battle with the heretics. For him, in contrast to Marcion's view of God, the Father is the Creator and not the evil Demiurge of Marcion. Ferguson summarizes:

> Irenaeus consistently identifies God the Father as the Creator. This was traditional, but the emphasis was dictated by the distinction that Marcion made between the Creator God of the Old Testament and the Father of Jesus Christ and by the Gnostics's demotion of the Creator (the Demiurge) to a lesser being than the supreme God. The Holy Spirit is presented as the one who prophesied the coming of Christ through the prophets, produced a recognition of the truth, led human beings in the path of justice, and in the new age was poured out in a new manner to renew humanity to God.[177]

Indeed, this kind of language litters Irenaeus's corpus. It may even be argued that the entire Demonstration of the Apostolic Preaching is an exposition of the *regula fidei*. The same approach continues in the use of the formula by Tertullian of Carthage.

In his helpful study of the use of the *regula fidei* in the work of Tertullian, Countryman begins by observing that "references to the *regula fidei* or 'rule of faith' as a criterion of Christian truth. Sometimes this

---

the "blessed presbyters" of Smyrna in their opposition to the anti-Trinitarian heretic Noetus of Smyrna (Kelly, *Early Christian Creeds*, 42). Kelly further argues that even more important is the Coptic creed, the *Epistula Apostolurum*, "an anti-Gnostic work probably written somewhere in Asia Minor shortly after the middle of the second century" (Kelly, *Early Christian Creeds*, 42).

177. Ferguson, *Rule of Faith*, 22. Fergusson further summarizes concerning Irenaeus's entire employment of the formula: "From the statements in Irenaeus, several points relative to the rule of faith may be determined. (1) The affirmation of its apostolic origin and its association with baptism (*Against Heresies* 1.9.4—1.10.1; *Demonstration* 6-7). The trinitarian structure likely derives from the baptismal formula (Matt 28:19) and the preceding confession of faith. (2) Although the wording reflects emerging creeds, the expanded article of Christ reflects the early *kerygma*. (3) The one God and one Lord pattern is early (1 Cor 8:6; cf. *1 Clement* 46.6 with the addition of 'one Spirit'). (4) The wording was flexible but followed a distinct outline. (5) The rule was often associated with Scripture and the apostolic tradition transmitted through Scripture. The rule was an epitome, the essential content, of the Scriptural tradition, an abstract of the biblical plan of salvation. (6) The formulation could focus on the two articles of the Father and the Son or on three articles with the inclusion of the Holy Spirit. The structure and traditional elements of the rule in Irenaeus indicate its contents preceded his polemical use of it (chapter 5)" (Ferguson, *Rule of Faith*, 22). See also Waszink, "Tertullian's Principles and Methods of Exegesis."

phrase makes sweeping reference to the whole content of Christian faith; at other times, however, it refers to a specific summary of the faith to which Tertullian appealed in the midst of controversy."[178] As such, in his usage of the formula, Tertullian means "much the same as St Irenaeus means by his 'canon of the truth,' i.e., the body of teaching transmitted in the Church by Scripture and tradition."[179] And, while there are many references of this formula in Tertullian's writings, these three are most significant: *Prescription Against Heretics* chapter 13, *The Veiling of Virgins* chapter 1, and *Against Praxeas* chapter 2. In the first of these, which is the earliest and very elaborate, Tertullian writes:

> Now, with regard to this rule of faith—that we may from this point acknowledge what it is which we defend—it is, you must know, that which prescribes the belief that there is one only God, and that He is none other than the Creator of the world, who produced all things out of nothing through His own Word, first of all sent forth; that this Word is called His Son, and, under the name of God, was seen in "*diverse manners*" by the patriarchs, heard at all times in the prophets, at last brought down by the Spirit and Power of the Father into the Virgin Mary, was made flesh in her womb, and, being born of her, went forth as Jesus Christ; thenceforth He preached the new law and the new promise of the kingdom of heaven, worked miracles; having been crucified, He rose again the third day; (then) having ascended into the heavens, He sat at the right hand of the Father; sent instead of Himself the Power of the Holy Ghost to lead such as believe; will come with glory to take the saints to the enjoyment of everlasting life and of the heavenly promises, and to condemn the wicked to everlasting fire, after the resurrection of both these classes shall have happened, together with the restoration of their flesh. This rule, as it will be proved, was taught by Christ, and raises among ourselves no other questions than those which heresies introduce, and which make men heretics.[180]

A casual reading of Tertullian's *regula fidei* here may lead to an incorrect conclusion—that Tertullian is binitarian. However, as Kelly argues, this is actually a trinitarian statement of faith because "the wording is extremely free throughout, and this excuses the inclusion of the

---

178. Countryman, "Tertullian and the Regula Fidei," 208.
179. Kelly, *Early Christian Creeds*, 83.
180. Tertullian, *Praescr.* 13.

belief in the Holy Spirit in a subordinate clause inserted into the lengthy Christology."[181] Tertullian repeats the formula, this time, in its short form, in *Virg.* 1. And, while, again, the Holy Spirit is not mentioned here, it is clear that he figures largely in the formula.

Finally, as noted above, the formula appears in *Adversus Praxaem* 2. Here, Tertullian writes:

> We, however, as we indeed always have done (and more especially since we have been better instructed by the Paraclete, who leads men indeed into all truth), believe that there is one only God, but under the following dispensation, or οἰκονομία, as it is called, that this one only God has also a Son, His Word, who proceeded from Himself, by whom all things were made, and without whom nothing was made. Him we believe to have been sent by the Father into the Virgin, and to have been born of her—being both Man and God, the Son of Man and the Son of God, and to have been called by the name of Jesus Christ; we *believe* Him to have suffered, died, and been buried, according to the Scriptures, and, after He had been raised again by the Father and taken back to heaven, to be sitting at the right hand of the Father, and that He will come to judge the quick and the dead; who sent also from heaven from the Father, according to His own promise, the Holy Ghost, the Paraclete, the sanctifier of the faith of those who *believe* in the Father, and in the Son, and in the Holy Ghost. That this rule of faith has come down to us from the beginning of the gospel, even before any of the older heretics, much more before Praxeas, *a pretender* of yesterday, will be apparent both from the lateness of date which marks all heresies, and also from the absolutely novel character of our new-fangled Praxeas.[182]

Here, it is evident, as with Tertullian's other usage of the formula, while it starts with what looks like a binitarian formulation, it ends with a brief Trinitarian creed. It is clear, as well, that Tertullian varies the wording of his *regula fidei* in order to fit the various polemical needs that he encounters. That is, whenever Tertullian is not engaging in any kind of polemics, his version of the *regula fidei* is a summary of the Christian teaching. But when he is using the formula for polemical reasons, it comes out more engaging. "The oneness of God," writes Kelly concerning Tertullian's usage of the formula, "for example, is set in high

---

181. Kelly, *Early Christian Creeds*, 85.
182. Tertullian, *Prax.* 2.

relief, and the suggestion of a second God is expressly denied; Jesus is identified with the Messiah of ancient prophecy and is declared to have experienced genuine human birth from Mary's womb; and the resurrection of the flesh is heavily underlined."[183] In other words, Tertullian uses this formula against such heretical groups as Marcionism, Praxeanism, and Docetism. For Tertullian, just as it is the case with Irenaeus, even though there is flexibility in the phrasing of the *regula fidei*, there is also a fixity that functions as the demarcation between *orthodoxy* and *heresy*. It functioned, in other words, as the oral bridge between early pre-creedal statements of the faith and the later creedalization of the same.[184]

CONCLUSION

This final section of the chapter has focused on what was known in the early church as the *regula fidei*. While there are multiple references to the *regula fidei* in the writings of many of the fathers from Clement of Rome (35–99 CE) to Origen of Alexandria (185–254 CE), the significant uses by Irenaeus of Lyons (d. 200 CE) and Tertullian of Carthage (155–220 CE) were dealt with in greater detail. Through these select usages, it was argued that, depending on the specific contexts, these church fathers chose any of the possibly three versions of the *regula fidei* that were circulating orally. As it was argued, when there was no need for the use of the longer version (for example, in the case of baptisms), the shorter version was utilized. However, in cases of polemics against the heretics, the longer version tended to be utilized.

Most significantly, it was argued that even though the phrasing of the formula showed flexibility and fixity, it was neither too fixed to be viewed as a concretized creed nor too broad as to include beliefs that were held by those groups that were considered heretical in their understanding of God the Father, his son Jesus Christ, as well as Jesus' work on the cross and its continued application. In this case, even with its flexibility, the *regula fidei* clearly served as the demarcation between *orthodoxy*

---

183. Kelly, *Early Christian Creeds*, 87.

184. See Williams, "Does It Make Sense." Williams perceptively observes concerning the *regula fidei*: "It may be that the very nature of the basic Christian narrative carries the notions of canon and orthodoxy with it, in the sense that it resists schematization in to a plan of salvation that can be reduced to a simple and isomorphic moment of self-recognition in response to illumination" (Williams, "Does It Make Sense," 16).

Determination of Orthodoxy and Heresy in Early Christianity 199

and *heresy*. As Köstenberger and Kruger correctly observe concerning the use of this formula in the determination of heresy, "the prevalence of the Rule of Faith in the writings of the second-century Fathers demonstrates the pervasive unity of the core Christian doctrines."[185] These "core Christian doctrines," as argued above, acted as the unifying themes of the early Christian communities scattered throughout the empire.[186] They comprised of what Jude refers to as the "faith that was once for all entrusted to the saints."

In sum, the *regula fidei* served as the means of establishing what was to be preached and taught as the summary of the *content* of the Christian faith. As Ferguson explains, the *regula fidei* "represented the *content* of the proclamation of the gospel and the instruction given to inquirers and potential converts."[187] And, as emphasized throughout, it served as a bulwark on the emerging heresies confronting the early church. Its use, in other words, was multifaceted. But it is historically erroneous to claim that the early church had no way of determining orthodoxy from heresy under the guise of the fluidity of these terms, as some scholars have contended.

---

185. Köstenberger and Kruger, *Heresy of Orthodoxy*, 59.

186. As Köstenberger and Kruger further contend, "Orthodox Christians, then, organized themselves into local assemblies remarkably early, established leadership (e.g., Acts 14:23; 20:28; Phil. 1:1; Titus 1:5; 1 Pet. 5:2), agreed on fundamental beliefs, and interacted regularly and frequently. These characteristics do not support Ehrman's portrait of an underdeveloped first- and second-century orthodoxy" (Köstenberger and Kruger, *Heresy of Orthodoxy*, 60). In other words, contra Ehrman, there were clear criteria for determination of orthodoxy and heresy this early.

187. Ferguson, *Rule of Faith*, 33.

CONCLUSION

Toward an Early Church Historiography

INTEREST IN THE HISTORY of earliest Christianity continues to rise with each and every emerging generation of church historians. However, modern fascination with diversity has led to an unbridled (and, sometimes, frankly anachronistic) projection of the same to the early church. Currently, this fascination has been dominated by the popularization of what has been designated the "Bauer-Ehrman thesis." And while, as Köstenberger and Kruger bluntly declare, this thesis is demonstrably "invalid," i.e., "Earliest Christianity was not infested with a plethora of competing heresies (or 'Christianities,' as Ehrman and other Bauer paragons prefer to call them); it was a largely unified movement that had coalesced around the conviction that Jesus was the Messiah and exalted Lord predicted in the Old Testament,"[1] the question of how early church historiography got to this point is itself quite fascinating.

The main purpose of this book is to trace how early church historiography has progressed from F. C. Baur's Hegelian approach to the "Bauer-Ehrman thesis" and beyond. The central claim that the work has sought to demonstrate is that, rather than seeing the entire historiography of Ehrman and others of the same ilk as of a recent origin, there is a traceable genealogical trajectory that stretches all the way back to the early church historiography of F. C. Baur (1792–1860). Of course, as it was stated several times, this trajectory was characterized by its own

---

1. Köstenberger and Kruger, *Heresy of Orthodoxy*, 233. For a helpful study as to how and why Christianity expanded so quickly as well as why it came to dominate the world of late antiquity, see Riley, *One Jesus, Many Christs*.

turns and twists (it would be the height of naivety to assume otherwise). But there are clear demonstrable genealogical connections.

While it is important to trace this trajectory, it is also equally needful to propose an early church historiography that, at the very least, provides a way to evaluate the available data on the development of doctrine (questions of orthodoxy and heresy) in the early church. While, obviously, the early church showed unity of message that emphasized that there is one God, the Father of our Lord Jesus Christ, and that Jesus Christ is the prophesied Messiah who is both Lord and Savior, and that he died for us at the cross, it is also clear that there was *legitimate* diversity and development in the comprehension and expression of these truths. As we saw, one of the best pieces of evidence for this is the phraseology of the *regula fidei* in the second century, which, as it was demonstrated, was neither so restrictive as to be equated with a codified creed nor so diverse as to include views that were deemed heretical. This understanding, therefore, calls for a workable early church historiography.

In his quest for a model that can meet these criteria, Bingham argues that an evangelical physiographical model of the early church "ought to reflect continuity with other theological commitments concerning diversity and development."[2] He identifies three models that he sees having the ability to meet these criteria. In my view, these are helpful models as they are derived from the writings of the fathers themselves. These are "bodily resurrection, the progress from old economy to new, and the immensity of the Creator but the frailty of the creature."[3] These three models appear in several places in the writings of key second-century thinkers.

Concerning the model of bodily resurrection, Bingham observes that it featured prominently in the thought of Irenaeus and Tertullian, who extrapolated it from Paul's seed metaphor (cf. 1 Cor 15:44). Owing to the significant study by Caroline Walker Bynum entitled *The Resurrection of the Body in Western Christianity*, Bingham notes that, for Irenaeus and Tertullian, the change of resurrection "highlights continuity: identity necessitates material continuity, 'what falls must rise,' substance remains although there is an alteration of quality."[4] Hence, to these fathers, this

---

2. Bingham, "Development and Diversity," 63.
3. Bingham, "Development and Diversity," 63.
4. Bingham, "Development and Diversity," 63–64. Bynum summarizes: "The transformation of the Pauline seed metaphor occurred against the background of other changes in ideas. By the early third century, polemicists for the resurrection of the flesh assumed a dualist anthropology that saw the human being as a union of the soul

metaphor emphasized doctrinal continuity even as it underwent change to suit the changing theological climates.

Concerning the second model, among their many understandings of God's work through the dispensations, early church fathers saw God's vision as coming in three stages. Bingham further elaborates concerning these: "The first is prophetic, figurative, and anticipative, given by the Spirit. The second is adoptive provided by the incarnate Son at his first coming. The third is paternal, eschatological, and consummative, when the glories of the Father are seen."[5] Hence, there is diversity and development even in God's unveiling of his program. Yet there is significant unity, as the program is laid out by the same God, and, significantly, the visions are only different in degree, not in substance.[6]

Lastly, there is also the model of the contrast between the Creator and his creation, a model that is also evident in the thought of the Bishop of Lyons. For Irenaeus, "there is tremendous distinction between Creator and creature, between the One who dwells in the heavens and those who dwell here below."[7] However, while there is this immense chasm between the Creator and his creation, there is also the understanding that the redeemed human creature is continuously progressing towards him. Thus, there is changelessness in God while there is "always growth, progress, increase."[8] The model, therefore, stresses both changelessness and change at the same time, a concept evident in early Christian doctrinal development.

All of these are great models as they highlight a theme that is consistent in the writings of the fathers: a commitment to neither be too

---

and body; they also assumed that soul was in some sense immortal although several of them held . . . immortality as a gift from God, not an inherent characteristic of soul. Nonetheless, neither body-soul dualism nor the assumption of immortality solved the problem of survival of self. A theory of bodily resurrection was, to these thinkers, essential . . . Changes in resurrection metaphors to stress rot and rupture, followed by regurgitation and impassibility, suggest that the body that rises is quintessentially the martyr's body, in danger not just from pain and mutilation, but also from scattering, dishonor, even cannibalism, after death. Resurrection is victory over partition and putrefaction; it is both the anesthesia of glory and the reunion of particles of the self" (Bynum, *Resurrection of the Body*, 57–58). See also Eijk, "Only That Can Rise Which Has Previously Fallen."

5. Bingham, "Development and Diversity," 64.
6. Bingham, "Development and Diversity," 64.
7. Bingham, "Development and Diversity," 64.
8. Bingham, "Development and Diversity," 64.

restrictive nor broad in their expression of the central beliefs of the church. However, it seems like any adopted model for early church historiography must insist on a prior commitment to holding onto the truthfulness of the key doctrines being espoused in the employment of the models. As Hartog comments concerning, for example, the treatment of the resurrection narrative in Matthew, "the text assumes that a proper understanding of the apostolic kerygma was integrated with the authority of the risen Lord, and that the diversity of responses reflected a multiplicity of subjective reactions to the singularity of an objective occurrence."[9] It this this assumption of the truthfulness of these historical events (as well as the doctrines derived from them), that allows for the employment of any of the above-mentioned models in the quest for a workable early church historiography.

---

9. Hartog, "From Völker to This Volume," 244. As Hartog further elucidates concerning this key observation: "For example, if one accepted the claim of Jesus's resurrection, then one would naturally believe that it could function as a benchmark of normativity. But if one believes that Jesus did not rise from the dead, then one would not believe that the purported event (since it never happened) could serve as a criterion of normativity. And if one believes that one cannot know whether or not the resurrection occurred, then one could not land firmly upon the claim as a point of reference in discussions of normativity, nor could one firmly dismiss the same possibility. One would naturally avoid assessing which Christologies of the era were proper but would only note which Christologies prevailed" (Hartog, "From Völker to this Volume," 246).

Bibliography

Alcorn, Randy. *If God Is Good: Faith in the Midst of Suffering and Evil.* Colorado Springs, CO: WaterBrook Multnomah, 2009.

Attridge, Harold W. "On Becoming an Angel: Rival Baptistmal Theologies at Colossae." In *Religious Propaganda and Misionary Competition in the New Testament World*, edited by Lukas Bormann, Kelly Del Tredici, and Angela Standhartinger, 481–98. Leiden: Brill, 1994.

Barbour, Robert S. "Theologians of Our Time: Xx. Ernst Käsemann and Günther Bornkamm." *The Expository Times* 76.12 (1965) 379–83.

Barnard, L. W. "The Heresy of Tatian—Once Again." *Journal of Ecclesiastical History* 19.1 (1968) 1–10.

Barth, Markus, and Helmut Blanke. *Colossians: A New Translation with Introduction and Commentary.* Edited by William Foxwell Albright and David Noel Freedman. The Anchor Bible. New York: Doubleday, 1994.

Bauer, Walter. *Orthodoxy and Heresy in Earliest Christianity.* Edited by Robert A. Kraft and Gerhard Krodel. 2nd German ed. Philadelphia: Fortress, 1971.

———. *Rechtgläubigkeit Und Ketzerei Im Ältesten Christentum.* Beiträge Zur Historischen Theologie 10. Tübingen: J. C. B. Mohr, 1934.

Bauer, Walter, and William F. Arndt. *A Greek-English Lexicon of the New Testament and Other Early Christian Literature.* Edited by Frederick W. Danker. 3rd ed. Chicago: University of Chicago Press, 2003.

Baur, Ferdinand Christian. *Ausgewählte Werke in Einzelausgabe.* Vol. 1. Stuttgart: Frommann-Holzboog 1855.

———. *Geschichte Der Christlichen Kirche.* Vol. 5. Tübingen: Fues, 1877.

———. *Paulus, Der Apostel Jesu Christi, Sein Leben Und Wirken, Seine Briefe Und Seine Lehre.* Edited by Eduard Zeller. 2nd ed. Leipzig: Fues's Verlag, 1866–67.

Bauspiess, Martin. "Preface to the German Edition." In *Ferdinand Christian Baur and the History of Early Christianity*, edited by Martin Bauspiess, Christof Landmesser, and David Lincicum. Oxford: Oxford University Press, 2014.

Behr, John. *The Way to Nicea.* The Formation of Christian Theology 1. Crestwood, NY: St. Vladimir's Seminary Press, 2001.

Bersee, Anthonius Nicolaas Johannes Maria. "Miracles in the Age of Science." PhD diss., Vrije Universiteit Amsterdam, 2020.

Betz, Hans Dieter. "Orthodoxy and Heresy in Primitive Christianity: Some Critical Remarks on Georg Strecker's Republication of Walter Bauer's *Rechtgläubigkeit Und Ketzerei Im Ältesten Christentum*." *Interpretation* 19 (1965) 299–311.

Bhabha, Homi K. *The Location of Culture*. London: Routledge, 1994.

Bingham, D. Jeffrey. "Development and Diversity in Early Christianity." *Journal of the Evangelical Theological Society* 49.1 (2006) 45–66.

———. *Pocket History of the Church*. Downers Grove: InterVarsity Press, 2002.

Blaising, Craig A. "Faithfulness: A Prescription for Theology." *Journal of Evangelical Theological Society* 49.1 (2006) 5–16.

Blowers, Paul M. "The *Regula Fidei* and the Narrative Character of Early Christian Faith." *Pro Ecclesia* 6.2 (1997) 199–228.

Bokedal, Tomas. "The Rule of Faith: Tracing Its Origins." *Journal of Theological Interpretation* 7.2 (2013) 233–55.

Bornkamm, Günther. *Jesus of Nazareth*. Translated by Irene McLuckey and James M. Robinson. New York: Harper, 1960.

Boyarin, Daniel, and Virginia Burrus. "Hybridity as Subversion of Orthodoxy? Jews and Christians in Late Antiquity." *Social Compass* 52.4 (2005) 431–41.

Bradley, James E., and Richard A. Muller. *Church History: An Introduction to Research Methods and Resources*. 2nd ed. Grand Rapids: William B. Eerdmans, 2016.

Bray, Gerald. *Holiness and the Will of God: Perspectives on the Theology of Tertullian*. Atlanta: John Knox, 1979.

Bultmann, Rudolf. *Das Urchristentum Im Rahmen Der Antiken Religionen* Zürich: Artemis, 1949.

———. *Die Geschichte Der Synoptischen Tradition*. Forschungen Zur Religion Und Literatur Des Alten Und Neuen Testaments, N.F. H. 12. Göttingen: Vandenhoeck & Ruprech, 1921.

———. *Die Religion in Geschichte Und Gegenwart: Handwórterbuch Für Die Theologie Und Religionswissenschaft*. Vol. 3. Tübingen: Mohr Siebeck, 1959.

———. *History and Eschatology: The Presence of Eternity*. Edinburgh: Edinburgh University Press, 1957.

———. *Jesus Christ and Mythology*. London: SCM, 1960.

———. *Kerygma and Myth: A Theological Debate*. Edited by Hans Werner Bartsch. London: SPCK, 1953.

———. "New Testament and Mythology." In *Kerygma and Myth: A Theological Debate*, edited by Hans Werner Bartsch, 1–16. London: SPCK, 1953.

———. *Primitive Christianity in Its Contemporary Setting*. Translated by R. H. Fuller. London: Thames and Hudson, 1956.

———. *Theology of the New Testament*. 2 vols Translated by K. Grubel. New York: Scribner's, 1951–55.

Burkitt, F. C. "Tatian's Diatessaron and the Dutch Harmonies." *Journal of Theological Studies* 25.98 (1924) 113–30.

Bynum, Carolyne Walker. *The Resurrection of the Body in Western Christianity, 200–1336*. New York: Columbia University Press, 1995.

Calhoun, David B. *Pleading for a Reformation Vision: The Life and Selected Writings of William Childs Robinson (1897–1982)*. Carlisle, PA: Banner of Truth, 2013.

Campbell, R. Alastair. "Identifying the Faithful Sayings in the Pastoral Epistles." *Journal for the Study of the New Testament* 54 (1994) 73–86.

Carson, D. A. *Exegetical Fallacies*. 2nd ed. Grand Rapids: Baker, 1996.

Castleman, Robbie F., Darian R. Lockett, and Stephen O. Presley, eds. *Explorations in Interdisciplinary Reading: Theological, Exegetical, and Reception-Historical Perspectives*. Eugene, OR: Pickwick, 2017.

Chadwick, Henry, and Molly Whittaker, eds. *Tatian: Oratio Ad Graecos and Fragments*. Oxford Early Christian Texts. Oxford: Clarendon, 1982.
Chalamet, Christophe, ed. *The Challenge of History: Readings in Modern Theology*. Minneapolis: Fortress, 2020.
Clouse, Robert D. "The Hellenization of Christianity: A Historiographical Study." *Canadian Journal of Theology* 8.1 (1962) 22–33.
Congdon, David W. *The Mission of Demythologizing: Rudolf Bultmann's Dialectical Theology*. Minneapolis: Fortress, 2015.
Conzelmann, Hans. *1 Corinthians: A Commentary on the First Epistle to the Corinthians*. Edited by George W. Dunkly. Translated by James L. Leitch. Hermeneia: A Critical and Historical Commentary on the Bible. Philadelphia: Fortress, 1975.
———. *Die Mitte Der Zeit: Studien Zur Theologie Des Lukas*. Tübingen: J. C. B. Mohr, 1954.
———. "On the Analysis of the Confessional Formula in 1 Corinthians 15:3–5." *Interpretation* 20.1 (1966) 15–25.
———. *An Outline of the Theology of the New Testament*. Translated by John Bowden. New York: Harper & Row, 1969.
Countryman, L. William. "Tertullian and the Regula Fidei." *The Second Century* 2 (1982) 208–27.
Cranfield, C. E. B. "Changes of Person and Number in Paul's Epistles." In *Paul and Paulinism*, edited by M. D. Hooker and S. G. Wilson, 280–89. London: SPCK, 1982.
Daley, Brian E. *The Hope of the Early Church: A Handbook of Patristic Eschatology*. Cambridge, UK: Cambridge University Press, 1991.
Decker, Rodney J. "The Rehabilitation of Heresy: 'Misquoting' Earliest Christianity." Paper presented at the Bible Faculty Summit, Central Baptist Seminary, Minneapolis, July 2007.
Desjardins, M. "Bauer and Beyond: On Recent Scholarly Discussions of Αἵρεσις in the Early Christian Era." *Second Century* 8 (1991) 65–82.
Dibelius, Martin, and Hans Conzelmann. *The Pastoral Epistles*. Translated by Philip Buttolph and Adela Yarbro. Hermeneia: A Critical and Historical Commentary on the Bible. Philadelphia: Fortress, 1972.
Dodd, C. H. *The Apostolic Preaching and Its Developments: Three Lectures with an Appendix on Eschatology and History*. London: Holder & Stoughton, 1936.
Dodd, C. H. *The Apostolic Preaching and Its Developments*. 2nd ed. London: Harper and Brothers, 1944.
Dunn, J. D. G. "The Colossian Philosophy: A Confident Jewish Apologia." *Biblica* 76 (1995) 153–81.
———. *Unity and Diversity in the New Testament. An Inquiry into the Character of Earliest Christianity*. 1990. Reprint, London: SCM, 2006.
Durst, Michaela. *Handbuch Der Bibelhermeneutiken: Von Origenes Bis Zur Gegenwart*. Edited by Oda Wischmeyer et al. De Gruyter Handbook. Berlin: De Gruyter, 2016.
Edsall, Benjamin, and Jennifer R. Strawbridge. "The Songs We Used to Sing? Hymn 'Traditions' and Reception in Pauline Letters." *Journal for the Study of the New Testament* 37.3 (2015) 290–311.
Ehrhardt, Arnold. "Christianity before the Apostles' Creed." *The Harvard Theological Review* 55.2 (1962) 73–119.

Ehrman, Bart. *Did Jesus Exist? The Historical Argument for Jesus of Nazareth*. New York: HarperOne, 2012.
———. *God's Problem: How the Bible Fails to Answer Our Most Important Question—Why We Suffer*. New York: HarperOne, 2008.
———. *How Jesus Became God: The Exaltation of a Jewish Preacher from Galilee*. New York: HarperOne, 2014.
———. *Jesus, Interrupted: Revealing the Hidden Contradictions in the Bible (and Why We Don't Know About Them)*. New York: HarperOne, 2009.
———. *Lost Christianities: The Battles for Scripture and the Faiths We Never Knew*. New York: Oxford University Press, 2003.
———. *Lost Scriptures: Books That Did Not Make It into the New Testament*. Oxford: Oxford University Press, 2003.
———. *Misquoting Jesus: The Story Behind Who Changed the Bible and Why*. San Francisco: HarperSanFrancisco, 2005.
———. *The Orthodox Corruption of Scripture: The Effect of Early Christological Controversies on the Text of the New Testament*. Oxford: Oxford University Press, 1993.
Eijk, A. H. C. van. "'Only That Can Rise Which Has Previously Fallen': The History of a Formula." *Journal of Theological Studies* 22.2 (1971) 517–29.
Ellis, Earl. *History & Interpretation in New Testament Perspective*. Leiden: Brill, 2001.
Eusebius, and Crusé Christian Frederic. *Eusebius' Ecclesiastical History: Complete and Unabridged*. Peabody, MA: Hendrickson, 1998.
Farmer, William. "Galatians and the Second-Century Development of the *Regula Fidei*." *The Second Century* 4.143–170 (1984).
Fascher, Erich. "Walter Bauer Als Kommentator." *New Testament Studies* 9 (1962–63) 23–38.
Fee, Gordon D. *1 & 2 Timothy and Titus*. Understanding the Bible Commentary Series. Grand Rapids: BakerBooks, 1988.
———. *Paul's Letter to the Philippians*. Edited by Ned B. Stonehouse et al. The New International Commentary on the New Testament. Grand Rapids: William B. Eerdmans, 1995.
Ferguson, Everett. *The Rule of Faith: A Guide*. Eugene, OR: Cascade, 2015.
Fichte, Johann Gottlieb. "Reden an Die Deutsche Nation, Achte Rede: 'Was Ein Volk Sei, in Der Hohem Bedeutung Des Worts, Und Was Vaterlandshebe: 'Vierzehnte Rede, 'Beschluss Des Ganzen.'" In *Ausgewählte Werke in Sechs Bänden*, edited by Fritz Medicus, 5.243–490. Darmstadt, Germany: Wissenschaftliche Buchgesellschaft, 1962.
Fischer, David Hackett. *Historians' Fallacies: Toward a Logic of Historical Thought*. New York: Harper & Row, 1970.
Flora, Jerry Rees. "A Critical Analysis of Walter Bauer's Theory of Early Christian Orthodoxy and Heresy." PhD diss., Southern Baptist Theological Seminary, 1972.
Frei, Hans W. *The Eclipse of Biblical Narrative: A Study in Eighteenth and Nineteenth Century Hermeneutics*. New Haven: Yale University Press, 1973.
Frend, W. H. C. "Church Historians of the Early Twentieth Century: Adolf Von Harnack (1851–1930)." *Journal of Ecclesiastical History* 52.1 (2001) 83–102.
Geertz, Clifford. *The Interpretation of Cultures: Selected Essays*. New York: Basic Books, 1973.

Gerö, Stephen. "With Walter Bauer on the Tigris: Encratite Orthodoxy and Libertine Heresy in Syro-Mesopotamian Christianity." In *Nag Hammadi, Gnosticism, and Early Christianity*, edited by C. W. Hedrick and R. Hodgson, 287–307. Peabody, MA: Hendrickson, 1986.

Gingrich, F. W. "Review of *the Formation of Christian Dogma* by Martin Werner. Translated by S. G. F. Brandon." *Journal of American Academy of Religion* 27.3 (1959) 251.

Glick, G. Wayne. *The Reality of Christianity: A Study of Adolf Von Harnack as Historian and Theologian*. Foundations of Historical Theology. New York: Harper & Row, 1967.

Goetz, Steven Norman. "An Historical Consideration of F. C. Baur, His Life, Works, and Theological Thought, Especially in Regard to His Church History and Historical Theology." Master's thesis, Portland State University, 1979.

Gustafson, James Walter. *The Quest for Truth: An Introduction to Philosophy*. 3rd ed. Needham Heights, MA: Ginn, 1992.

Grant, Robert M. "The Heresy of Tatian." *Journal of Theological Studies* 5 (1954) 62–68.

Green, Jay D. *Chrstian Historiography: Five Rival Versions*. Waco, TX: Baylor University Press, 2015.

Grenz, Stanley J., David Guretzki, and Cherith Fee Nordling. *Pocket Dictionary of Theological Terms*. Downers Grove: InterVarsity Press, 1999.

Gupta, Nijay K., and Jonah M. Sandford, eds. *Intermediate Biblical Greek Reader: Galatians and Related Texts*. Newberg, OR: George Fox University Library, 2018.

Guthrie, Donald. *New Testament Theology*. Leicester, U.K.: Inter-Varsity, 1981.

———. *The Pastoral Epistles: An Introduction and Commentary*. Vol. 14. Tyndale New Testament Commentaries. Downers Grove: IVP Academic, 1990.

Hannah, John D. *Our Legacy: The History of Christian Doctrine*. Colorado Springs: NavPress, 2001.

Harnack, Adolf. *Das Wesen Des Christentums* Leipzig: J. C. Hinrichs, 1902.

———. *History of Dogma*. Vol. 1. Translated by Neil Buchanan. Boston, MA: Roberts Brothers, 1894–1899.

———. *History of Dogma*. Vol. 2. Translated by Neil Buchanan. Boston, MA: Roberts Brothers, 1897.

———. *History of Dogma*. Vol. 7. Translated by Neil Buchanan. Edited by Neil Buchanan et al. Eugene, OR: Wipf and Stock, 1894–1899.

———. *Lehrbuch Der Dogmengeschichte*. 3 vols. Freiburg, Germany: Akademische Verlagsbuchhandlung von J. C. B. Mohr, 1886–1890.

———. *Marcion: The Gospel of the Alien God*. Durham, NC: Labyrinth, 1990.

Harrington, Daniel J. "The Reception of Walter Bauer's Orthodoxy and Heresy in Earliest Christianity During the Last Decade." *Harvard Theological Review* 73.1–2 (1980) 289–98.

Harris, Horton. *The Tübingen School: A Historical and Theological. Investigation of the School of F. C. Baur*. Grand Rapids: Baker, 1990.

Harrisville, Roy A. "The Life and Work of Ernst Käsemann (1906–1998)." *Lutheran Quarterly* 21.3 (2007) 294–319.

Harrisville, Roy A., and Walter Sundberg. *The Bible in Modern Culture: Baruch Spinoza to Brevard Childs*. 2nd ed. Grand Rapids: William B. Eerdmans, 2002.

Hartog, Paul. "From Völker to This Volume: A Trajectory of Critiques and a Final Reflection." In *Orthodoxy and Heresy in Early Christian Contexts: Reconsidering the Bauer Thesis*, edited by Paul A. Hartog, 235–48. Cambridge, UK: James Clarke, 2015.

———. "The 'Rule of Faith' and Patristic Biblical Exegesis." *Trinity Journal* 28.1 (2007) 65–86.

Harvey, Van A. "D. F. Strauss's Life of Jesus Revisited." *Church History* 30 (1961) 191–211.

Hawthorne, Gerald F. *Philippians*. Edited by David A. Hubbard and Glenn W. Barker. Word Biblical Commentary 43. Waco, TX: Word Books, 1983.

Hedrick, Charles W. "Introduction: Nag Hammadi, Gnosticism, and Early Christianity—a Beginner's Guide." In *Nag Hammadi, Gnosticism and Early Christianity*, edited by Charles W. Hedrick and Robert Hodgson Jr., 1–11. Peabody, MA: Hendrickson, 1986.

———. "Liberator of the Nag Hammadi Codices: *In Memoriam*: James McConkey Robinson June 30, 1924–March 22, 2016." *Biblical Archaeology Review* 42.4 (July/August 2016) 51–54.

Hefner, Philip, trans. *Albrecht Ritschl: Three Essays*. Philadelphia: Fortress, 1972.

Hege, Brent. *Rudolf Bultmann on Myth, History, and the Resurrection in German Protestant Theology*. Eugene, OR: Pickwick, 2017.

Hegel, Georg W. F. *The Philosophy of History*. Translated by J. Sibree. Great Books in Philosophy. Buffalo, NY: Prometheus Books, 1991.

Heick, O. W., and J. L. Neve. *A History of Christian Thought, Vol. 2: History of Protestant Theology*. Philedelphia, PA: The Muhlenberg, 1946.

Hodgson, Peter C., ed. *Ferdinand Christian Baur on the Writing of Church History*. New York: Oxford University Press, 1968.

———. *The Formation of Historical Theology: A Study of Ferdinand Christian Baur*. New York: Harper & Row, 1966.

———. "The Rediscovery of Ferdinand Christian Baur: A Review of the First Two Volumes of His Ausgewählte Werke." *Church History* 33.2 (1964) 206–14.

Hoekema, Anthony A. *The Bible and the Future*. Grand Rapids: William B. Eerdmans, 1994.

Holmes, Michael W., ed. and trans. *The Apostolic Fathers: Greek Texts and English Translation after the Earlier Work of of J. B. Lightfoot and J. R. Harmer*. 3rd ed. Grand Rapids: Baker, 2007.

Holmes, Stephen R. *The Quest for the Trinity: The Doctrine of God in Scripture, History and Modernity*. Downers Grove: IVP Academic, 2012.

Hooker, M. D. "Were There False Teachers in Colossae?" In *Christ and Spirit in the New Testament: Studies in Honour of Charles Francis Digby Moule*, edited by Barnabas Lindars and Stephen S. Smalley, 315–31. Cambridge, UK: Cambridge University Press, 1973.

Hultgren, A. J. *The Rise of Normative Christianity*. Minneapolis: Fortress, 1994.

Hultgren, Arland J., and Steven A. Haggmark, eds. *The Earliest Christian Heretics: Readings from Their Opponents*. Minneapolis: Fortress, 2008.

Hunt, Emily J. *Christianity in the Second Century: The Case of Tatian*. Routledge Early Church Monographs. London: Routledge, 2003.

Hunter, A. M. "The Sure Sayings." In *Probing the New Testament*, 126–29. Richmond: John Knox, 1971.

Hunter, Archibald M. *Paul and His Predecessors*. London: SCM, 1961.

Hurtado, Larry W. *How on Earth Did Jesus Become a God? Historical Questions about Earliest Devotion to Jesus*. Grand Rapids: Wm. B. Eerdmans, 2005.

———. "Jesus as Lordly Example in Philippians 2:5–11." In *From Jesus to Paul: Studies in Honour of Francis Wright Beare*, edited by P. Richardson and J. C. Hurd, 113–26. Waterloo, Canada: Wilfrid Laurier University Press, 1984.

Irenaeus. *Against Heresies*. Edited by Alexander Roberts and James Donaldson. The Ante-Nicene Fathers: Translations of the Writings of the Fathers Down to AD 325 1. Grand Rapids: Eerdmans, 1885–1887.

Jenkins, Philip. *Hidden Gospels: How the Search for Jesus Lost Its Way*. Oxford: Oxford University Press, 2002.

Jeremias, Joachim. *The Eucharistic Words of Jesus*. London: SCM, 1966.

Jerome, and W. H. Fremantle. *The Principal Works of St. Jerome: Letters and Selected Works*. The Nicene and Post-Nicene Fathers 6. Grand Rapids: Eerdmans, 1954.

Johnson, Luke Timothy. *The First and Second Letters to Timothy*. The Anchor Yale Bible Commentaries 35A. New York: Doubleday, 2001.

Johnson, S. E. "Unsolved Questions about Early Christianity in Anatolia." In *Studies in New Testament and Early Christian Literature*, edited by D. E. Aune, 181–93. Novum Testamentum 33. Leiden: Brill, 1972.

Käsemann, Ernst. "Das Problem Des Historischen Jesus." *Zeitschrift für Theologie und Kirche* 51 (1954) 125–53.

———. *Essays on New Testament Themes*. Translated by W. J. Montague. London: SCM, 1964.

———. *Jesu Letzter Wille Nach Johannes 17*. Tübingen: Mohr, 1966.

———. *New Testament Questions for Today*. Translated by W. J. Montague. Philadelphia: Fortress, 1969.

———. *The Testament of Jesus: A Study of the Gospel of John in the Light of Chapter 17*. Translated by Gerhard Krodel. Philadelphia: Fortress, 1968.

Kegley, C. W., ed. *The Theology of Rudolph Bultmann*. New York: Harper and Row, 1966.

Kelly, J. N. D. *A Commentary on the Pastoral Epistles*. Harper's New Testament Commentaries. 1968. Reprint, Peabody, MA: Hendrickson, 2009.

———. *Early Christian Creeds*. New York: McKay, 1972.

Kerr, Fergus. "The Theology of Ernst Käsemann—I." *New Blackfriars* 62.729 (1981) 100–113.

Kloppenborg, John. "An Analysis of the Pre-Pauline Formula 1 Cor 15:3b–5 in Light of Some Recent Literature." *The Catholic Biblical Quarterly* 40.3 (1978) 351–67.

Knight, George. *The Faithful Sayings in the Pastoral Letters*. Grand Rapids: Baker, 1979.

Koester, Helmut. "Apocryphal and Canonical Gospels." *The Harvard Theological Review* 73.1/2 (1980) 105–30.

———. "Gospel Traditions in the Apostolic Fathers." In *Trajectories through the New Testament and the Apostolic Fathers*, edited by Andrew Gregory and Christopher Tuckett, 27–68. Oxford: Oxford University Press, 2006.

———. "An Intellectual Biography of James M. Robinson: Speech at the Occasion of His Retirement." In *From Quest to Q: Festschrift James M. Robinson*, edited by Jon Ma Asgeisson, Kristin de Troyer, and Marvin W. Meyer, xiii–xxi. Bibliotheca Ephemeridum Theologicarum Lovaniensium. Leuven: Leuven University Press, 2000.

———. *Synoptische Überlieferung Bei Den Apostolischen Vätern*. Texte Und Untersuchungen Zur Geschichte Der Altchristlichen Literatur. Berlin: Akademie-Verlag, 1957.

Koltun-Fromm, Naomi. "Re-Imagining Tatian: The Damaging Effects of Polemical Rhetoric." *Journal of Early Christian Studies* 16 (2008) 1–30.

Köpf, Ulrich. "Ferdinand Christian Baur and David Friedrich Strauss." In *Ferdinand Christian Baur and the History of Early Christianity*, edited by Martin Bauspiess, Christof Landmesser, and David Lincicum, 3–43. Oxford: Oxford University Press, 2017.

Köstenberger, Andreas, Darrell Bock, and Josh Chatraw. *Truth Matters: Confident Faith in a Confusing World*. Nashville: B&H, 2014.

Köstenberger, Andreas J. "Diversity and Unity in the New Testament." In *Biblical Theology: Retrospect and Prospect*, edited by Scott J. Hafemann, 144–58. Downers Grove: InterVarsity, 2002.

Köstenberger, Andreas J., and Michael J. Kruger. *The Heresy of Orthodoxy: How Contemporary Culture's Fascination with Diversity Has Reshaped Our Understanding of Early Christianity*. Wheaton, IL: Crossway, 2010.

Ladd, George. *A Theology of the New Testament*. Grand Rapids: Eerdmans, 1993.

Laing, Stefana Dan. *Retrieving History: Memory and Identity Formation in the Early Church*. Evangelical Ressourcement: Ancient Sources for the Church's Future. Grand Rapids: Baker Academic, 2017.

Land, Darin H. "Synthesis Searching: The Continuing Influence of F. C. Baur." *Mediator* 10.1 (2014) 23–55.

Lindbeck, George. *The Nature of Doctrine: Religion and Theology in a Postliberal Age*. Philadelphia, PA: Westminster, 1984.

Livingston, James C. *Modern Christian Thought, Vol. 1: the Enlightenment and the Nineteenth Century*. 2nd ed. Minneapolis: Fortress, 2006.

Livingston, James C., et al. *Modern Christian Thought, Vol. 2: The Twentieth Century*. 2nd ed. Minneapolis: Fortress, 2006.

Lohse, Eduard. *Colossians and Philemon: A Commentary on the Epistles to the Colossians and to Philemon*. Translated by Eduard Lohse. Hermeneia—a Critical and Historical Commentary on the Bible. Philadelphia: Fortress, 1971.

Lyman, Rebecca. "Hellenism and Heresy." *Journal of Early Christian Studies* 11 (2003) 209–22.

———. "Justin and Hellenism: Some Postcolonial Perspectives." In *Justin Martyr and His Worlds*, edited by Sara Parvis and Paul Foster, 160–68. Minneapolis: Fortress, 2007.

———. "Natural Resources: Tradition without Orthodoxy." *Anglican Theological Review* 84 (2002) 67–80.

———. "The Politics of Passing: Justin Martyr's Conversion as a Problem of Hellenization." In *Conversion in Late Antiquity and the Early Middle Ages: Seeing and Believing*, edited by Kenneth Mills and Anthony Grafton, 36–60. Rochester, NY: University of Rochester Press, 2003.

Mackay, Robert William. *The Tübingen School and Its Antecedents: A Review of the History and Present Condition of Modern Theology*. Edinburgh: Williams and Norgate, 1863.

Marshall, I. Howard. *New Testament Theology*. Downers Grove: IVP Academic, 2014.

———. "Orthodoxy and Heresy in Earlier Christianity." *Themelios* 2.1 (1976) 5–14.

Martin, Brice L. "Some Reflections on the Unity of the New Testament." *Studies in Religion/Sciences* 8.2 (1979) 143–52.
Marxen, Willi. *Der Evangelist Markus. Studien Zur Redaktionsgeschichte Des Evangeliums.* Göttingen: Vandenhoeck & Ruprecht, 1959.
Matlock, Barry R. *Unveiling the Apocalyptic Paul: Paul's Interpreters and the Rhetoric Criticism.* London: Bloomsbury Academic, 1996.
McCue, J. "Bauer's Rechtgläubigkeit Und Ketzerei." In *Orthodoxy and Heterodoxy*, edited by Johann-Baptist Metz and Edward Schillebeeckx, 28–35. Edinburgh: T. & T. Clark, 1987.
———. "Orthodoxy and Heresy: Walter Bauer and the Valentinians." *Vigiliae Christianae* 33.2 (1979) 118–30.
McKnight, Scot. *The Letter to the Colossians.* The New International Commentary on the New Testament. Grand Rapids: William B. Eerdmans, 2018.
Medley, George H. "History Is Divine Art: Schelling's *Spätphilosophie* as Orthodox Romantic Theology." *Zeitschrift für neuere Theologiegeschichte* 22.1 (2015) 59–76.
Meinecke, Friedrich. *Historism: The Rise of a New Historical Outlook.* Translated by J. E. Anderson. New York: Herder and Herder, 1972.
Mellink, Albert Osger. *Death as Eschaton: A Study of Ignatius of Antioch's Desire for Death.* Amsterdam: University of Amsterdam, 2000.
Morgan, Robert C. "Strauss, David Friedrich." In *Historical Handbook of Major Biblical Interpreters*, edited by Donald K. McKim, 364–68. Downers Grove: InterVarsity Press, 1998.
Moss, Candinda. *The Myth of Persecution: How Early Christians Invented a Story of Martyrdom.* New York: HarperCollins, 2013.
Mounce, Bill. *Pastoral Epistles.* Word Biblical Commentary 46. Nashville: Thomas Nelson, 2000.
Muller, Richard. *Post-Reformation Reformed Dogmatics: The Rise and Development of Reformed Orthodoxy, ca. 1520 to ca. 1725.* 4 vols. 2nd ed. Grand Rapids: Baker Academic, 2003.
Munslow, Alan. *Deconstructing History.* 2nd ed. London and New York: Routledge, 1997.
Mutie, Jeremiah. *Death in Second-Century Christian Thought: The Meaning of Death in Earliest Christianity.* Eugene, OR: Pickwick, 2015.
Myllykoski, M. "Wild Beasts and Rabid Dogs: The Riddle of the Heretics in the Letters of Ignatius." In *The Formation of the Early Church*, edited by J. Ádna, 342–77. Tübingen: Mohr Siebeck, 2005.
Nagata, Takeshi. "Philippians 2:5–11: A Case Study in the Contextual Shaping of Early Christology." PhD diss., Princeton Theological Seminary, 1981.
Neill, Stephen, and Tom Wright. *The Interpretation of the New Testament, 1861–1986.* 2nd ed. Oxford: Oxford University Press, 1988.
Neufield, Vernon H. *The Earliest Christian Confessions* Grand Rapids: Wm. B. Eerdmans, 1963.
Norris, F. W. "Asia Minor before Ignatius: Walter Bauer Reconsidered." In *Studia Evangelica Vii*, edited by E. A. Livingstone, 365–77. Berlin: Akademie-Verlag, 1982.
———. "Ignatius, Polycarp, and 1 Clement: Walter Bauer Reconsidered." *Vigiliae Christianae* 30 (1976) 23–44.

O'Brien, Peter T. *Colossians, Philemon*. Edited by David A. Hubbard and Glenn W. Barker. Word Biblical Commentary 44. Waco, TX: Word, 1982.

———. *The Epistle to the Philippians*. Edited by I. Howard Marshall and W. Ward Gasque. The New International Greek Testament Commentary. Grand Rapids: William B. Eerdmans, 1991.

Oden, Thomas. *First and Second Timothy and Titus*. Interpretation: A Bible Commentary for Teaching and Preaching. Louisville, KY: John Knox, 1989.

Osborn, Eric. "Reason and Rule of Faith in the Second Century AD." In *The Making of Orthodoxy: Essays in Honour of Henry Chadwick*, edited by R. Williams, 40–61. Cambridge, UK: Cambridge University Press, 1989.

Packer, J. I. "Orthodoxy." In *Evangelical Dictionary of Theology*, edited by Walter A. Elwell, 875. Grand Rapids: Baker, 2001.

Pagels, Elaine. *Beyond Belief: The Secret Gospel of Thomas*. New York: Random House, 2003.

———. *The Origin of Satan: How Christians Demonized Jews, Pagans, and Heretics*. New York: Vintage Books, 1995.

———. *Why Religion?: A Personal Story*. New York: Ecco, 2018.

Paget, James Carleton. "The Reception of Baur in Britain." In *Ferdinand Christian Baur and the History of Early Christianity*, edited by Martin Bauspiess, Christof Landmesser, and David Lincicum, 307–54. Oxford: Oxford University Press, 2017.

Pelikan, Jeroslav. *The Christian Tradition: A History of the Development of Doctrine. Volume 1: The Emergence of the Catholic Tradition (100–600)*. The Christian Tradition. Chicago: University of Chicago Press, 1971.

———. *Credo: Historical and Theological Guide to Creeds and Confessions in the Christian Tradition*. New Haven: Yale University Press, 2003.

Pfleiderer, Otto. *Lectures on the Influence of the Apostle Paul on the Development of Christianity*. London: William and Norgate, 1885.

———. *Paulinism: A Contribution to the History of Primitive Christian Theology*. London: Williams and Norgate, 1877.

———. *Philosophy of Religion on the Basis of Its History*. Translated by Allan Menzies. London: Williams and Norgate, 1888.

———. *Primitive Christianity: Its Writings and Teachings in Their Historical Connections*. Edited by W. D. Morrison. Translated by W. Montgomery. London: Williams and Norgate, 1906.

Porter, Stanley E. "A Dead End or a New Beginning? Examining the Criteria for Authenticity in Light of Albert Schweitzer." In *Jesus Research: An International Perspective: The First Princeton-Prague Symposium on Jesus Research, Princeton 2005*, edited by James H. Charlesworth and Petr Pokorný, 16–35. Grand Rapids: Wm. B. Eerdmans, 2009.

Randall Jr., John Herman. *The Making of the Modern Mind: A Survey of the Intellectual Background of the Present Age*. New York: Columbia University Press, 1926.

Rensberger, David K. "As the Apostle Teaches: The Development of the Use of Paul's Letters in Second Century Christianity." PhD diss., Yale University, 1981.

Reumann, John. *Philippians: A New Translation with Introduction and Commentary*. Edited by John J. Collins. The Anchor Yale Bible 33B. New Haven: Yale University Press, 2008.

Rick, K. W. "Heresy." In *Evangelical Dictionary of Theology*, edited by Walter A. Elwell, 550–51. Grand Rapids: Baker, 2001.

Riley, Gregory J. *One Jesus, Many Christs: How Jesus Inspired Not One True Christianity, but Many: The Truth about Christian Origins*. Minneapolis: Fortress, 2009.

Ritschl, Albrecht. *The Christian Doctrine of Justification and Reconciliation*. Vol. 3. Translated by H. R. Mackintosh and A. B. Macaulay. Edinburgh: T. & T. Clark, 1902.

Robinson, James M., ed. *Das Geschichtsverständnis Des Markus-Evangeliums*. Abhandlungen Zur Theologie Des Alten Und Neuen Testaments 30. Zürich: Zwingli-Verlag, 1956.

———. "Introduction: The Dismantling and Resembling of the Categories of New Testament Scholarship." In *Trajectories through Early Christianity*, by James M. Robinson and Helmut Koester, 1–19. Philadelphia, PA: Fortress, 1971.

———, ed. *The Nag Hammadi Library in English*. Leiden: E. J. Brill, 1997.

———. *The Nag Hammadi Library: Translated and Introduction by Members of the Coptic Gnostic Library Project of the Institute for Antiquity and Christianity*. San Francisco: HarperOne, 1990.

———. *A New Quest of the Historical Jesus and Other Essays*. Philadelphia: Fortress, 1983.

———. "Theological Autobiography." In *The Sayings Gospel Q: Collected Essays*, edited by Christoph Heil and Joseph Verheyden, 3–34. Bibliotheca Ephemeridum Theologicarum Lovaniensium 189. Leuven: Leuven University Press, 2005.

Robinson, James M., Paul Hoffmann, and John S. Kloppenborg, eds. *The Critical Edition of Q. Synopsis Including the Gospels of Matthew and Luke, Mark and Thomas with English, German, and French Translations of Q and Thomas*. Leuven: Peeters, 2000.

Robinson, James M., and Helmut Koester. *Trajectories through Early Christianity*. Philadelphia: Fortress, 1971.

Robinson, Thomas A. *The Bauer Thesis Examined: The Geography of Heresy in the Early Christian Church*. Lewiston, NY: Edwin Mellen, 1988.

Rowe, William V. "Adolf Harnack and the Concept of Hellenization." In *Hellenization Revisited: Shaping a Christian Response within the Greco-Roman World*, edited by Wendy Helleman, 68–98. Lanham, MD: University Press of America, 1994.

———. "Harnack and Hellenization in the Early Church." *Philosophia Reformata* 57.1 (1992) 78–85.

Royalty, Robert M. "Dwelling on Visions. On the Nature of the So-Called 'Colossians Heresy.'" *Biblica* 83.3 (2002) 329–57.

Rudolph, Kurt, ed. *Gnosis: The Nature and History of Gnosticism*. Translated by P. W. Coxon and K. H. Kuhn. San Francisco: HarperSanFrancisco, 1987.

———, ed. *Historical Fundamentals and the Study of Religions: Haskell Lectures Delivered at the University of Chicago*. New York: Macmillan, 1985.

Salvatorelli, Luigi. "From Locke to Reitzenstein: The Historical Investigation of the Origins of Christianity." *Harvard Theological Review* 22.4 (1929) 263–369.

Sappington, Thomas J. *Revelation and Redemption at Colossae*. Journal for the Study of the New Testament Supplement 53. Sheffield, UK: JSOT Press, 1991.

Schelling, Friedrich Wilhelm Joseph. *Vorlesungen Über Die Methode Des Akademischen Studium*. Stuttgart and Tübingen: J. G. Cotta, 1803.

Schleiermacher, Friedrich. *On Religion: Speeches to Its Cultured Despisers*. Translated by John Oman. New York: Harper and Row, 1958.

Schlier, Heinrich. *Religionsgeschichtliche Untersuchungen Zu Den Ignatiusbriefen*. Beihefte Zur Zeitschrift Für Die Neutestamentliche Wissenschaft 8. Giessen: Töpelmann, 1929.

Schoedel, W. R. "Polycarp of Smyrna and Ignatius of Antioch." In *Aufstieg Und Niedergang Der Römischen Welt (Anrw) Ii.27.1*, edited by Hildegard Temporini and Wolfgang Haase, 272–358. Berlin: de Gruyter, 1993.

Schreiner, Thomas. *New Testament Theology: Magnifying God in Christ*. Grand Rapids: Baker Academic, 2008.

Schweitzer, Albert. *The Mysticism of Paul the Apostle*. Translated by William Montgomery. Baltimore: Johns Hopkins University Press, 1930.

———. *The Quest of the Historical Jesus: A Critical Study of Its Progress from Reimarus to Wrede*. Translated by William Montgomery. New York: Macmillan, 1968.

Shauf, Scott. *Theology as History, History as Theology: Paul in Ephesus in Acts 19*. Beihefte Zur Zeitschrift Für Die Neutestamentliche Wissenschaft Se 133. Berlin: Walter de Gruyter, 2005.

Shaw, Mark. *The Kingdom of God in Africa: A Short History of African Christianity*. Grand Rapids: Baker, 1996.

Smith, Ian. *Heavenly Perspective: A Study of the Apostle Paul's Response to a Jewish Mystical Movement at Colossae*. The Library of New Testament Studies 326. London: T. & T. Clark, 2006.

Smith III, James D., and Philip Sellew, eds. *The Fabric of Early Christianity: Reflections in Honor of Helmut Koester by Fifty Years of Harvard Students*. Eugene, OR: Pickwick, 2007.

So, Ky-Chun. "James M. Robinson's Impacts on Korean New Testament Scholarship." *Korea Presbyterian Journal of Theology* 9 (2009) 23–52.

Strauss, David Friedrich. *The Christ of Faith and the Jesus of History: A Critique of Schleiermacher's Life of Jesus*. Translated by Leander E. Keck. Philadelphia: Fortress, 1977.

———. *Die Christliche Glaubenslehre in Ihrer Geschichtlichen Entwicklung: Und Im Kampfe Mit Der Wissenschaft Dargestellt*. Tübingen: C. F. Osiander, 1840–1841.

———. *Gesammelte Schriften Von David Friedrich Strauß. Nach Des Verfassers Letztwilligen Bestimmungen Zusammengestellt. Eingeleitet Und Mit Erklärenden Nachweisungen Versehen Von Eduard Zeller*. Vol. 5. Bonn: Emil Strauß, 1877.

———. *Life of Jesus Critically Examined*. Translated by George Eliot. 4th ed. London: Swan Sonnenschein & Co, 1902.

Strecker, Georg. "Appendix 2: The Reception of the Book." In *Orthodoxy and Heresy in Earliest Christianity*, edited by Robert Kraft and Gehard Krodel, 286–316. Philadelphia: Fortress, 1971.

Svensson, Leif. "A Theology for the Bildungsbürgertum: Ritschl in Context." PhD Diss., Umeå University, 2018.

Svigel, Michael J. "Second Century Incarnational Christology and Early Catholic Christianity." PhD diss., Dallas Theological Seminary, 2008.

Swete, H. B. "The Faithful Sayings." *The Journal of Theological Studies* 18.69 (1916) 1–7.

Swinson, L. Timothy. "Πιστὸς Ὁ Λόγος: An Alternative Analysis." *Southeastern Theological Review* 7.2 (2016) 57–76.

Tanner, Kathryn. *Theories of Culture, a New Agenda for Theology*. Guides to Theological Inquiry. Minneapolis: Fortress, 1997.

Tertullian, Alexander Roberts, and James Donaldson. *Latin Christianity: Its Founder, Tertullian: I. Apologetic; Ii. Anti-Marcion; Iii. Ethical.* Edited by A. Cleveland Coxe. Ante-Nicene Fathers: The Writings of the Fathers Down to AD 325 3. Peabody, MA: Hendrickson, 1994.

Thomassen, Einar, ed. *Canon and Canonicity: The Formation and Use of Scripture.* Copenhagen: Museum Tusculanum, 2010.

———. *The Coherence of "Gnosticism."* Hans-Lietzmann-Vorlesungen. Berlin: De Gruyter, 2020.

———. "How Valentinian Is the Gospel of Philip?" In *The Nag Hammadi Library after Fifty Years*, edited by John D. Turner and Anne McGuire, 251–79. Nag Hammadi and Manichaean Studies 44. Leiden: Brill, 1997.

———. "Orthodoxy and Heresy in Second-Century Rome." *Harvard Theological Review* 93 (2004) 241–56.

———. *The Spiritual Seed: The Church of the "Valentinians."* Nag Hammadi and Manichaean Studies 60. Leiden: Brill Academic, 2008.

———. "The Tripartite Tractate from Nag Hammadi: A New Translation with Introduction and Commentary." PhD Diss., Unversity of St. Andrews, 1982.

Trebilco, Paul. "Christian Communities in Western Asia Minor into the Early Second Century: Ignatius and Others as Witnesses against Bauer." *Journal of the Evangelical Theological Society* 49.1 (2006) 17–44.

———. *Jewish Communities in Asia Minor.* Society for New Testament Studies Monograph Series 69. Cambridge, UK: Cambridge University Press, 1991.

Trueman, Carl R. *Histories and Fallacies: Problems Faced in the Writing of History.* Wheaton, IL: Crossway, 2010.

Turner, H. E. W. *The Pattern of Christian Truth: A Study of the Relations between Orthodoxy and Heresy in the Early Church.* London: A. R. Mowbray, 1954.

Varner, William. "Baur to Bauer and Beyond: Early Jewish Christianity and Modern Scholarship." In *Orthodoxy and Heresy in Early Christian Contexts: Reconsidering the Bauer Thesis*, edited by Paul A. Hartog, 89–113. Eugene, OR: Pickwick, 2015.

Vinzent, Markus. *Writing the History of Early Christianity: From Reception to Retrospection.* Cambridge, UK: Cambridge University Press, 2019.

Völker, Walther. "Walter Bauer's Rechtgläubigkeit Und Ketzerei Im Ältesten Christentum." *Zeitschriftfur Kirchengeschichte* 54.628–31 (1935).

———. "Walter Bauer's *Rechtgläubigkeit Und Ketzerei Im Ältesten Christentum*." *Journal of Early Christian Studies* 14.4 (2006) 399–405.

Waszink, J. H. "Tertullian's Principles and Methods of Exegesis." In *Early Christian Literature and the Classical Intellectual Tradition*, edited by William Schoedel and Robert Wilken, 17–31. Paris: Beauchesne, 1979.

Welch, Claude. *Protestant Thought in the Nineteenth Century, Vol. 2 (1870–1914).* New Haven: Yale University Press, 1985.

Werner, Martin. *Die Entstehung Des Christlichen Dogmas: Problemgeschichtlich Dargestellt.* Bern: Leipzig, 1941.

———. *The Formation of Christian Dogmas: An Historical Study of Its Problems.* Translated by S. G. F. Brandon. New York: Harper, 1957.

Wettflaufer, Ryan D. "An Interpretative Discusion of Preformed Creedal Texts in the New Testament and Their Relevance to the Theology of the Earliest Church through an Exegetical Case Study of the Pastoral Epistles." Master's thesis, Gordon-Cornwell Theological Seminary, 2002.

White, Hugh G. Evelyn. *The Sayings of Jesus from Oxyrhynchus: Edited with Introduction, Critical Apparatus and Commentary*. Cambridge, UK: Cambridge University Press, 1920.

Williams, Rowan. "Does It Make Sense to Speak of Pre-Nicene Orthodoxy?" In *The Making of Orthodoxy: Essays in Honour of Henry Chadwick*, edited by Rowan Williams, 1–23. Cambridge, UK: Cambridge University Press, 1989.

Wolterstorff, Nicholas. "Tertullian's Enduring Question." In *Inquiring about God*, edited by Terence Cuneo, 1.283–303. Cambridge, UK: Cambridge University Press, 2010.

Wrede, Wiliam. *Das Messiasgeheimnis in Den Evangelien Zugleich Ein. Beitrag Zum Verständnis Des Markusevangeliums*. Göttingen: Vandenhoeck & Ruprecht, 1901.

Wyman, Walter E. "The Kingdom of God in Germany: From Ritschl to Troeltsch." In *Revisioning the Past: Prospects in Historical Theology*, edited by Mary Potter Engel and Walter E. Wyman, 257–77. Minneapolis: Fortress, 1992.

Yamauchi, E. M. "Gnosticism and Early Christianity." In *Hellenization Revisited: Shaping a Christian Response within the Greco-Roman World*, edited by W. E. Helleman, 29–61. Institute for Christian Studies. New York: University Press of America, 1994.

Yarbrough, Robert W. *Clash of Visions: Populism and Elitism in New Testament Theology*. Edited by J. V. Fesko and Matthew Barrett. Reformed Exegetical and Doctrinal Studies. Fearn, UK: Christian Focus, 2019.

———. *The Salvation Historical Fallacy: Reassessing the History of New Testament Theology*. History of Biblical Interpretation Series 2. Leiden: Deo, 2004.

Zahl, Paul F. M. "A New Source for Understanding German Theology: Käsemann, Bultmann, and the 'New Perspective on Paul.'" *Sewanee Theological Review* 39.4 (1996) 413–22.

———. "A Tribute to Ernst Käsemann and a Theological Testament." *Anglican Theological Review* 80 (1998) 382–94.

Zahn, Thedor. *Forschungen Zur Geschichte Des Neutestamentlichen Kanons Und Der Altkirchlichen Literatur: 1. Theil: Tatian's Diatessaron*. Erlagen: Andreas Deichert, 1881.

Zeller, Eduard. *David Friedrich Strauss in His Life and Writings*. London: Smith, Elder & Co, 1874.

INDEX

Note: References following "n" refer notes.

A

Abgar V, 80
Acts, 27–28, 126, 167
   1:8, 104
   2:41, 174
   5:17, 155
   8:37, 111
   9:21, 104
   14:23; 20:28, 199n186
   15:5, 155
   20:7, 174
   ii. 30, 40
   iii. 22, 40
   vii. 37, 40
Adv. Haer.
   1.3.6, 193
   1.10, 193, 194
   1.10.1, 189
   1.28.1, 12
   3.4.2, 193
   4.33.7, 193
Against Heresies
   2.14.7; 3.3.3, 168n61
Alcorn, Randy, 124n10
Alexandria, 81, 113
   Athanasius of, 144, 150
   Christian, 82
Antioch, 78
apethanen, 162
Apocalypses, 117, 126
Apocryphal Gospels, 81
Apocryphon of John, 81
apologists, 12, 58n57, 141, 142, 143

Apology/Apologies (Justin Martyr), 15, 80, 143, 144
apostasy, 13, 14, 85
Apostle(s), 129, 172–173, 193
Apostles' Creed, 98–100
Arianism, 18
Arians, 145–146, 147
Arnold, G., 110
Asia Minor, 78, 79, 100, 116, 119
   Jewish syncretism in, 184n138
   Pauline influence in, 115
Athanasius, 86, 144–147
   of Alexandria, 144, 150
   deal with Arianism, 145
   interaction with Arians, 145–146
Augustine, 56

B

baptismal hypothesis, 190n160
Barnard, L. W., 15–17
   reconstruction of Tatian's life, 16
Barth, Karl, 30, 48, 101
Barth, Markus, 180, 181
Bauer, Walter, 9n8, 48, 112–119, 127, 128, 137–138, 144, 166, 168
   attention to lexicography, 83–84
   and centrality of Rome, 149
   and Conzelmann, 86–90
   critics of, 157
   early church historiography, 89
   Edessene Chronicle, 80
   education, 74–75

(Bauer, Walter continued)
   fallacy of historical anachronism, 118
   Greek-English Lexicon of the New Testament and Other Early Christian Literature, 76, 100
   hypothesis, 73–74
   under influence of Holtzmann, 76
   life and thought, 74–120
   misidentified Ignatius's opponents, 114–115
   New Testament documents, 158
   orthodoxy and heresy, 153–154
   Orthodoxy and Heresy in Earliest Christianity, 77, 156
   presentation of Rome, 117
   reconstruction of Edessan church history, 80–81
   reversed doctrinal development in early Christianity, 78–79
   teaching at Marburg, 76
   and work of Ignatius of Antioch, 79
Bauer thesis, 22, 72, 73, 77, 83, 90, 98, 148
   Baur's Hegelian approach to, 200
   Bultmann and, 85–86
   effective popularizer in America, 5
   emergence of, 5
   proponents of, 84, 107
   radical, 78
   reliance on, 97
   Thomassen and, 149
   Turner's criticism of, 111
Baur, F. C., 9, 21, 22–45, 78, 108, 121, 127
   Bauspiess' views on, 24–25
   Bengel's influence upon, 28–29
   Chalamet's views on, 25
   contemporaries of, 26
   disagreement with Strauss, 36–37
   early church historiography, 73, 200–201
   Hegelianism, 4, 5
   Hegel's influence upon, 33–34
   historical theology, interest in, 29
   historiography, 36, 95
   interaction with Schleiermacher, 31–32
   "Jewish-Pauline" controversy, 26
   life, work, and thought of, 27–45
   New Testament, 36
   prehistory of, 24–45
   Roman Catholic view of history, 36
   and Roman Catholic view of history, 35
   Theologiae, 25n11
   thesis-synthesis-antithesis cycle, 131
   Tübingen hypothesis, 25–26, 27
   Welch's views on, 24
Bauspiess, Martin, 24
Behr, John, 153, 159
Bengel, Ernst, 28
Bengel, Johann Albrecht, 28
Bhabha, Homi
   hybridity and mimicry, postcolonial theories of, 141–142, 144
   The Location of Culture, 140
Bingham, Jeffrey, 7, 8, 61, 73, 83, 107, 138
   and evangelical physiographical model of church, 152, 201–202
Blaising, Craig, 132, 133
Blanke, Helmut, 180, 181
Blowers, Paul, 160, 189, 191–192
Bock, Darrell, 123
Bokedal, Tomas, 189
Book of Jeu, 81
Bornkamm, Günther, 95
Bousset, Wilhelm, 76
Boyarin, Daniel, 5, 144, 146, 147–148, 149
Brown, Herbert, 95
Bultmann, Rudolf, 5, 47, 59, 62–72, 84, 97, 98, 100, 119
   anthropology, 92
   and Bauer's thesis, 85–86, 90
   conception of kerygma, 66, 93
   concept of mythology, 67–69
   demythologization, 67–69
   Die Geschichte der synoptischen Tradition, 62
   Entmythologisierung, 63
   Kerygma and Myth, 66–67
   Marburg New Testament theology of, 101

New Testament, 64, 66, 68, 84, 85, 87
Primitive Christianity in Its Contemporary Setting, 65
Synoptische Überlieferung bei den Apostolischen Vätern, 104–105
Burkitt, F. C., 80
Burrus, Virginia, 5, 144, 146, 147–148, 149
Bynum, Caroline Walker, 201

C

Calvin, John, 30
Campenhausen, Hans von, 168
Carson, Donald, 4
Catholicism, 34, 35, 46
  concretization of, 158
  vs. Gnosticism, 100
catholiques manqués, 11
Chalamet, Christophe, 25, 30, 48, 62
Chatraw, Josh, 123
Christian Congregation, 85
Christian God, 21n53
Christianity, 4–5, 71, 106–107
  Church dogma, 54, 56–57
  Colossian, 184n138
  de-eschatologized, 70
  diversity in, 7–8
  Divine Providence and, 17
  Edessan, 110n168
  in Egypt, 81
  Gentile, 34, 84
  Germany's supremacy in study of, 76
  Gnosticism and, 65
  Greek philosophy and, 70
  Hegelian historiography of, 47
  Hegelianized, 20
  Hellenic culture for, 54, 55
  Hellenization of, 64, 65
  historical-critical approaches to, 26
  Jewish, 26, 34, 81
  Kantian-Hegelian-Ritschlian interpretation of, 58
  Kantianized, 20
  Pauline, 26, 46
  progress of early, 60–61
  rise in early, Tübingen hypothesis and, 25–26
  in Rome, 137, 138, 139, 157
  secularization of, 58
  in Smyrna, 115
  Syrian, 76
  triumph of, 145
  universality of, 53
Christological hymns, 177, 179–181
Christology, 116, 124, 125, 179, 197
  doctrines of, 175
  New Testament, 66
  orthodoxy to matters of, 154
Christuslob, 181n124
Church dogma, 54, 56–57
church historiography, classical theory of early, 9–20
  chronology, 11
  church of Jerusalem, virgin, 10
  Hegesippus, 10–11
  heresy and orthodoxy, 10–13
  Irenaeus, 12–13
  Marcionism, 19
  Tertullian church, 17
  Turner on, 9–10
Church of Jerusalem, 10
Church of Rome, 117
Church of the Heavenly Rest in New York, 133
Claremont Graduate University, 103, 104
Clash of Visions: Populism and Elitism in New Testament Theology (Yarbrough), 23
classic historicism, 106–107
Clement, 17, 118, 141, 188
  42:1–4, 11–12
  46.6, 193
Clement of Alexandria, 13
Clement of Rome, 11, 198
Cohen, Hermann, 75
Colossians, 170, 182, 184n138, 185n139, 186, 187, 188
  1:15, 177, 179
  1:15–18, 179
  1:15–20, 161, 177, 179, 180, 181, 188
  1:19, 179

(Colossians continued)
   2:4, 182
   2:6, 111
   2:8, 182, 185n139, 186
   3:15, 181
Commission on Faith and Order of the World Council of Churches in Montreal, 97
concordia discors, 80
Confessing Church, 90, 91n83
Conzelmann, H., 86–90, 119, 162, 165
Corinthians, 117, 160
   4:1–5, 173
   11:4, 85
   11:19, 155
   11:23, 159
   15, 85
   15:1–11, 99, 163
   15:2, 161
   15:44, 201
   15:3b–5, 163
   XV. 1, 99
   XV. 1 f, 99
Countryman, William, 193n169, 195
Credner, Karl August, 26
creedal formula, 6
Crescens, 15, 16
Crete, 78, 78, 168, 169

D

Daley, Brian, 17
Das Messiasgeheimni (Wrede), 102
Das Wesen des Christentums (*The Essence of Christianity*), 54
Defense of My Life of Jesus against the Hegelians (Strauss), 42
Demiurge of Marcion, 195
demythologization, 67–69
Dibelius, Martin, 165
Die Mitte der Zeit (Conzelmann), 86
Dionysius of Helicarnassus, 172
Divine Providence, 17
divine simplicity, 52
Docetism, 114
Doctrine of Addai (Syriac), 80
Dodd, C. H., 176
Donatist schism, 18

dualism, 185
   eschatological, 64
   Gnostic, 65n90

E

The Earliest Christian Confession (Neufield), 170
Ebeling, Gerhard, 95
ecclesiologia perennis, 95
Edessa, 78, 80, 81, 82, 113
   Christianity in, 110n168
egêgertai, 162
Egypt, 78, 81
   Christian, 82
   Gospel of Peter, 127
   Gospel of Thomas, 127
EH
   2.22.1–2, 167
Ehrhardt, Arnold, 90, 119
   Apostles' Creed, 98–100
Ehrman, Bart, 5, 9n8, 21, 43, 59, 120, 121–150, 151, 165
   and Bauer thesis, 130, 131, 133
   and Christianity, 7–8
   Christology, 125
   contemporaries of, 133–140
   cosmology, 124–125
   discrepancies in Gospels, 128–129
   doctrine of Christ, 125
   early church historiography, 73, 83, 121–133
   early years, 122–123
   on Gospel writers, 128–129
   Jesus, Interrupted, 122
   left Christianity, 123–124
   Lost Christianities, 124, 126
   Lost Scriptures: Books That Did Not Make It into the New Testament, 126
   Misquoting Jesus, 122
   in Moody Bible Institute, 123
   New Testament, 124, 126, 131, 158
   Orthodoxy and Heresy in Earliest Christianity, 83, 128
   on Tübingen hypothesis, 27
Elaine Pagels, Elaine, 148
Ellis, Earl, 170

empty deceit, 183
Engelhardt, Moritz von, 53
Enteschatologisierug, 60, 63
Ephesians, 170
   15.3, 193
   18.2, 193
Epistles, 126
Eschenmayer, Adam Karl August von, 43n88
Essenes, 183
Eusebius, 14, 15–16, 80, 129
   EH 2.22.1–2, 167
   HE 3.32.8, 11n16
   HE 4.16.7, 15
   heresy on Tatian by, 16
Evangelische Kirchenzeitung, 43n88

F

Farmer, William, 190n159
Fee, Gordon, 168, 169, 177
Ferguson, Everett, 195, 199
Fichte, Johann Gottlieb, 92
Fischer, David Hackett, 2, 3
Flora, Jerry, 74, 75, 76n20, 83, 120
The Formation of Christian Dogma, 59
Fourth Gospel, 71, 76, 82, 95, 111
Fourth World Conference on Faith and Order (1963), 95
Frei, Hans, 132
Frend, W. H. C., 48, 53
Fuchs, Ernst, 95
Funk, Robert, 103, 105

G

Galatians
   1:11, 192
   1:12, 161
   6:16, 189
Genesis, 41n82, 136n68
Gentiles
   1:6–9, 85
Gestapo, 91n82
Gingrich, F. W., 59
Gnostic dualism, 65n90

Gnosticism, 4, 16, 19, 23n3, 56, 64, 82, 88, 113, 114, 166
   vs. Catholicism, 100
   Christian, 65, 72, 85, 127
   early church and origins of, 21
   gospel interacted with, 55
   libertine forms, 130n41
   Pastoral Epistles and, 168
Gnostic myth of redemption, 71–72
God, 11, 20, 33, 194n175, 195, 201
   beliefs about, 134
   Christian, 21n53
   Fatherhood of, 54
   Greek Orthodox priests and, 8
   Jesus as, 52n24
   kingdom of, 12, 50, 51–52, 60, 63n80
   Spirit in Nature, 32
   Spirit of, 55
   vision, 202
Goetz, Steven, 28–30, 32
Gospel, 27, 31, 38, 57, 103, 126, 159n30
   foreign structure of, 54
   Fourth, 71, 76, 82, 95
   The Gospel According to the Egyptians, 81
   The Gospel According to the Hebrews, 81
   The Gospel of Peter, 81
   of Jesus Christ, 66, 70
   Jesus' teaching in, 46
   with Nag Hammadi, 135–136
   narratives, 40–41
   Synoptic, 43n88
   translation of, 53
   truth of, 71
Gospel of John, 97, 136n68
Gospel of Mark, 103, 123
Gospel of Peter, 127
Gospel of Thomas, 127, 135, 136n68
Gray, James A., 121
Greek philosophy, 20, 21, 24, 56, 70, 142, 183
Grenz, Stanley, 154, 155n17
Gunkel, Hermann, 108n160
Gupta, Nijay, 155
Guretzki, David, 155n17

H

Haggmark, Steven A., 157
Hanarckian historiography, 190
Hannah, John, 50
Harnack, Adolf von, 4–5, 24, 47–72, 75, 78, 134
   education of, 48–49
   Hellenistic historiography of, 47
   Hellenization of faith, 55
   historiography, 5, 48–59
   Lehrbuch der Dogmengeschichte (History of Dogma), 49, 53, 56, 57–58
   overview, 47–48
   regula fidei, 190
   and Ritschlian school of Protestantism, 49–53
   What Is Christianity?, 5
Harnack, Theodosius, 48
Harris, Horton, 36
Hartog, Paul, 109, 110, 192, 203
Harvard Divinity School, 104
Harvey, Van, 42, 46
HE
   3.32.8, 11n16
   4.16.7, 15
   v.13, 16
   v.28, 16
Hebrews
   11:11, 173
Hedrick, Charles W., 127
Hege, Brent, 67
Hegel, Georg Wilhelm Friedrich, 20, 28, 29, 30, 46
   dialectic philosophy, 33, 34
   historiography, 32–34, 35, 45
   idealism, 41, 42
   influence on Baur, 32
   The Philosophy of History, 33
Hegesippus, 10–11
Heick, O. W., 26, 41n81
Hellenism, 47, 54, 64, 144, 183
Hellenization, 71, 140, 149
   of Christianity, 64, 65
   of faith, 55
heresy, 5, 6, 10–13, 78, 90, 106, 119, 128. *See also* orthodoxy
   of Arians, 145
   in Asia Minor, 113
   Christological, 182
   Colossian, 182, 184n138, 185n139, 188
   criteria for determination, 169–170
   definition of, 155, 156
   early conceptions of, 153–158
   in Ephesus, 113
   identification of, 182, 188
   Irenaeus' accusation of, 13, 16
   and orthodoxy, 10–12
   overview, 151–153
   the problem of, 10
Hermann, Wilhelm, 75
Hilgenfeld, Adolf, 36
Hippolytus, 14
History of Dogma, 48, 56, 57
Hodgson, Peter, 28
Holtzmann, H. J., 76
Holy Spirit, 175, 176, 194n175, 195, 197
Holy Trinity, 152–153
homologia, 171
Hultgren, Arland J., 82, 157
Hunt, Emily J., 14, 16
Hurtado, Larry, 178–179
hybridity, postcolonial theory of, 141–149
   early church historiography of, 144
   Hellenization and syncretism to, 140
   imperialized, 150

I

Ignatian corpus, 193
Ignatius, 79, 114, 193
   opponents in Asia Minor, 113–115
Imperial Council for Studies in Stuttgart, 41n81
Institute for Antiquity and Christianity, 103
Irenaeus, 12–17, 141, 188, 190, 193, 201, 202
   1.28.1, 12
   theology, 17
Irenaeus of Lyons, 198

Index

J

Jenkins, Philip, 126
Jerusalem, 129
Jesus Christ, 11, 31, 45, 54, 57, 68–69, 79, 111, 125, 135, 154, 173–174, 185, 201, 203n9
   apostles of, 126
   beliefs about, 134
   birth, 39n77
   Davidic descent of, 176
   deity of, 179, 181
   eschatological message, 60
   faithfulness to, 132
   faith in, 84
   gospel of, 66, 70
   historical, 68, 91, 93
   interpretations of, 157
   life of, 39–40
   message of, 66
   Messiah-Son-of-Man, 64
   miracles of, Strauss argued, 38
   as Savior, 175
   Son of God, 194n175
"Jesus Seminar," 103, 120
Jews, 146–148
Johannine Letters, 116
Johannine tradition, 136
John, 43n88, 84, 87, 113
   4.2, 3, 171
   6:69, 89
   9.22, 171
   11:27, 111
   19:14, 39n77, 129
   vii. 42, 40
Josephus, 183
Judaism, 65n90, 145, 185n139
Judaizers, 114
Jülicher, Adolf, 75
Justin Martyr, 12–17, 141, 147
   Apology/Apologies, 15, 144
   death of, 15–17
   early Christianity, 26
   failure to mention Paul, 166
   heresiology truth, 143n96
   martyrdom of, 15
   orthodoxy, 14
   and postcolonial theory of hybridity, 142–144

K

Kaftan, Julius, 63n80
Kähler, Martin, 93
Kant, Immanuel, 31, 56, 74
Kantianized Christianity, 20
Kantian tradition, 52
Käsemann, E., 90–97, 119
   dependence on Bauer, 97
   early church historiography, 95–96
   Essays on New Testament Themes, 94
   historiography, 95
Kelly, J. N. D., 193, 194, 196, 197
Kerygma, 66, 163, 165
kerygma, 176–177, 192
King, Karen, 5, 120
Kloppenborg, John, 161, 162, 163
Knight, George, 171–172, 175, 177
Koester, Helmut, 5, 101–108, 119, 135n66, 144
   classical historicism of, 140
   Nag Hammadi documents, publication of, 103–104
   obsolete categories in New Testament scholarship, 106–107
   reviewed *Das Geschichtsverständnis des Markus-Evangeliums*, 102
   Trajectories through Early Christianity, 100, 101, 104, 105
konseqent-eschatologisch, 59
Köpf, Ulrich, 37, 43n88
Köstenberger, Andreas, 73, 76, 77, 78, 84, 106, 111, 112, 123, 152, 154, 200
   and Christological hymn, 178
   New Testament evidence, 157
   and *regula fidei*, 192
Köstlin, Karl Reinhold, 36
Kruger, Michael J., 73, 76, 77, 78, 84, 106, 111, 112, 152, 154, 200
   and Christological hymn, 178
   New Testament evidence, 157
   and *regula fidei*, 192
Kümmel, W. G., 76n20

L

Land, Darin, 36
Leben Jesus, 44
Lehrbuch der Dogmengeschichte, 53
Lessing, G. E., 39
Lindbeck, George, 132
Livingston, James C., 24, 30, 43n88, 48, 49, 50, 62
The Location of Culture (Bhabha), 140
Lohse, Eduard, 180, 183, 185–186
Luke
    4:13, 87
    23:34, 163
    24:1–52, 39n77, 129
    i. 32, 40
Luther, Martin, 55, 57
Lyman, Rebecca, 5, 140–144, 148
    Logos Spermatikos, 142

M

Macedonia, 78
MacRae, George, 135n66
Magnesia, 114, 115
Marcion, 138, 139, 166
    view of God, 195
Marcionism, 19, 113, 114, 198
Mark
    6:23, 39n77, 129
    6:35, 39n77, 129
    8:29, 111
    14:12, 39n77
    14:22, 39n77
    15:25, 39n77
Marshall, I. H., 112, 120
Mary Magdalen, 127n26
Matthew, 203
    9:18, 39n77, 129
    12:13–23, 39n77, 129
    14:33, 111
    28:1–20, 39n77, 129
    ii. 5 f., 40
    xxii. 42, 40
McKnight, Scot, 180, 181n124, 182–183
McRae, George, 103, 105
Metzger, Bruce M., 123

Middle Platonism, 185
mimicry, postcolonial theory of, 141–149
    early church historiography of, 144
    Jewish, 147
Moody Bible Institute, 123
Munslow, Alan, 3
myth, 41
    Mandean form of, 71–72, 72n113
    of *salvator salvandus*, 72n114
mythology, 67–69
    and Gnosticism, 70
mythos, 66

N

Nag Hammadi Codices, 149
Nag Hammadi documents, 103
Nag Hammadi Library, 104, 126, 127, 130n41
Nazis, 91n83
Neill, Stephen, 27, 41n82, 43n88, 48, 66, 102
Neo-Protestantism, 52n24
Neufield, Vernon, 163, 164
    The Earliest Christian Confession, 170
Neve, J. L., 26, 41n81, 62
New Testament, 6, 11, 39, 103, 112
    Baur's historiography and, 36
    "Baur-Wrede-Bultmann" approach to, 27
    Bultmann and, 64, 66, 68
    canonical, 126, 152
    canonization of, 136
    Christology, 66
    church, 97, 99
    complex issues in, 120
    creedal formulae in, 99, 100
    creedal statements in, 159
    crisis in, 105–106
    demythologizing, 69, 84
    at Göttingen University, 86
    Hegelian historiography of, 47
    historical-critical approaches to, 26
    liturgical material predating, 177–187
    mythical interpretation, 42

as mythos, 70
Pastoral Epistles of, 163
Paul and John in, 84
pre-creedal formulations in, 158–177
scholarship, 'obsolete' categories in, 106
static historiographies of, 106
theology, 24n5, 25, 76
Nicene-Constantinopolitan creed, 159n30
Nordling, Cherith Fee, 155n17
Norris, Frederick, 78, 113, 114, 115, 117, 119, 120

O

Object (antithesis), 35
Oedipus, 41n82
Old Testament, 54, 125
On Religion: Speeches to Its Cultured Despisers (Schleiermacher), 31
On Speeches: Addressed to Its Cultured Despisers (Schleiermacher), 30
Oratio (Tatian), 15, 17
Origen, 18
Origen of Alexandria, 198
orthodox minorities, 114–115
orthodoxy, 21, 82, 85, 88, 90, 106, 119, 128, 149. *See also* heresy
  Christological, 182
  conceptions in documents of New Testament, 158–187
  criteria for determination, 169–170
  definition of, 154–155, 156
  in early Christianity, 117
  early conceptions of, 153–158
  heresy and, 10–12
  identification of, 188
  overview, 151–153
  Roman, 138–139
  roots of, 116n194
  of Tatian, 12–13
Osborn, Eric, 190n156
An Outline of the Theology of the New (Conzelmann), 86–87
Oxyrhynchus Logia, 81

P

Packer, J. I., 154
Pagels, E., 5, 9, 120, 133–137, 149, 151
  and Bauer thesis, 134, 136
  Beyond Belief: The Secret Gospel of Thomas, 133
  gnostic Gospels, discovery of, 135
paradidonai, 161
paralambanó, 160
Pastoral Epistles (PE), 116, 163–169, 171, 172, 175, 187
  authenticity of, objection to, 168, 169
  Bauer's reconstruction, 166
  five-fold occurrences of, 174–175
  paraenetic letters, 169
  Pauline authorship of, 165, 167
Paul, 26, 53, 56, 84, 87, 160–174, 182–187
  2:6–11, 162
  2:11–12, 185
  15:3–8, 159
  in Colossians 2:8, 186
  declaration on Jewish Messiah, 181
  declares Jesus image of God, 180
  2:6f, 183
  in Galatians, 183
Pelikan, Jeroslav, 82
Pentecost, 152
Peter, 45–46, 166
  5:2, 199n186
pfarrer (pastor), 91
Pfarrernotbund, 90n82
Pfleiderer, Otto, 75
Pharisees, 183
Philadelphia, 114, 115
Philippians
  1:1, 115, 199n186
  2:6, 179
  2:6–8, 178
  2:6–11, 161, 161n35, 177, 179, 188
  2:9–11, 179
  2.11, 171
  2:11, 111
  4:1, 168n61
The Philosophy of History (Hegel), 33
Pistis Sophia, 127n26

pistos logos, 163
Planck, Karl Christian, 36
Plato, 19
Platonism, 143
    Middle, 185
    Pythagorean, 143
Polycarp, 114, 115, 117, 168
    of Smyrna, 79–70
Praxeanism, 198
pre-performed creedal texts (PCT), 164, 165n48, 170, 172, 174 175
    and *kerygma*, 176
pro hoc, 4
propter hoc, 4
Protestantism, 35, 48, 57
    German, 90n82
    idealistic, 92
Protestant Reformation, 35, 52, 55
Pythagorean Platonism, 143

Q

Quest, 60

R

redeemed Redeemer, 71, 72n13
regula fidei, 130n41, 160, 169, 199, 201
    in *Adv. Haer.* 1.10, 194
    catholic, 190n159
    and "Christian" identity, 191
    Demonstration of the Apostolic Preaching, 195
    emergence and functions of, 188–198
    orally-transmitted, 175
    origin of, 189
    pre-creedal, 177
Reimarus, Hermann, 39n77, 127, 128, 129
Rensberger, David, 26, 166–167
The Resurrection of the Body in Western Christianity (Bynum), 201
Rick, K. W., 155
Ristchlianism, 49–51, 53, 58, 63n80
Ritschl, Albrecht, 36, 48, 49–53, 56
    objection to classical theology, 53
    rejection of classical theism, 52
Ritschlian, Berlin, 47
Ritschlian school of Protestantism, 48–49
Robinson, James M., 5, 95, 100–113, 119, 144
    The Bauer Thesis Examined: The Geography of Heresy in the Early Christian Church, 112
    classical historicism of, 140
    Das Geschichtsverständnis des Markus-Evangeliums, 102
    A New Quest of the Historical Jesus, 103
    obsolete categories in New Testament scholarship, 106–107
    returned to Princeton Theological Seminary, 102
    success in Nag Hammadi Library, 104
    "Theological Autobiography," 100–101
Robinson, T., 112, 120
Robinson, William Childs, 101
Romans
    3. 12f, 69
    6. 11ff, 69
    6:1–14, 187
    6:10, 161
    10.8–10, 171
    10:9, 111
    10:9b, 163
    I.3 f, 99
Roman Hellenism, 141, 142, 153
    intellectual movement within, 149
    universalism and traditions within, 144
Rosenmüller, G., 26
Rule of Faith, 188–189, 191, 193–94

S

Sadducees, 183
salvator salvandus, 72n114
Sandford, Jonah, 155
Satan, 66–67
Sayings Gospel (Q), 104

Schelling, Fredrick von, 28, 29–30
   idealism, 32
   influence on young Baur, 29
Schlatter, Adolf, 25n11
Schleiermacher, Friedrich Daniel
      Ernst, 28, 29, 30–37, 40, 44, 48
   Baur's interaction with, 31–32
   Brief Outline of Theology as a Field
      of Study, 31
   Der christliche Glaube, 31
   and German romanticism, 32
   Protestant Reformers, 30
   religion, definition of, 31
   On Religion: Speeches to Its Cultured
      Despisers, 31
   on Ritschlian school of theology,
      50–51
   On Speeches: Addressed to Its
      Cultured Despisers, 30
   works of, 30–31
Schwegler, Albert, 36
Schweitzer, Albert, 9n8, 59, 60, 93
   consistent eschatology of, 61
Seldom, 91n83
Seventh-Day Adventists, 8
Shauf, Scott, 87
Shaw, Mark, 1
Sitz im Leben, 163
Smith, Ian, 186–187
Smyrna, 115
So, Ky-Chun, 101
Society for Biblical Literature, 103
soteriology, 125
   doctrines of, 175
   orthodoxy to matters of, 154
St. Jerome, 18
Steudal, J. C. F., 41n81
stoicheia, 186
Strathmann, Hermann, 62
Strauss, D. F., 37–45, 46
   Baur's teaching on, impact of,
      37–38
   Defense of My Life of Jesus against
      the Hegelians, 42
   disagreement with Baur, 36–37
   free New Testament studies, 39
   and Hegelian idealism, 41–42
   Life of Jesus, 36, 38, 72

Strecker, Georg, 156
Stroth, F. A., 26
Subject (thesis), 35
Swinson, Timothy, 159n31
syncretism, 8, 65, 81, 88, 108, 140, 149
   Hellenistic, 61n69
   Jewish, 184n
Synoptic Gospels, 43n88
Syria, 119
Syrian Christianity, 76

T

Talmudic heresiology, 146
Tanner, Kathryn, 132–133
   "free Word of God," 133
Tatian, 12–17
   apostasy, 14
   biographical chronology, 16
   life of, chronological issues in, 15
   Oratio, 15, 17
   orthodoxy of, 14
   turned to heresy, 13
Tertullian, 11, 17–20, 188, 193, 194,
      195–196, 201
   Against Marcion, 189–190
   Praescr, 20n49, 190
   Against Praxeas, 196
   Prescription Against Heretics, 196
   regula fidei, 196–198
   The Veiling of Virgins, 196
Theodore of Mopsuestia, 174n89
Theologischen Literaturzeitung, 48
Theories of Culture: A New Agenda for
      Theology (Tanner), 132
Thessalonians, 170
   4:14, 163
   5: 5–8, 69
Thomassen, Einar, 5, 137–140, 148,
      149
   and Bauer thesis, 138
   orthodoxy and centralization in
      church, 139
Timothy I, 170
   1: 3, 168
   1:12, 173
   1:15, 175, 176n99
   3:16, 177

(Timothy I continued)
   4:1–5, 168n61
   4:8, 175
   4:9, 159, 171
   6.12, 171
   6.13, 171
   1:15a, 159, 171
   2:11a, 159
   3:1a, 159, 171
Timothy II
   2:11–13, 175, 176n99
Titus, 170
   1:5, 199n186
   1:9, 172
   3:4–7, 176n99
   3:8, 159
Torah, 146
Trajectories through Early Christianity (Koester), 100
Tralles, 114, 115
Trebilco, Paul, 113, 116, 120
Trinity, 19
true believers, 164
Trueman, Carl R., 3n9
Tübingen hypothesis, 25–26
Turner, H. E. W., 17, 18, 22, 58, 59, 61, 71, 80, 81, 120
   Bultmann, introduced, 62
   classical theory of early church historiography, 9–10
   Gnosticism, 56
   Harnack's historiography, introduced, 53
   orthodoxy of Gospel, 82
   The Pattern of Christian Truth, 9, 18n42
   The Pattern of Christian Truth (lectures), 109
   Rule of Faith, 188–189

U

Una Sancta Apostolica, 96
unity and diversity, 130n41

V

Valentinus, 19, 138, 139, 166
Varner, William, 25, 27–28, 74, 119
Völker, W., 109–111, 120
   criticism of Bauer, 109–110
Volkmar, Gustav, 36

W

Watorp, Paul, 75
Weiss, Johannes, 59, 60, 63n80, 75
Welch, Claude, 24, 45
Werner, M., 47, 59–61, 65, 70, 85
   Enteschatologisierug, 60, 63
   The Formation of Christian Dogma, 59–60
   Jesus' catastrophic eschatology, 60–61
Wettlaufer, Ryan, 164, 168, 169, 170, 174
What Is Christianity? (Harnack), 5
White, Evelyn, 81
Wissenschaft, 45
Wolterstoff, Nicholas, 20
Wrede, William, 102–103
Wright, Tom, 27, 41n82, 43n88, 48, 66, 102

Y

Yarbrough, Robert W., 23–24
   Clash of Visions: Populism and Elitism in New Testament Theology, 23
   Ferdinand Christian Baur and the History of Early Christianity, 27

Z

Zahl, Paul, 91n83
Zeitschriftfur Kirchengeschichte, 109
Zeller, Eduard, 36, 38n72